Total
Piano
tutor

THIS IS A CARLTON BOOK

Copyright © Carlton Books Limited 2004, 2010

This edition published in 2010 by
Carlton Books Limited
a division of the Carlton Publishing Group
20 Mortimer Street
London W1T 3JW

First published in 2002

A CIP catalogue record for this book is available from the British Library

Hardback ISBN 978 1 84732 537 2
Paperback ISBN 978 1 84732 667 6

Commissioning editor: Claire Richardson
Art direction: Clare Baggaley
Production: Janette Burgin
Design: The Orgone Company
Music editor: Mike Flynn

Photographs by Laura Wittenden and Terry Burrows unless otherwise credited.

Printed in Dubai

Total
Piano
tutor

The ultimate guide to learning
and mastering the piano

TERRY BURROWS

CARLTON
BOOKS

PART ONE
INTRODUCING THE PIANO

HOW TO USE THIS BOOK

In an ideal world, every person that wanted to learn to play a musical instrument would find themselves an excellent teacher, and take regular one-on-one lessons. The teacher would work from a well-established methodology, and set the student measurable goals that would give a clear indication of progress, and motivate the student to attain the next level. Unfortunately, there are many reasons why this approach is not possible for some: good piano tuition doesn't come cheaply; there may not be a piano teacher in your area, and if there is, he or she may not be appropriate to your needs; you may not want to take your piano playing to a particularly high level, but merely want an occasional hobby; or you may dread the idea of formal learning with a teacher. If any of the above are true, this is the ideal course for you. Some may question how effectively any "art" can be taught via an instruction book. There's no question that personal tuition from the right individual is the most effective way of learning to play the piano, but it isn't the only way. Using the combination of text, photographs, diagrams, compact disc and notated music, the student is given a clear picture of the most appropriate playing and fingering techniques, as well as developing the important skill of sight-reading in tandem with acquiring playing skills. Throughout the course, the student is given complete pieces of music to play – many of these are special arrangements of works by some of the most famous composers ever to have lived. Above all, the playing techniques shown are all absolutely standard: if on completing the course the student wants to take lessons with a professional tutor, they shouldn't have to unlearn any of those easily acquired bad habits.

WHAT DO YOU REALLY WANT?

Since you're reading this we would imagine that you want to learn how to play the piano. But what do you hope to achieve? What kind of music do you want to play? Classical? Jazz? Rock? Pop? Do you want to play solo pieces, or do you want to play with other musicians? How much work are you prepared to put in? If you want to play to a very high standard, you could be talking about committing yourself to several hours of practice each day. Are you up for that? These are all questions that only you can answer, yet they will play a fundamental part in how you approach a course like this.

There's an unashamedly "classical" leaning to this course. After all, we're using standard playing techniques and teaching standard music theory. This is *by no means* to say that the course is only aimed at those wanting to play classical music. Absolutely everything you learn from the eight lessons that follow is applicable to any form of music. A practical knowledge of note intervals (as you'll soon get bored of hearing) is fundamental to understanding melody and harmony: add rhythm to these two elements and you have the three basic components of all music. This is just as true for Beethoven's piano sonatas as it is for music by the Black Eyed Peas or Lady Gaga. What's more, if your interests are less formal, after the final lesson has ended, you will find an extensive dictionary of chords. If you can play these in their various positions, you should be able to come up with a simple accompaniment for almost any song you hear.

WHAT WILL YOU LEARN, THEN?

Let's start off with a brief list of some of the things you should have achieved by the end of the eight lessons in this book.

1. You'll have a good basic understanding of music theory. This will include:
    *   The different note names
    *   The different key signatures
    *   The different time signatures
    *   How to work out the timing and rhythm of music
    *   The names and sounds of the intervals between any two notes
    *   Combining those intervals to produce scales
    *   Combining notes to create chords
    *   The terminology that describes the performance instructions on any piece of music
    *   All of the symbols used in standard music notation.

2. You should be able to understand almost ANY piece of written music.

3. You'll be able to play some reasonably demanding pieces of music using both hands.

4. You'll begin to gain an understanding of the historical developments in piano music over the past three centuries, including a basic knowledge of some of the greatest performers, composers, and their works.

5. Enough practical knowledge and experience to enable you to take your piano or keyboard playing in any musical direction you choose.

6. You'll (hopefully) derive fun and satisfaction while you're doing all of the above.

APPROACHING YOUR STUDY

The advantage of teaching yourself using a course like this is that you can work at your own pace. A sensible and methodical approach to using *Total Piano Tutor* is to set yourself a timetable and stick to it. Although working through a single lesson may only take you a few hours or so, you should perhaps consider restricting yourself to working through no more than a single lesson each week. In between times, keep practising those exercises until you're happy with your performance. Whatever approach you take, however, before you go on to the next lesson, review the one you've just completed and ENSURE THAT YOU'VE UNDERSTOOD IT THOROUGHLY.

As you will discover, the way music "works" is quite simple to understand and you may have a naturally musical "ear", finding that you can work through a single lesson very quickly. A word of warning, however: no matter how well you *understand* written music, the facility for sight-reading the ability to see a piece of music and immediately sing or play it back will only come with time and practice. A useful tip is to get hold of some published sheet music (most reasonable libraries hold at least a small stock) and apply the lessons you have taught yourself to "real" examples of written music. If possible, take some photocopies so that you can mark up the music with a pen. At first, mark up the note names and timings, and try to "play" them through in your head.

USING THE CD

Although you can learn keyboard techniques from the photographs, diagrams and notated music shown throughout the book, *Total Piano Tutor* also includes a 54-minute compact disc. The system is very simple to use. Wherever you see the CD symbol, set your CD player to the track number shown alongside. Altogether there are 63 tracks on the CD.

23 ▶ = Instruction to play track 23

The contents of the CD can be grouped into two categories. Many of the tracks are there to provide aural reinforcement of new ideas. For example, if you see a piece of music containing a string of notes, you will be able to hear exactly how the sequence should sound. This helps to forge an immediate link between the notation and the music. This recognition of note and rhythm patterns is crucial to attaining sight-reading skills.

In addition, all of the "repertoire" pieces shown throughout the book can also be heard in full on the CD.

THE PIANO AND ITS ANCESTORS

The best-known and most popular keyboard instrument, the piano enjoys a high-profile position not only in the world of classical music, but in modern forms such as jazz, rock, pop and country. However, in spite of its pre-eminence, you may be surprised to learn it was not until the early part of the eighteenth century that the instrument even came into being.

THE PIANO AND ITS ANCESTORS

Who were the first musicians? We can guess that at some point in the early part of our evolution, ancient man might have discovered that by plucking a thong stretched between the horns of a dead animal, or a forked branch, it created a sound. Later, the hunter will have been aware that the string of his bow produced the same sound every time he fired an arrow, and that by altering the length and and thickness of the string, other sounds – or notes – were possible. Once two or more parallel strings were added to the bow, we have a rudimentary harp – the first stringed instrument.

THE ORGAN

Although the piano is clearly a stringed instrument, in order to trace the period leading up to its development we must look back to before the birth of Christ, to the godfather of all keyboard instruments – the organ. The earliest known organ was the *hydraulis*, which is purported to have been invented in the region of 300BC by Ctesibius of Alexandria. The instrument came about from an experiment to apply a mechanical wind supply to a giant set of panpipes.

However, it was in Europe that the organ evolved, and where from the eighth century it exerted a strong influence over the early development of Western music. Strangely, though, it was not for another five hundred years that the "chromatic" keyboard was developed and applied to the organ. Initially, the notes of the keyboard were designed around the modes that were used as the basis of music at this time, meaning that the early organs only used the keys that we now call the "white notes". The accidentals (the "black" notes) were gradually added to reflect changes in approach to music composition. Since the fourteenth century, keyboards have remained much the same – except for the colour, which at the time was the reverse of the black and white keys that we are familiar with today.

STRINGED KEYBOARD INSTRUMENTS

During the early sixteenth century, other keyboard instruments began to appear, the most notable of which was the harpsichord. Each time a key on the harpsichord is pressed, a connected quill plucks the string, creating the sound. For the next two hundred years, the harpsichord was one of the most important of European musical instruments.

Coexisting alongside the harpsichord during this period was the clavichord. This instrument appears as a small, rectangular cabinet with a keyboard built into one of the long sides, and strings traversing from left to right. When a key is pressed, a brass blade strikes the string, remaining in contact until pressure is taken off the key. Unlike the harpsichord, the clavichord allows the player a high degree of dynamic control, however the "soft" sound and low volume meant that it could only be used in small spaces.

THE FIRST PIANO

The story of the piano begins in 1709, in Florence, when the Italian harpsichord-maker Bartolomeo Cristofori constructed what he called *Gravicembalo col piano e forte* (literally "harpsichord with soft and loud"). Cristofori had replaced the plucking mechanism with a series of hammers, so that when the note was pressed, the hammer struck the string creating the note. One major difference, however, was in the

One of the two remaining Cristofori instruments.

The Silbermann pianoforte—fully approved by Johann Sebastian Bach.

dynamic control offered by the new instrument: unlike the harpsichord, the *pianoforte* (as it was abbreviated) allowed the player to vary the volume of the sound depending on how hard the keyboard was pressed. But while Cristofori received brief attention for his endeavours, interest quickly waned. He had produced about twenty pianos by this time, after which he is presumed to have returned to manufacturing harpsichords. Only two of the original models are now known to exist.

THE SILBERMANN MODELS

One of the few historical references to the Cristofori piano came in a 1709 article about the pianoforte, written by Scipione Maffei. In 1725, the Court Poet at Dresden published a translation of Maffei's text, which aroused the interest of clavichord-maker Gottfried Silbermann (1683–1753). He immediately began to build pianofortes based on the Cristofori design. Initially, however, Silbermann's pianos were received with some hostility, which led him to lose interest in the instrument.

Christian Ernst Friederici, a pupil of Silbermann, continued the venture, devising a small "square" piano which he named a *fortbien*. Although not widely recognised, Friederici embarked on many such experiments, some of which offered a glimpse of the piano's later development.

All of the instruments produced up until this period could more accurately be described as variations on a *dulcimer* (a stringed instrument plucked with a quill plectrum) with keyboard and dampers. Few of these instruments worked especially well, but they did arouse the interest of a number of significant figures. The most prominent harpsichord composer of the period, François Couperin, acknowledged the importance of this innovation: "The harpsichord is perfect as to its compass and brilliant in itself, but as one can neither swell nor diminish its sounds, I will be forever grateful to those who with infinite pains guided by taste succeed in rendering the instrument capable of expression".

By 1750, Silbermann's instrument had gained the approval of no less a figure than Johann Sebastian Bach. A close friend of Silbermann, Bach had not liked the instrument at first, but the scope for dynamic control eventually won him over. However, it was one of Bach's sons who would prove to be the first significant musical figure associated with the piano.

Carl Philip Emmanuel Bach (or C. P. E. Bach, as he is usually known) wrote one of the first important keyboard tutors. Although directed mainly at harpsichord players, Bach's *Versuch über die wahre Art das Klavier zu spielen* (*Essay on the True Art of Keyboard Playing*) remains an influential work. It was here, for the first time, that the piano was acknowledged as an instrument of the future. Indeed, Bach could accurately be described as the founder of modern piano-playing. By the time of his death in 1788, the piano was universally accepted as the superior instrument in the clavier family: the harpsichord's time had passed.

JOHANNES ZUMPE

The first significant wave of popularity enjoyed by the piano began in 1760 after the arrival in England of the so-called "twelve apostles" – a group of Dutch and German instrument-makers who settled in London having fled the German Seven Years War. Among their number was Johannes Christoph Zumpe. A former apprentice of Silbermann, Zumpe set up a workshop in Hanover Square, London, in 1761 to produce a new kind of "square" piano. Zumpe believed that the instrument – previously only affordable to the very wealthy – could attract the middle classes if suitably priced. His square piano was small, light and could be carried on the back of a single porter, and sold for £50. So successful was the square piano that during the second half of the eighteenth century, it became known simply as the "Zumpe". The instrument remained popular until the middle of the nineteenth century when the "upright" piano began to find its way into an increasing number of homes.

Zumpe's instrument made its professional debut in 1767 when it was used as an accompaniment to a performance of *The Beggar's Opera* at Covent Garden. The player was Charles Dibdin. However, the first pianist of any real consequence was yet another member of the Bach family – Johann Christian. Long a resident of London, and the youngest son of Johann Sebastian, he was popularly referred to as "the English Bach".

Johannes Christoph Zumpe's famous "square" piano.

SHUDI, BROADWOOD AND STODART

Hailing from a family of Swiss wood craftsmen, Burkat Shudi arrived in London in 1718, at the age of 16, where he became an apprentice in the Soho harpsichord workshop of Hermann Tabel. Ten years later, by then widely acknowledged as one of the great instrument-makers of his generation, Shudi successfully went into business on his own. In 1769, a Scottish cabinet-maker named John Broadwood made his way to London in search of his fortune. Marrying Shudi's daughter, Broadwood joined his father-in-law's workshop. Together they produced the most distinguished instruments of the period. On Shudi's death in 1773, Broadwood took over the company, and began to experiment with Zumpe's designs for the piano.

Four years later, Broadwood joined forces with another Scot, William Stodart. Their innovative work created the blueprint for the modern grand piano. Indeed, that year Stodart obtained a patent for the "English grand action" – the first documented evidence we have of the word used in conjunction with the piano. In 1782, the company took Broadwood's name. Among the significant developments that followed were the design of the damper and soft pedals.

John Broadwood and Sons remains a prestigious manufacturer of pianos, having held a Royal Warrant since the reign of King George II. The company has produced instruments for every British monarch since.

NINETEENTH-CENTURY EVOLUTION

Although as early as 1739 the Italian Domenico del Mela had experimented with the idea of an instrument that was strung vertically rather than horizontally, the first true upright piano was built in 1800 by John Isaac Hawkins, an Englishman living in the United States. The Hawkins piano was build so that strings ran below the keyboard with the tuning hitchpins

A modern concert grand piano.

at the base. From the 1830s onward, the "upright" became the most popular domestic piano.

Another very significant name in the history of the piano is that of Heinrich Englehard Steinweg. Having built his first grand piano in his hometown of Seesen, Germany, in 1836 (which surprisingly has survived and is now housed at the New York Metropolitan Museum of Art), in 1850 he emigrated to New York where he "became" Henry Steinway and formed the most important company in the instrument's history.

It was his two sons, Henry Jr. and Theodore, who were responsible for many of the technical breakthroughs and refinements for which Steinway pianos are famed. These include "crossing" strings for the highest and lowest notes to create a fuller sound, the use of an iron frame, modifying the tone of the piano to maximise string vibrations for a richer sound, and improving many of the instrument's mechanical functions.

Interestingly enough, like Steinway and Sons, many of the companies founded by the greatest innovators of the nineteenth century are still in operation in one form or another – albeit often under the ownership of impersonal multinational corporations. But through these companies, celebrated names such as Ignaz Bösendorfer, Dwight Hamilton Baldwin, Jonas Chickering and Carl Bechstein are able to live on, a testament to their enduring achievements.

THE DECLINE OF THE DOMESTIC PIANO

The upright piano typically formed the centrepiece of communal family life in many homes throughout Europe and America until well into the twentieth century. It wasn't until after the end of the Second World War that other forms of home entertainment – radio, television and gramophone records – started a gradual decline in its popularity.

When the rock-and-roll era arrived in the mid-1950s, the piano found it increasingly hard to compete with the glamour and volume of the modern electric guitar. The new young "beat groups" rarely found an exclusive place for the piano in their line-ups, preferring instead to use offspring such as the electronic piano or Hammond organ – or, in many cases, ignore keyboard instruments altogether.

Nonetheless, the piano has remained a popular and well-loved instrument. It is arguably the most revered of instruments in the classical world, and still somehow manages to find a place for itself whatever new musical trends may appear. For many years now, trained pianists have been using synthesizers and other electronic equipment. And the development of MIDI and the rapid growth of dance music and digital sampling have once again placed those with basic piano skills at the very centre of contemporary music.

THE PIANO: SOME KEY DATES

1700 First evidence of Cristofori's piano experiments, in the inventory of musical instruments belonging to Prince Ferdinand. The pianoforte uses a hammer mechanism rather than the plucked string action of the harpsichord.

1709 Cristofori reveals his pianoforte for the first time in public.

1728 Gottfried Silbermann, a clavichord-maker, produces two refinements on the "harpsichord with hammers" theme without commercial success.

1753 C. P. E. Bach publishes the first book to include reference to piano technique.

1760 German and Dutch piano-makers (known as the "Twelve Apostles"), including Johannes Zumpe, arrive in England having fled the German Seven Years War.

1768 First solo piano performances in England when J. C. Bach uses a Zumpe instrument.

1771 John Broadwood launches his first square piano.

1777 William Stodart of London obtains the patent for the "English Grand Action", which will be used by American and English manufacturers. This is the first use of the word "grand".

1795 Stodart designs a new type of upright grand piano – the "bookcase" piano.

1797 *Pianoforte*, the first magazine devoted to the piano, begins publication in London.

1800 Matthias Muller and John Isaac Hawkins develop the first upright pianos with strings running down to floor level.

1828 Ignaz Bosendorfer takes over management of the Brodmann instrument workshop in Vienna.

1859 H. Steinway Jr. patents overstrung grand piano.

1874 Steinway perfects the *sostenuto* pedal.

HOW THE PIANO WORKS

The principles on which the piano creates its unique sound are quite straightforward. However, the mechanisms that bring the hammers into contact with the strings each time a key is pressed are extremely sophisticated. Indeed, an average concert grand piano has in excess of 10,000 moving parts.

INSIDE THE PIANO

A standard concert grand piano has 88 keys, giving it a range of over seven octaves. A piano makes sounds when its pre-tuned strings are struck by small hammers. All of the keys have their own hammers and strings. Each time a key is pressed it activates a mechanism which swings the hammer at the appropriate string (or strings). At the same time, a related mechanism lifts a damper pad away from the strings, allowing them to vibrate. When the key is released the hammer falls back into place and the damper is returned to the strings to prevent them from being vibrated.

Each of the strings is stretched tightly across a "bridge", mounted on a large flat piece of spruce called the "soundboard". The vibrations of the strings are transferred to the soundboard, which disturbs the surrounding airwaves, thus amplifying the sound.

THE CASE

The outer wooden cabinet that houses all the components is known as the "case". To add more strength, most piano cases are made up of a laminated construction of hard woods. The most commonly used woods are maple, mahogany and luan. The traditional varnished finish is known as a "high polish".

THE KEYS

Piano manufacture has altered little over the past century, although both economic and ecological factors have resulted in some changes.

The black keys were traditionally made from ebony; scarce and expensive, it is now used only on the most exclusive pianos. The white keys were once made from a hard wood covered with an ivory veneer. Other materials used have included bone, mother-of-pearl and tortoiseshell. For reasons of conservation there is now an embargo on the use of ivory for piano keys, so they are generally now made from a synthetic covering.

THE STRINGS

The piano strings are attached to a cast-iron frame, known as the "plate". This has to be sufficiently durable to withstand in excess of 20 tons of pressure from the tension in the strings. It is the heaviest part of the piano and can weigh up to 600 pounds.

Each string is tuned to predefined pitch. Steel is used to make the treble strings. The bass strings are also made from steel, but are wound with copper. Although there are 88 different keys, there are many more strings. This is because the middle and treble strings are arranged in "courses" – groups of two or three strings tuned to the same note. This is necessary because as the strings get shorter (and the pitch higher) so they diminish in volume. The greater number of strings redresses this imbalance.

WHAT IS A PIANO?

Musical instruments can be classified according to the way their sounds are created. The first formal system of classification was devised in the nineteenth century by Charles Mahillon. His four categories were: autophones (instruments made from a sonorous material that vibrates to produce a sound – such as cymbals); membranophones (instruments where a stretched skin creates sound by vibration, e.g. drums); aerophones (instruments that create sound by vibrating a column of air, e.g. wind instruments); and chordophones, which covers all stringed instruments.

In the early twentieth century, German musicologists Erich von Hornbostel and Curt Sachs added a fifth class – electrophones, catering for a new breed of instrument where sound vibrations were created by oscillating electric circuits. They also created subdivisions within each of the five categories.

Although we tend naturally to group the various keyboard instruments together, it's possible for them to fall into different categories. Since the piano is essentially a series of wires struck with a hammer, according to the Hornbostel and Sachs system, it is a "struck zither" within the "chordophone" family; the organ, on the other hand, is a "free aerophone," since its sound is created from air passing through a series of pipes.

ELECTRONIC KEYBOARDS

Technology has not been kind to the traditional piano. Whereas once you could find one in almost any self-respecting household, today the instrument has more specialised appeal. As our living environments become ever smaller, fewer of us can justify the space and expense of owning a real piano. As electronics become increasingly advanced, digital keyboards capable of producing convincing piano-like sounds have become more appealing. They are smaller, lighter, cheaper, can be packed away after use, and can often create a wide range of alternative sounds. Their appeal is clear. But in direct competition with the sound created by a traditional acoustic piano, they are in every way inferior.

THE ELECTRONIC AGE

Although we may think of electronic instruments as a modern phenomenon, experimentation with the idea of harnessing electricity for musical uses has been going on for over 200 years. However, it wasn't until Alexander Graham Bell invented the telephone in 1876 that a real breakthrough arrived. Bell showed that sound could be converted to electrical impulses and back again, creating a basic principle on which future electronic instruments would operate. From that point onward, a wide variety of strange and exotic electronic instruments appeared.

THE ELECTRIC PIANO

The concept of an amplified piano was first developed during the 1920s. The initial idea was to fit magnetic pickups to the strings of a traditional piano. The Wurlitzer company, famed for its cinema organs of the 1930s, owned the patent to this idea. In 1954 the first production-line electric piano was launched.

The Wurlitzer EP 100 was based on the idea of a set of vibrating metal reeds. A simplified piano hammer mechanism was used to strike a reed each time a key was pressed. The vibration of the reed passed through a transducer turning it into electrical impulses, which could then be amplified. The pitch of a note was dependent on the length of the metal reed. Fine tuning the early Wurlitzers required each reed to be carefully filed until the pitch was correct.

In 1959, the most famous electric piano of them all came on to the market. The Fender Rhodes was both more reliable and playable than the Wurlitzer. Although it still didn't sound much like a "real" piano, it had a similar feel. During the 1960s and 1970s, both pianos thrived in the worlds of rock, pop and jazz.

THE DIGITAL AGE

In the 1960s, Dr Robert Moog's synthesizer captured the imagination of many keyboard players. However, although these early models were capable of creating piano-like sounds, they had one major drawback – they could only play one note at a time. It wasn't until the late 1970s that polyphonic synthesizers began to appear.

It was the launch of the Yamaha DX7 "polysynth" in 1983 that more or less killed off the electric piano industry overnight.

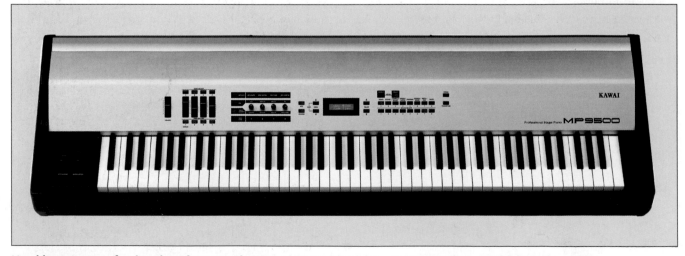

Used by many professional performers, the Kawai Stage Piano has an outstanding sound and playability.

Using a revolutionary new FM synthesis, realistic approximations of other acoustic or electric instruments were possible – at least in the hands of a skilled programmer.

THE ELECTRONIC PIANO

It was the advent of digital sampling (*see below*) that would soon give birth to a new form of piano. The old electric pianos only relied on technology to amplify the low-volume acoustic sounds they made. *Electronic* pianos differ in that they are not mechanical devices. When you press a key this simply switches on a sound; when you release the key, it turns it off. The big difference is that the sound is not synthesized at all. It doesn't use a series of oscillators and filters like Dr Moog's system; it plays back digital recordings of a real piano. The sound can be made more realistic by using multi-samples, each note on the piano consisting of different samples of the original instrument. Thus, pressing the key harder on the digital piano plays back a digital sample of the original piano being played with the same pressure – rather than the same note being played back at different volumes, which was the case with early models.

In truth, with the right kind of amplification, it can be hard to detect the difference between a digital piano and the real

Some modern digital pianos even look like the real thing.

thing. Sound is one thing, but from a player's point of view, it's impossible (or at least impractical) to electronically recreate the "feel" of a concert grand piano. No matter how much invention goes into making the keys respond like an acoustic piano, or the volume and sound react to the most delicate of touches, the result will always be second best.

DIGITAL SAMPLING

One of the most important technical developments in the musical sphere over the past 25 years was the birth of digital sampling. At its simplest, a keyboard equipped with sampling facilities can play back a digital recording of a real instrument. For example, if you feed in a recording of a piano playing Middle C, it can be programmed to replay every time you press Middle C on the keyboard.

Sampling has dominated many areas of modern music since its inception. However, its history can be traced back to the 1960s, and the British-built Mellotron keyboard. This worked in fundamentally the same way as a sampler except that each key of the instrument was linked to a cartridge holding a loop of magnetic tape that contained a recording of a real instrument playing the same note.

The first digital sampling system to reach the commercial market was the Fairlight CMI system, developed in Australia in 1979. Although it was used extensively, at a cost of over $150,000 for a full system, only the wealthiest producers and musicians could afford it.

With the passing of time and rapid developments in technology, it was inevitable that the major Japanese synthesizer manufacturers would develop their own cheaper, user-friendly versions. Nowadays, most sampling functions are carried out on a computer using dedicated sampling software or "plug-in" modules. For example, anyone with a reasonably powerful laptop could run a plug-in module like the East West Bosendorfer 290 Grand Piano *(see below)* which contains multi-samples from one of the most famous pianos ever made. In the context of a recording, with careful use even the keenest ear would be hard-pressed to tell that it wasn't the "real thing" – and, of course, in a sense it *is* the real thing as the musician is triggering recordings of a Bosendorfer Piano.

THE GREAT PIANISTS

Before we embark on the playing section of the book, here is a small selection of some of the most important piano players ever to have lived and worked. We are fortunate in that all of those musicians who were active from the 1920s onward have had their work captured on audio recordings or film of concert performances. But we can only begin to guess at how someone like Franz Liszt – reputed to be the most spectacular soloist the instrument has ever known – might have sounded at his peak. There are, of course, numerous other great instrumentalists not included in this list.

CHARLES-VALENTIN ALKEN *(1813–1888)*

A child prodigy from a musical family, Alken entered the Paris Conservatoire at the age of six, and made his concert debut at twelve. By his early twenties he was widely recognised as France's leading pianist. He could count Chopin among his friends, and was admired by Liszt – it was said that Alken was the only pianist before whom Liszt became nervous of performing.

In 1838, Alken vanished from public view in order to concentrate on composition for the piano. He emerged six years later with some remarkable works, among them the first known musical depiction of a railway train, *Le Chemin de Fer*. After a brief triumphant return to the concert stage, he once again turned his back on performance.

Daniel Barenboim—from child prodigy to virtuoso.

Alken was unfortunate in that much of his finest work was published around the time of the French Revolution, when most of the influential figures in the music world had left Paris. Unlike Liszt, Alken did not use his virtuoso talents to promote his own music, and by the time of his accidental death in 1888, he had already drifted into obscurity.

CLAUDIO ARRAU *(1903–1991)*

Widely regarded as the finest pianist of the twentieth century, Claudio Arrau was born in Chile, and began performing professionally at the age of five. So impressed was the Chilean government that it gave a grant for his entire family to move to Berlin, enabling him to train with the finest teachers. Here he came under the tuition of Martin Krause, a former pupil of Liszt.

Arrau first gained a wider audience in 1927 when he won the famed International Geneva Prize. In the early part of his career he was best known for his Bach renditions, however he is now widely remembered as perhaps the greatest interpreter of Beethoven. His vast discography includes all 32 Beethoven piano sonatas, and five piano concertos, the two Brahms concertos, and the complete works for piano and orchestra by Chopin.

VLADIMIR ASHKENAZY *(b. 1937)*

While a student at the Moscow Conservatory, Ashkenazy took prizes in the 1955 Warsaw Chopin competition, and the Queen Elizabeth in Brussels the following year. It was his victory in the 1962 Tchaikovsky that turned him into an international concert star. The darling of the formidable Soviet music system, in 1963 he caused outrage when he defected to the West. Since the early 1970s his principal achievements have been as an orchestral conductor.

DANIEL BARENBOIM *(b. 1942)*

Born in Buenos Aires in 1942, Barenboim started piano lessons at the age of five with his mother, continuing to study with his father, who remained his only other teacher. He gave his first professional concert at the age of seven, made his debut in Vienna at the age of 10, produced his first gramophone recordings at the age of 14, and a year later made his New York debut under Leopold Stokowski. By his early twenties he had recorded the complete cycles of the piano sonatas of Mozart and Beethoven as well as concertos by Mozart, Beethoven and Brahms.

One of the major names active in the music world today, although Barenboim continues to give concert performances, he is now highly rated for his skills as a conductor.

FREDERIC CHOPIN *(1810–1849)*

It is almost impossible to separate Chopin the composer from Chopin the pianist. All of his music was either written for solo piano, or placed the piano in a central role. As a performer, he was admired for his improvisational ability, and his compositions were often a direct result of this experimentation.

Chopin was able to conjure new sounds from the piano, exploring the full expressive range of the instrument. But although his reputation as a virtuoso pianist is only exceeded by that of Liszt, he was not popular with Paris audiences of his day. The most common criticism was that he played too softly. At the time it was claimed that this was a result of his frailty, but this argument falls down under even the slightest scrutiny. At a time when concert audiences valued showmanship, volume and bluster, Chopin viewed this as vulgarity. His subtlety was simply not appreciated. Having given barely thirty concert performances he retired from the stage, devoting the rest of his life to composition. Dying at the age of 39, his legacy was arguably the greatest body of work ever written for the piano.

MUZIO CLEMENTI *(1752–1832)*

Born into a poor Italian musical family, Clementi was adopted by an English aristocrat who recognised his brilliance on the harpsichord and organ. In 1770 he created a sensation with his London piano debut.

Although the piano was still a relatively new instrument by the turn of the century, Clementi was the first significant player to break with conventions regarding the use of legato and dynamics. Although his own works are largely neglected, as a composer he was an influence on some of the most important names of the century that followed – not least of whom was Beethoven.

To some scholars, Clementi was the godfather of the piano. He was an important teacher, his students included John Field and Giacomo Meyerbeer. His 1817 book of studies *Gradus ad Parnassum* is still in use today. And he even turned his hand to music publishing and also manufactured a range of pianos that bore his name.

Skilful in his business affairs, unlike many of the great pianists of the nineteenth century, Clementi died a very wealthy man.

Not only a great virtuoso, Frédéric Chopin was also one of the piano's most significant composers.

ALFRED CORTOT *(1877–1962)*

One of the piano's most important figures in the early part of the twentieth century, Alfred Cortot enjoyed an unusually industrious career. In 1907, at the age of 30, he was appointed professor at the Paris Conservatoire; twelve years later he founded his own school, the Ecole Normale de Paris. At this time he was the most prominent teacher in the world – his students included some of the best-known pianists of the century. In a related sphere, he prepared some eighty editions of the music of Schumann, Liszt, Chopin and many others. These are filled with annotations and helpful hints for overcoming technical problems.

As a pianist, Cortot was also massively popular around the world's great concert halls. An elegant, yet unpredictable musician, his busy life meant that he seldom had time to practise; his performances were sometimes criticised as sloppy, even if they rarely failed to thrill.

During the Second World War, Cortot accepted the post of High Commissioner of Fine Arts in the Vichy government. Branded as a "collaborator" after the war, it was not until the 1950s that Cortot was able resume all of his musical activities.

JOHN FIELD (1782–1837)

An important composer of the early Romantic period, John Field also enjoyed considerable success as a concert pianist. In 1793, Field entered an apprenticeship with Muzio Clementi. Although he received valuable training in piano technique and composition, his treatment during this time was perhaps questionable: Field was forced to work as a sales demonstrator in Clementi's piano warehouse, and had several of his early compositions published anonymously by his master.

In 1802, Clementi took Field on an extended continental tour, where his playing deeply impressed the discerning audiences of Paris and Vienna. But although the two of them performed on the same concert programmes, Clementi would generally claim the entire performance fee for himself.

It was while performing in St Petersburg, that Field freed himself of the burden of Clementi's exploitation. Here he met his first important patron, General Marklovsky, and chose to remain in Russia. He was immediately embraced by the upper echelons of Russian society. By the time Clementi visited St Petersburg four years later, he was surprised to find that his former apprentice was now a performer and composer of great celebrity. Indeed Mikhail Glinka – known to many as "the father of Russian music" – declared Field's playing to be "like great drops of rain, poured over the keys like pearls on velvet".

Earl Hines, the father of jazz piano.

GLENN GOULD (1932–1982)

One of the most intriguing figures in the modern history of classical music, Canadian pianist Glenn Gould had the extraordinary ability to thrill and outrage audiences almost in equal measures. At the age of three it became clear that he possessed exceptional musical aptitude, and his formal studies began. At the age of ten, he began lessons at the Royal Conservatory of Music in Toronto.

Following his first public recital in 1947, one reviewer hailed him as a genius. Throughout the 1950s he developed a reputation as a provocative interpreter of the standard piano repertoire. His 1955 recording of Bach's *Goldberg Variations* was a best-seller, and established him as a fully mature international artist. Then, in 1964, his concert career seemingly flourishing, Gould announced that he would make no further public appearances.

His sudden decision created a reputation for eccentricity. In fact, Gould did not even think of himself primarily as a pianist; he was equally committed to writing, broadcasting, composing, conducting and experimenting with technology.

EARL HINES (1903–1983)

Earl "Fatha" Hines has been described as the first modern jazz pianist. Emerging in Chicago in the early 1920s, his style differed from other pianists of the period in his use of what were then considered unusual rhythms and accents. As far as sheer

Glenn Gould, one of music's most interesting figures.

technique was concerned, he was as far ahead of his rivals as his friend and collaborator, Louis Armstrong, was on the trumpet.

In 1928, Hines recorded his first ten piano solos. These stand as milestones in the art of jazz piano. That same year, Hines debuted with his first big band. He would continue as a bandleader until 1948, introducing the world to such talents as vocalist Billy Eckstine and bebop pioneers Dizzy Gillespsie and Charlie Parker.

Hines is remembered for his awesome technique and talent for improvisation – his horn-like phrasing and rhythms influenced popular jazz through the swing era.

JOSEF HOFMANN (1876–1957)

One of the most noted (and exploited) of all child musical prodigies, Hofmann was purported to have been equally gifted in the realms of mathematics, science and mechanics. By the age of seven he had already toured the world as a pianist. In 1887 he visited Thomas Edison's laboratory, where he became the first ever professional musician to have a performance recorded.

His considerable playing talent was harnessed when, in 1892, he became the sole pupil of Anton Rubinstein. Although Hofmann enjoyed a successful concert career with a fanatical following (no less a figure than Rachmaninov regarded him as the greatest living pianist), such a varied mind had no intention of focusing wholly on the piano. He was also a prolific – if hardly gifted – composer, publishing his work under the pseudonym Michel Dvorsky; an important teacher, becoming the first director of the now prestigious Curtis Institute of Music in Philadelphia; and he also found time to patent more than 70 inventions, including a design for the first windshield wiper.

VLADIMIR HOROWITZ (1904–1989)

Ukrainian virtuoso Horowitz made his solo debut recital in Kiev in 1920. With a vast repertoire at his disposal, in 1924 he is reputed to have given 25 professional recitals in Leningrad alone, never once repeating a single work. He established an international reputation in 1926 when he was given the opportunity to perform Tchaikovsky's *Piano Concerto No. 1* with the Hamburg Philharmonic – having been given barely an hour's notice. By the time he reached Paris later that year, he was a sensation, his concerts selling out immediately.

As a performer, one of the regular criticisms to be levelled at Horowitz was his over-willingness to please audiences. This, it was said, could sometimes lead to astonishing displays of technique for its own sake.

His concert repertoire tended to concentrate on the traditional "virtuoso" works of Chopin, Schumann, and Liszt. However, he was also one of the first important players of the twentieth century to champion "modern" composers, most notably Prokofiev, Rachmaninov and Barber.

The breathtaking virtuoso, Vladimir Horowitz.

FRANZ LISZT (1811–1886)

When discussing the history and development of the piano – and in particular, playing technique – one name towers above all others: Franz Liszt. The greatest of the nineteenth-century composer-virtuosi, by the time of his death in 1886, Liszt had written over 1,300 works and had carved out a reputation as a performer that remains second to none. He was the first artist to carry the instrument's potential to its limits.

Born in Hungary in 1811, Liszt began to study the piano at the age of six. With the financial assistance of a number of Hungarian aristocrats for whom the young child had performed, he and his family moved to Vienna, where he studied under Carl Czerny. Following the death of his father, at the age of 16, Liszt took up long-term residence in Paris, where his playing was beginning to attract notice.

In 1831, Liszt saw a performance by the violinist Niccolo Paganini. The experience had a profound impact on the young pianist; he resolved to apply the same levels of showmanship and pyrotechnics to the piano. He withdrew for a short period, devoting himself to a practice regime of obsessive proportions, sometimes playing for up to fourteen hours a day. He emerged as arguably the greatest technician ever to have lived.

Thereafter it can be difficult to separate the musician from the mythology. Liszt's private life in particular seems to have been lifted straight from the pages of *Don Juan*. His appetite for brief liaisons was seemingly insatiable. And his affairs with Countess Marie d'Agoult (with whom he fathered three children) and the Russian Princess Carolyne Sayn-Wittgenstein created a scandal. Even as a concert performer, Liszt was evidently able to induce near-hysteria among the women in his audiences.

In 1847, at the age of 35, he astonished the music world by announcing his retirement from the concert platform. He took up a position as court conductor in Weimar, where he concentrated on composition and teaching. In 1861, he went to Rome to take religious studies, and in 1865 he was ordained as Abbé Liszt. Given his former proclivities, this development must have surprised many.

As a performer, Liszt was every bit the "pop star" of his day. It was he more than anyone else who created the template for the modern concert pianist.

DINU LIPATTI *(1917–1950)*

Another of the instrument's great child prodigies, although Lipatti had virtually no formal education, his childhood feats – he was giving charity performances by the age of four – brought him to the attention of professors at the Bucharest Conservatory, who gave him private tuition. It was not until 1934 that he played outside his native Romania, when he entered an international competition in Vienna. One of the judges, French pianist Alfred Cortot *(see page 17)*, was so impressed that he resigned from the jury in protest when Lipatti was awarded only second prize. He subsequently invited the young pianist to study with him at the Ecole Nationale de Musique in Paris.

Over the next decade Lipatti's reputation continued to grow as he became widely appreciated for the sensitivity of his interpretations. Preparing for a concert tour of America in 1948 he was diagnosed as suffering from leukemia. Two years later he was dead. Hailed by the French composer Poulenc as "an artist of divine spirituality", Lipatti's passing at the age of 33 robbed the music world of a unique voice.

IGNACE PADEREWSKI *(1860–1941)*

Arguably the most popular concert pianist of all time, by 1900, Paderewski was a household name throughout Europe and the United States. His reputation as a performer rests on his sensitive interpretations of the works of fellow countryman, Chopin. An ardent patriot, he briefly headed Polish governments in 1919 and 1940. He amassed a huge fortune – in 1914 alone he earned the equivalent of £1,250,000 for a ninety-date tour – most of which he donated to the service of Poland and Jewish refugees.

SERGEI RACHMANINOV *(1873–1943)*

Rachmaninov studied under the austere tutelage of Nikolai Zverev at the Moscow Conservatory, from where he graduated at the age of 19 with the highest possible honours in composition. His *Prelude in C sharp minor*, written that year, made him almost an overnight sensation. He was also a superb pianist, attributable in part to his unusually large hands – he had a stretch of one-and-a-half octaves, and much of his own piano music reflected this ability.

Massively successful as a composer-performer, his career was upturned by political events in his homeland. After the Bolshevik Revolution of 1917 he and his family were forced into exile. Not well-known outside of Russia – he had made one successful concert tour of the United States in 1909 – Rachmaninov, at the age of 44, relaunched himself as a concert pianist. For the first time in his professional life he found

Sergei Rachmaninov – composer turned concert pianist.

himself predominantly playing the works of other composers.

His personalised interpretations were not appreciated by some critics, but he was extraordinarily popular with concert audiences. Almost all of his important recordings from the 1930s are still widely available.

ANTON RUBINSTEIN *(1829–1894)*

A seminal figure in the history of Russian music, Rubinstein was an outstanding concert pianist – in fact he was widely regarded as second only to the great Liszt. Born and schooled in Russia, Rubinstein's formal music training then shifted to Vienna. But unable to settle outside of his homeland, he soon returned to St. Petersburg from where he launched a dazzling concert career. His international reputation was sealed in 1872 with a fabulously successful tour of the United States.

Rubinstein was Russia's first internationally successful musician, and the first to achieve equal status as a pianist and a composer. During his lifetime, his own works enjoyed great popularity and critical acclaim, although are quite obscure.

His enduring claim to fame lies in his critical importance to the development of music education within Russia. He was responsible for laying the groundwork for Russia's noted tertiary educational system for the training of musicians, and founded the St. Petersburg Conservatory. He also established the use of Western structural forms in Russian music.

ARTUR RUBINSTEIN *(1887–1976)*

Born in the Polish city of Lodz, Artur Rubinstein studied in Warsaw and Berlin, making an astonishing debut in 1900 with the Berlin Philharmonic. His long and distinguished concert career came to an end in 1976 when, at the age of 89, he gave his farewell performance.

Naturally gifted and possessing an extraordinary memory, the young Rubinstein was a passionate and temperamental player. Never scared to take risks, if a few notes suffered en route he viewed it as a price worth paying. Late on in his career, he remarked: "On stage I will take a chance. There has to be an element of daring in great music-making. These younger ones, they are too cautious. They take the music out of their pockets instead of their hearts".

For many, Rubinstein was the century's finest interpreter of Chopin, although, typically, neither was he without his detractors. He was also a tireless champion of many contemporary composers – Stravinsky, Prokofiev and Villa Lobos all benefited from his patronage. Famously, when one audience booed him after he had performed Ravel's evidently controversial *Valses nobles et sentimentales*, he responded by repeating the piece in full during his encore.

In an altogether too "serious" musical age, Rubinstein stood out for the sheer joy in his playing. He loved the piano, he loved the music he played, and he was always able to communicate his passion to his audience.

ANDRAS SCHIFF *(b. 1953)*

Born in Budapest, Hungary, Schiff began piano lessons at the age of five with Elisabeth Vadász and continued his studies at the Liszt Academy under Professor Pál Kadosa. His recordings of the works of Bach, Mozart and Schumann are among the finest to emerge during the age of digital recording.

Widely honoured, in 1991, Schiff was awarded the Bartók Prize, followed by the "Claudio Arrau Memorial Medal" in 1994. Two years later, he received the highest Hungarian distinction, the "Kossuth Prize".

ARTUR SCHNABEL *(1882–1951)*

"The notes I handle no better than most pianists. But the pauses between the notes… ah, that is where the art resides". Born in Lipnick, Poland, Artur Schnabel enjoys a reputation as one of the "intellectuals" of the piano. Beginning his concert career at the end of the nineteenth century, a period in which audiences still looked for dazzling virtuoso performances, the highly individualistic Schnabel instead chose to concentrate on Beethoven and Schubert. The latter was a particularly bold step in that Schubert at this time was a largely forgotten figure. (In 1928, on the centenary of Schubert's death, no less a figure than Rachmaninov claimed not only had he never heard nor played Schubert's piano sonatas, he was not even aware of their existence!)

Although extremely highly rated by other musicians, initailly, Schnabel was not popular with audiences, preferring to keep

The infectious passion and joy of Artur Rubinstein.

Hungarian star András Schiff is one of the most respected pianists to have emerged over the past two decades.

them at a distance. His concerts were serious events, with no crowd-pleasing favourites and no encores. He is famously quoted as saying that there are only two different types of audience… "one that coughs and one that doesn't".

His uncompromising stance made him a major influence on the generation of pianists that followed. His pupils have claimed that they learned as much from him about life as playing the piano. He remains something of a cult figure among lovers of piano music.

CLARA SCHUMANN *(1819–1896)*

The daughter of noted teacher Freidrich Wieck, Clara Schumann was the first woman to establish a major international career as a concert pianist. By her 25th birthday she had performed at most of the major concert houses across Europe. Inevitably, at a time when women enjoyed considerably less individual freedom, her marriage to the great composer Robert Schumann meant the subordination of her career to his. She was not able to practise when her husband was composing, and there is certain evidence that he was somewhat envious of her public success.

Nevertheless, she played an important role in popularising much of his music. She was also an important role model for many female performers that followed: four of her pupils – Natalie Janotha, Ilona Eibenschütz, Fanny Davis and Adelina de Lara – all enjoyed some success during the late nineteenth century.

ART TATUM *(1910–1956)*

The 1930s saw the emergence of jazz music's greatest keyboard virtuoso. Almost blind from birth, Art Tatum started out as a stride player in the style of ragtime player Fats Waller. But his gifts were remarkable: not only did he have perfect pitch, but from only a single listen he could evidently play back any tune he heard in any key. The most awesome aspect of his playing was a startling technique that placed him in the same league as Liszt. A typical Tatum solo saw the most basic of melodies embellished with fearsome complexity.

In 1953 – three years before his death – Tatum embarked on a major series of recordings which resulted in the 13-album set, *The Tatum Solo Masterpieces*. This contains some of the finest examples of unaccompanied piano ever recorded.

PART TWO
PLAYING THE PIANO

GETTING PREPARED

By the time you've worked your way through Part Two of *Total Piano Tutor* you will have achieved the following: a firm grasp of all of the essential piano-playing techniques; the ability to read any piece of written music; and a good grasp of music theory. The first section of Part Two covers some important basic ground which really should be addressed before you actually begin playing: selecting the right instrument, adopting a correct playing posture, and the fundamentals of reading music. This is followed by eight self-contained, easy-to-follow lessons, each one illustrated by examples from classic works by such noted composers as Beethoven, Mozart, Offenbach, Schubert, Schumann, Handel and Bach, many of which have been specially arranged for this book.

GETTING THE RIGHT HARDWARE

There was once a time when no self-respecting household was complete without a piano sitting in the corner of the living room. Before the advent of television, hi-fi and computer games, families would gather around the piano to provide entertainment for each other. But times change. With space at an ever-increasing premium for most town and city dwellers, the idea of having a great big wooden box taking up a sizable chunk of a small room is no longer something that can be taken for granted. All of this means that most people who now want to learn to play the piano have to go out and buy one for themselves.

The first elementary decision you have to face is whether to buy a traditional acoustic piano or some kind of electronic keyboard. Deciding what kind of instrument to choose can be a tough experience for a beginner, so whatever direction you choose, it's always a good idea if you involve someone who has experience in these matters – especially if you intend buying second-hand.

SOUND

A good-quality piano will *always* sound better than even the best digital approximation. *But*, a cheap, ancient, badly-neglected upright piano may sound dreadful – the playing action may be inconsistent, and the strings may be in such poor condition that it cannot be tuned properly.

ENVIRONMENT

What kind of place do you live in? Can you afford to devote permanent space to a piano?

BUDGET

A brand new, modern upright piano will cost you more than the most expensive digital piano on the market. Second-hand pianos may be bought for reasonable prices, but MUST be chosen with great care (*see opposite page*). If you're considering a grand piano, first take a careful look at your bank balance: this type of piano is for the well-healed. Even the cheapest new grand piano will set you back around the same cost as a decent sports car. And don't forget the hidden costs. Transporting a piano is a notoriously perilous job. It can take three experienced removal men to carry even the smallest piano up a flight of stairs. Moving a grand piano is a highly specialised skill that will cost hundreds (maybe even thousands) of pounds.

VERSATILITY

What do you want to do with your piano skills? If you are interested in playing pop, rock, or electronic dance music then a good digital workstation (*see opposite page*) may be a more practical option than a dedicated piano (or even a digital piano that can only produce piano sounds). Since few music venues can be guaranteed to provide a piano these days, it also makes the possibility of performing in public that much more practical.

CHOOSING A PIANO

First decide on your budget. The best advice here is to spend as much as you can reasonably afford. You may be able to pick up a broken-down old upright piano for virtually nothing, but if the keys don't work properly and it doesn't stay in tune, then you might as well not bother: even good players will make a terrible sound on such an instrument.

Assessing the value of a piano is something of a skill, so when viewing a potential purchase you really should take someone who at least knows a little about the instrument. If you're buying second-hand, here are a few points that are worth considering:

APPEARANCE

You can tell a lot from an instrument's external appearance. While a scratched or broken piano will look horrible as a piece of furniture – which is usually a consideration for most homes – it can also provide you with a clue that the instrument might have been abused.

SOUND

Play each of the keys independently. They should provide a uniform feel throughout. When you apply different levels of pressure to each key you should be able to detect the volume changing consistently. You should also listen out for rattling and scratching noises when you work through the notes. These can indicate that something is wrong with the hammer mechanisms.

TUNING

Try to ascertain if the piano is in tune. You can do this by taking a standard tuning device and testing out the pitch of the note A below Middle C. Pianos rarely go out of tune in a consistent manner, but if a piano has been subjected to extremes of cold and damp, the strings can easily rust, making it impossible to achieve concert tuning.

ELECTRONIC KEYBOARDS

One of the hardest things to accept when deciding to buy an electronic keyboard is the rate at which new technology loses its value: a brand new thousand-pound keyboard may well have a resale value of less than half of that amount within just a few months. For this reason alone, novices are advised to start out with a second-hand instrument. If you don't like that idea, there are plenty of new bargains to be found when music stores sell off last year's models at "knock-down" prices.

Since there are so many different types of electronic keyboards (*see below*), the buyer is often spoilt for choice. A good starting point is to buy a music technology magazine. Not only do they review new equipment, but they will also get you accustomed to the language of music technology. Advertisements are also useful in that they can provide you with a good feel for the instruments and features you can expect for your budget; you can also gauge resale prices from the second-hand pages.

ELECTRONIC KEYBOARDS

Electronic keyboards come in a wide variety of shapes and sizes, so you need to ensure that anything you buy matches your requirements in full. They can be broadly grouped into four categories: home keyboards; digital pianos; polyphonic "workstation" synths; and monophonic synths. You can immediately discount the last of those options: since a monophonic keyboard can only play one note at a time it won't be much use for learning to play the piano.

DIGITAL PIANOS have largely replaced acoustic instruments in the home. They usually contain a limited range of piano-based voices that are created by digital samples – recordings of an acoustic piano. This means they are capable of producing very realistic sounds. Additionally, the best models are built with weighted or wooden keys to give the effect of playing a real piano. Some, like the Kawai featured on page 15, even look quite convincing.

HOME KEYBOARDS represent the cheapest option, but may not be the best route to follow. A typical home keyboard offers a variety of preset sounds, which are usually cheap, synthesized takes on acoustic instruments. They usually also feature a built-in amplifier and speaker. This means that everything you need to make music is in place. However, more often than not, the keys themselves have a cheap, plastic feel to them that makes playing anything too demanding an impossibility. The amplification system also usually leaves much to be desired.

WORKSTATION SYNTHESIZERS are the most useful keyboards from an all-round point of view. Some models feature multiple programmable sounds, digital samples of acoustic instruments and even on-board sequencing facilities. However, most pianists tend to find the quality and "feel" of the keyboard unsatisfactory.

THE RIGHT POSTURE

Before you start to play it's important that you adopt an appropriate posture. Although to some degree this may be affected by the type of music you play, there are basically just two possibilities: either you sit down or you stand up. Although playing keyboards from the standing position is commonplace in rock, pop and other types of electronic music, you'll never find a classical pianist working in this way.

THE SITTING POSITION

Sitting down is by far the best way to play effectively. It gives maximum control over the hands and fingers, and allows the feet freedom of movement over the pedals. The key to getting the right posture is in sitting at the correct height in relation to the piano keyboard. An adjustable stool is a worthwhile purchase for this purpose. For the perfect position, when seated with both feet flat on the floor, your thighs should be in a broadly horizontal position.

A piano has a fixed height (3 feet 2 inches in the case of a concert grand), however, an electronic keyboard can be operated in any position, from a table, chair or sofa to a bed. Although versatile, this is not necessarily to be recommended. Try to get in the habit of having your keyboard in the same position whenever you play it. This will help your fingers to acquaint themselves instinctively with the fingerboard. For this reason, if you have an electronic keyboard it's also a good idea to acquire a sturdy, purpose-built, adjustable stand. Set it up so that when you are sitting, your forearms are in a horizontal position when your fingers touch the keyboard. This is an ideal angle for relaxing the elbows and wrists as well as controlling the movement of the hands.

STANDING UP

Whether standing or sitting, most keyboard players leave their instruments set up at the same height. This means that when playing in the standing position, the forearm is naturally higher and so the wrist has to be bent back at an angle. This method can place undue strain on the wrist muscles. Of course it would be possible to raise the overall height of the keyboard or alter its angle so that the keys lean away from the player, but this can look unusual or obscure the musicians in a live situation, which has to be a consideration in pop and rock gigs.

OTHER CONSIDERATIONS

Give some thought to the kind of clothing you wear when playing keyboards. Bulky or excessively loose clothing can easily restrict your movement. Although rings and other such jewellry shouldn't cause any obstruction, they may create an imbalance in weight among the fingers.

FINGER POSTURE

The precise manner in which the fingers strike the keys is largely a matter of choice. The approach shown at the top of the page is fairly standard in that the fingers are very slightly clawed but – most important of all – they touch the keys with the pads of the finger. Because of the way the human hand has evolved, the thumb has to come into contact with the piano keys using the side of the pad – but it still falls short of touching the nail.

The fingers should come into contact with the keyboard at an angle of 20–30°: less than that, and it can be difficult to control pressure; if it's more, then the fingernails may start rattling against the keys, which is obviously not ideal.

RELAXATION

It's quite common among novices to adopt a very tense posture. But to get yourself into the ideal state for playing it's important to relax the muscles. As Frédéric Chopin was known to have told his students: *souplesse avant tout* – "suppleness before everything".

It can be extremely tiring sitting at a keyboard for long periods, and consequently very easy for the back and shoulders to become hunched. You should do your utmost to avoid this type of posture. When playing, always try to sit straight, with firm shoulders pulled back and the chest pushed forward. This creates an ideal sense of balance at the piano.

Before you begin playing, it's always a good idea to relax your arms and hands before bringing them in position on the keyboard. On the right you will find a selection of simple exercises aimed at relaxing the muscles.

- Sit down at your keyboard.
- Close your eyes.
- Slowly breathe in through your nose, and then exhale quickly through the mouth.
- Repeat ten times.
- Drop your arms to your side so that they hang loosely from the shoulder.
- With your arms still in position, slowly stretch your fingers out as widely as you can and hold them in position for ten seconds before releasing them to their natural positions.
- Repeat this exercise ten times.
- Now wriggle your hands quite vigorously from your wrists for about ten seconds.
- Let your arms hang loosely from your shoulders again for about ten seconds

THE PEDALS

All "real" pianos have at least two foot pedals. Often these are referred to as being either "loud" or "soft", but in truth this is not strictly accurate.

The most important pedal is the SUSTAIN, which is usually controlled by the right foot. When the pedal is held down, the dampers on the piano strings are lifted up so that the notes are allowed to ring for longer.

The SOFT pedal on a grand piano is technically known as *una corda* ("one string"). When no pedals are being pressed, and a hammer strikes a note, it actually plays a number of different strings which have all been tuned to the same pitch. The soft pedal shifts the entire mechanism of the piano – including the keyboard and hammers – to the right, so that the hammers strike one string less. Although by definition the sound is lower in volume, the main purpose of this pedal is to alter the tonal quality of the notes being played. (Since the piano is a highly responsive instrument, a note's volume is governed by the pressure with which the key is pressed.)

On a concert grand piano, a third pedal is fitted between the other two. This is called the SOSTENUTO, and is an alternative sustain pedal.

It's important to understand that these pedals are not simple "on-off" switches. They can be used to varying degrees to produce a wide array of very subtle effects.

Foot pedals can also be used on some electronic keyboards. These are usually crude approximations of the two principal piano pedals: the sustain pedal simply lets notes linger while the pedal is pressed; at best, the soft pedal "dulls" the tone of sound.

One foot pedal, however, which is unique to certain electronic keyboards – most commonly electronic organs – is the VOLUME pedal. Rather than simply being activated by pushing the foot down, this pedal has a rocking motion that can be fixed in any position by removing the foot. As the name suggests, it simply controls the overall output level.

NOISE CONTROL

Although it often seems to be a low priority for many people, one thing you really should consider is the issue of how much noise you are making. No matter how satisfying you find learning the piano, you can be sure that it's going to be a good deal less fun for those around you. (Come on, would you *really* want to listen to someone struggling to play a C major scale for hours on end?) So try to keep your family, neighbours or flatmates in mind when you are playing.

You can avoid becoming Public Nuisance Number One by keeping your practising to civilised hours. But if you live in a building with paper-thin partitioning walls, and you *really* have to play until the early hours of the morning, make sure that you do it on an electronic keyboard with the volume at a considerate level – or better still, use a pair of headphones.

READING MUSIC

Music is notated using a system of lines and symbols. If you are completely new to the idea of written music, the next four pages will give you a brief overview of what it's all about. It may seem a bit daunting at first, but don't panic – music works in an *extremely* logical way. (Indeed, the German philosopher and mathematician Gottfried Wilhelm Leibniz [1646–1716] famously noted: "The pleasure we obtain from music comes from counting, but counting unconsciously. Music is nothing but unconscious arithmetic.")

THE NOTE NAMES

Before we start to look at written music, we first need to clarify the most basic of principles. Think of a simple song that everyone knows, for example "When The Saints Go Marching In". If you sing the first line of the tune – "Oh, when the saints…" – you will notice that it contains four different notes. This is because each note has a different PITCH. Each of these notes can be scientifically defined in terms of the frequency of its soundwaves. This means that the pitch of any note is fixed.

OCTAVE INTERVALS

All Western music is made up of twelve different notes – that means twelve fixed pitches. These are best viewed as the notes of a piano keyboard (*see below*). Notes increase in pitch as you move from left to right along the keyboard. The white notes on the keyboard are named from A to G. Each of the black notes can have two possible names, depending on their musical context – we'll talk some more about those in a moment.

If you look at the way the notes are named you will see that these sequences repeat themselves. When you get to G, the next white note along the keyboard is once again called A. Although this has the same name, it clearly has a higher pitch than the previous A in the sequence. If you play both notes, one after the other, you will hear that in spite of the different pitches, they are in fact the same note. This special relationship is called an OCTAVE – scientifically speaking, doubling the frequency of any note creates the same note one octave higher in pitch.

WEBSITES

If you have access to the Internet, you may find some of the sites listed below of interest. They variously contain tips on playing and practising, as well as MIDI files of many of the most famous piano works ever composed.

The Classical Music Archives
www.classicalarchives.com/index.html
Piano 300
www.piano300.si.edu
The Piano Page
www.ptg.org
Piano Technicians' Guild
www.ptg.org/
Practicespot
http://www.practicespot.com/home.php

SHARP AND FLATS

The interval between any two adjacent notes is called a SEMITONE. This represents one-twelfth of an octave. In terms of the white keys, B and C are a semitone apart, as are E and F. However, the other white keys are two semitones apart. This is usually referred to as a TONE. If you move a semitone in either direction from these notes, you will play a black key. These can be given names relative to the notes on either side. For example, the black note between F and G can

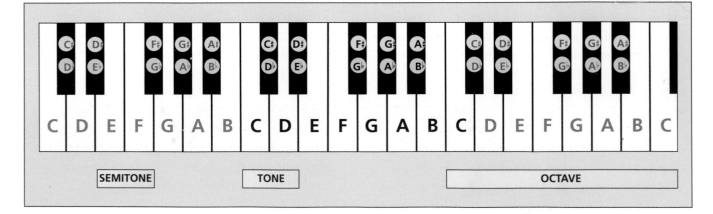

be called "F sharp" (which is written as F♯) or G flat (notated as G♭). The term "sharp" means to raise the pitch of a note by a semitone, thus F♯ is the note F raised by a semitone. Similarly, the term flat means to lower a note by a semitone – so G♭ is the note G that has been lowered by a semitone. Notes such as these can be referred to as ENHARMONIC. It is also possible to have double sharps and double flats; these raise or lower the note by a tone respectively.

STANDARD MUSIC NOTATION

Music is traditionally written on a five-line grid known as a STAFF (or a STAVE). A variety of symbols can be positioned on and between the lines of the staff to indicate the pitch and duration of a single note.

Musical instruments such as the piano have a very wide range of notes – a concert grand can encompass over seven octaves. As such, these notes cannot all be fitted within a single five-line staff. Therefore, a staff can be given a unique range of notes by positioning a symbol at the start of the music. Notes that are predominantly above Middle C on a piano are positioned on a "treble" staff, which is prefixed by a treble clef (𝄞); notes predominantly below Middle C are positioned on a staff prefixed by a bass clef (𝄢). For this reason, piano music is invariably written over two concurrent staves.

THE TREBLE CLEF

The clef defines the notes on and between each line on the staff. For a treble clef, the notes on the lines are fixed as E, G, B, D and F. The notes between the lines are F, A, C and E. If you look at the two staves below you can see that each of these notes is represented by a circular symbol. You will later discover that the appearance of these symbols will change in accordance with the length of the note, although it is the position of the circle – the HEAD of the note – on the staff that always defines the pitch of the note.

We can see how the white notes are shown on the staff, but what about the enharmonic black notes? These appear on the line or space after which they are named and are shown with either a flat or sharp symbol to the immediate left of the head of the note.

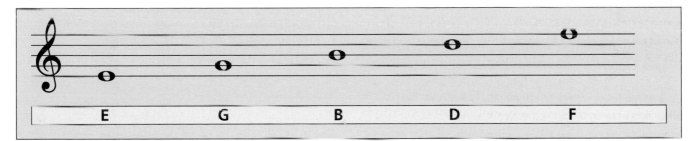

REMEMBERING THE NOTE NAMES

Learning the names of the notes on the lines and spaces of the staff is fundamental to being able to read music. At first it may take a while to get used to interpreting the positions of these symbols – later they will become instinctive.

A commonly used trick to memorise the notes on the lines and spaces of the treble clef is to use a mnemonic phrase. This is an easy-to-remember expression in which the first letter of each word represents each note. For the notes on the lines, use the phrase "Eat Good Bread Dear Father." For the spaces in between you can use the word "FACE." (Remember that they refer to the note names from the bottom of the staff upward.)

EAT	=	E	F
GOOD	=	G	A
BREAD	=	B	C
DEAR	=	D	E
FATHER	=	F	

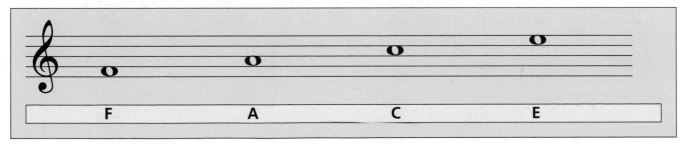

THE BASS CLEF

By replacing the treble clef with a bass clef, the notes on the lines and spaces of that staff take on different names and pitches. By definition, the notes on the bass clef are lower in pitch than their treble counterparts: the note E on the third space of the bass clef (*see below*) is exactly one octave below the note E on the first line of the treble clef. You can remember the notes on the lines

of the bass clef using the phrase "GOOD BOYS DESERVE FUN ALWAYS", and the spaces with "A COW EATS GRASS".

GOOD	=	G		**A**	=	A
BOYS	=	B		**COW**	=	C
DESERVE	=	D		**EATS**	=	E
FUN	=	F		**GRASS**	=	G
ALWAYS	=	A				

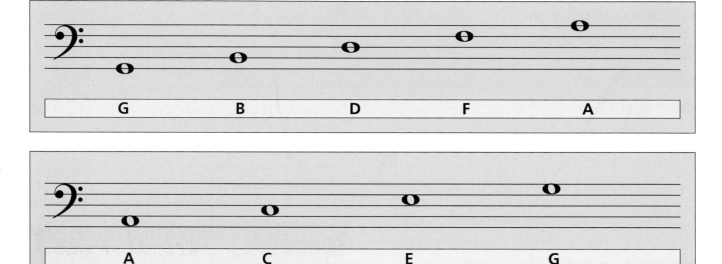

CONCERT PITCH AND MIDDLE C

Sound is produced by the vibration of air waves. The pitch of any note is defined by the number of vibrations that take place every second. The standard unit of measurement for vibrations-per-second is the hertz (Hz).

If you sit at the middle of a piano and look down, the note "C" before you is known as MIDDLE C. It's so called because it's notated on the first ledger line beneath the treble staff, and the first ledger line above the bass staff. In musical terms, the pitch of any note is governed by its relationship to a reference source. Since Western music works in semitone intervals that reference pitch is critical only in ensuring that the different instruments are in tune with one another. However, since 1939, the US and Western Europe have agreed an absolute value for Middle C of 256 Hz. This is because the reference note known as CONCERT PITCH – which is A above Middle C – is measured as 440 Hz.

Why 440 Hz? The measurement is arbitrary. Over the past five centuries it has varied between 400 Hz and 455 Hz. Even today, the norm in Eastern European is 444 Hz.

BEYOND THE STAVES

Because the piano has a wider range of notes than any other musical instrument, works composed specifically for the piano or other keyboards are nearly always written over two concurrent staves. A BRACKET joins the two staves indicating that they are to be played simultaneously. As a general rule, the left hand is used to play the notes on the bass staff, while the right hand plays the notes on the treble staff, although this is by no means always the case.

LEDGER LINES

The problem with the staves as you've seen them so far is that they can only represent a range of nine pitches: from E on the bottom line to F on the top line of the treble clef; and from G on the bottom line to A on the top line of the bass clef. It should be immediately obvious that even the simplest music may well require notes outside of these ranges.

This problem can be overcome using LEDGER LINES – short lines added to notes that run "over the edge" of the staff.

To see how this works, look at the two staves across the page. These illustrate the way in which the additional ledger lines can be extended above and below the five treble staff

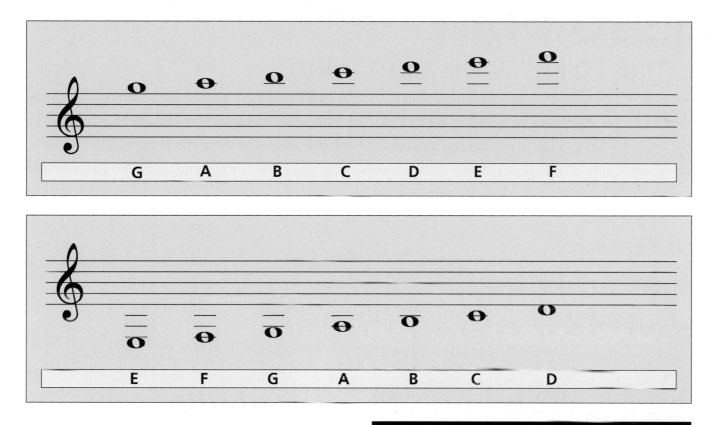

lines to cover a range of more than two octaves. The same principles can also be applied to the notes on the bass clef.

ALTERNATIVES TO LEDGER LINES

Although ledger lines are useful, they can be confusing if they are used with lengthy sequences of notes. It may be that an entire movement or piece of music shifts into a completely different REGISTER, or octave range. When this happens, music can become difficult to interpret if ledger lines are used. There are several solutions to this problem.

Where notes intended to be played with the left hand appear well above the normal range of the bass clef, the most common practice is simply to insert a treble clef on to the staff. This has the effect of redefining all of the notes that follow. When the music resumes its normal register, a bass clef is positioned at the start of the sequence of notes. The same principle can be adopted for music when notes on the treble clef fall into the range of the bass clef.

Another common alternative is to use the *ottava* symbol. This is shown as either **8** or **8v,** and is followed by a dotted line marking out the range of notes. If it appears above the notes, they have to be raised by an octave; if it appears below the notes then they should be lowered by an octave. An example of this can be found in Tchaikovsky's "The Dance of the Sugar Plum Fairy" from the *Nutcracker Suite* (*see pages 126–129*), during which several sequences are played over two octaves above Middle C.

HANDLING MUSIC THEORY

There is nothing fundamentally difficult about music theory: it doesn't really amount to much more than simple arithmetic. For most people, learning to read music is rather like learning a language that uses an unfamiliar alphabet. When Westerners encounter Russian or Japanese for the first time, they may be able to pick up some basic phrases within a few days, but the skill of being able to recognise those words when they are written down takes a good deal longer. Similarly, the ability to SIGHT-READ – that's the skill of being able to see a piece of music and immediately sing or play it back – will only come with time. And that inevitably means practice. If you want your sight-reading abilities to develop alongside your piano playing you will need to take on some additional study.

Don't try to race your way through the book. Space out your lessons. In between times, try to get hold of some published sheet music and apply the things you have taught yourself to "real" examples of written music. You'll be surprised by how quickly you can develop your sight-reading skills in this way. All it takes is as little as FIVE MINUTES A DAY reading through ANY piece of written music, marking down the note names and their time values.

LESSON ONE
GETTING TO KNOW THE RIGHT HAND

The aims of the exercises and examples shown in this lesson are threefold: first, to get your fingers moving; second, to get your brain recognising notes; and third, to get you making some vaguely musical sounds. Getting your fingers used to moving correctly is essential if you are to play the piano to any reasonable level. Taking short cuts at this stage can be a false economy – you may think you're progressing but you may also find that you have to "unlearn" bad habits later on.

THE RIGHT HAND

We'll start off with a very simple exercise: you're going to play a sequence of five different notes using the thumb and four fingers of your right hand.

Begin by looking at the picture of the hand on the right. Look carefully at the numbers attached to each digit. You are probably accustomed to referring to your hand as having a thumb and four fingers – with the fingers being numbered from one to four. When playing the piano, think of your thumb as being finger number "1"; your index finger (first finger) as number "2," and so on. This is significant because written music sometimes includes fingering notation.

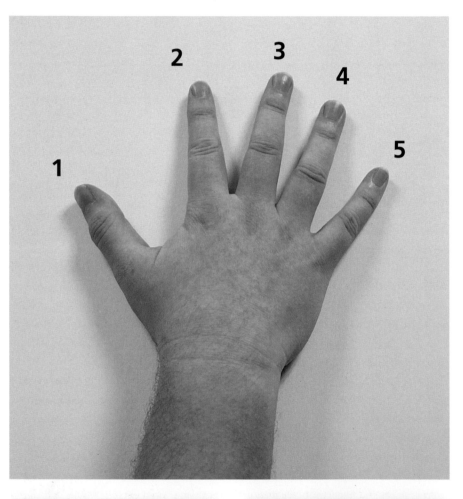

ONE NOTE FOR EACH FINGER

The diagrams below and across the page show you how to play the notes C, D, E, F and G. Each box contains a keyboard diagram with a single note highlighted

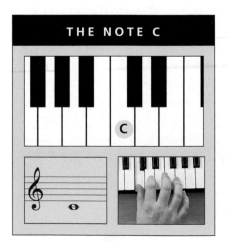

THE NOTE C

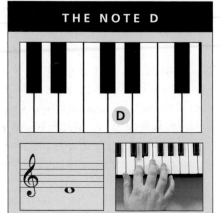

THE NOTE D

THE NOTE E

with its name. Beneath the keyboard you can see how the note is written on the staff alongside the treble clef. The photograph shows you the finger (or thumb) with which you need play the note.

This very simple set of exercises illustrates one of the fundamental aspects of keyboard playing – making use of the most appropriate fingers. The five keyboard diagrams show the notes C to G being played by the thumb and four fingers respectively. Clearly, it would be possible to play all of these notes using the same finger. Indeed, rather like novices

encountering a computer keyboard, when you are learning you will probably find it more natural to play just using the strongest finger, probably your index finger. However, if you become used to a restricted range of fingers you will later find it difficult to play sequences of notes or chords effectively.

Start off by playing the note C with the thumb. Exert a delicate touch – you don't need to poke at the keyboard, just press down firmly. Repeat this exercise, playing the notes D, E, F and G with the first, second, third and fourth fingers respectively.

YOUR FIRST SEQUENCE

Now you can play all five notes one after the other. The notated music is shown below. Directly beneath the staff you'll find the note names, and below those, the fingers you should use to play the notes.

To get you accustomed to the idea of playing in time, slowly count a beat out

loud, repeating in cycles of one to four (one-two-three-four-one…etc.) Start by playing each note only on the first beat of each sequence (the count of "one"). Now play notes on the count of "one" and "three", Finally, try to play a new note on every beat.

You can hear the sequence played on the first track of the CD.

PIANO DOGMA

What the exercises shown on these pages are definitely *not* telling you is that the note C should *always* be played by the thumb, D by the first finger, E by the second finger, and so forth. The practice being illustrated is simply that *adjacent notes in a sequence are best played by adjacent fingers*: if the sequence goes C–D–E you should use the thumb and first two fingers; if the sequence is C–E–G then you could use the thumb, second and fourth fingers. As you will see over the coming pages, this kind of approach to fingering can be adapted easily to any set of circumstances.

All the exercises in Lesson One are intended to played by the right hand only – we'll be dealing with the left hand later (*see page 52*).

As you play each key, pay special attention to the position of the note on the staff. It's critically important that you begin to recognise their names as soon as possible. It should help to think back to those little mnemonic phrases we encountered on pages 29 and 30: <u>E</u>at <u>G</u>ood <u>B</u>read <u>D</u>ear <u>F</u>ather for the lines; and <u>F A C E</u> for the spaces.

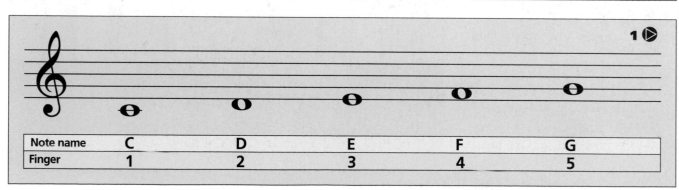

NOTES ON THE TREBLE STAFF #1

Here are three more exercises for you to try. These are more demanding in that these notes are not all being played in ascending pitch sequence. Once again, use the thumb (1) and fingers (2 to 5) to play the notes. You can make the exercises more demanding by covering the blue panel beneath each staff, leaving you to work out the notes for yourself.

Since you won't yet be used to the names of the notes on the keyboard, you could mark them on your piano with removable sticky labels. Simply write the note name on the sticker and fix it to your keyboard.

This exercise is about learning the note names and working the fingers. Once again: we're not saying that the same fingers will always be used to play the same notes.

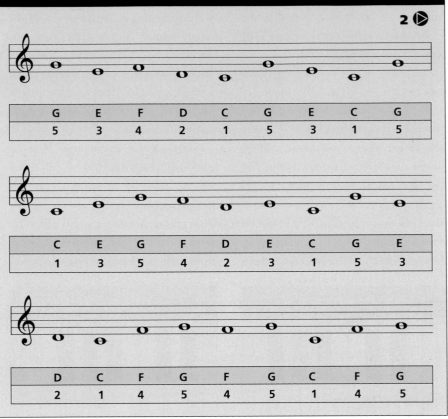

G	E	F	D	C	G	E	C	G
5	3	4	2	1	5	3	1	5

C	E	G	F	D	E	C	G	E
1	3	5	4	2	3	1	5	3

D	C	F	G	F	G	C	F	G
2	1	4	5	4	5	1	4	5

INCREASING THE RANGE OF NOTES

Using the thumb and four fingers to play notes independently, as we've seen on the previous three pages, is all well and good if you only need to play a range of five notes – C to G, for example. But in practice this is never likely to happen. So what do we do when a piece of music calls for us to continue playing the white notes on the keyboard below C or above G?

ASCENDING SEQUENCES

The most important aspect of developing even the most basic powers of keyboard dexterity is in having your hand and fingers in the correct position so that they are always ready to play the next note.

Let's look at an example. If you are playing a sequence of successive white notes running from C up to A, it's not very much use playing the penultimate

note (G) with your "little" finger (the fourth finger). There isn't another finger free to play the note A without moving your entire hand (or making a *very* awkward crossing motion with the third finger). You may not have time to move your hand if the music is in the middle of a phrase, or calls for notes to be played in fast succession.

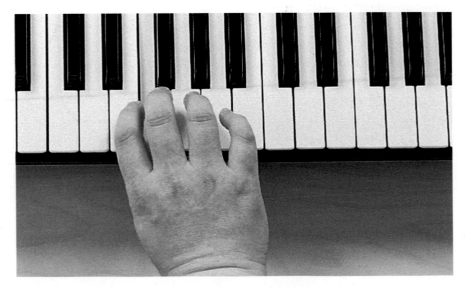

If you place your right hand down on the keyboard, with the thumb on C, you have a range of notes that easily covers between C and G without having to spread your fingers too far. If you now move your entire hand to the right, so that the thumb covers the note F, your range of notes has shifted to between F and C. To move smoothly between both ranges

YOU MUST USE THE THUMB AS A PIVOT FOR THE WHOLE HAND. This can usually be done when following on from notes played by the first three fingers.

Here is an example of how this can work in practice. If, within a piece of music, the note E is being played by the second finger, and you know that the next note to be played is F, you have the choice of playing that note with the third finger – as was the case in the previous exercises – OR YOU CAN BRING YOUR THUMB BEHIND THE FIRST AND SECOND FINGERS TO PLAY THE NOTE. (This is shown clearly in the photograph at the foot of the opposite page.)

DESCENDING SEQUENCES

Moving between ranges by tucking the thumb only works WHEN YOU ARE PLAYING NOTES THAT ARE ASCENDING IN PITCH. When you are playing a descending sequence a similar principle is used, but this time the hand pivots on the first or second fingers and CROSSES OVER the thumb.

If the note D is being played by the thumb, and the next note to be played is the C below, then the first or second finger can be crossed over the thumb to play that note. Which finger you use will depend on the note that follows immediately after: if pitch rises, use the first finger, leaving the second or third free to play the higher-pitched note; if the pitch falls, use the second finger, leaving the first to play the lower note.

THE LEFT HAND

Although we're not concerned with the left hand until Lesson Three, it's worth noting that the two techniques used for ascending and descending sequences work in reverse when used with the left hand: when descending, you tuck the thumb; when ascending, you cross the fingers.

THE FULL SEQUENCE OF EVENTS

Whatever kind of music you want to play, tucking the thumb and crossing the fingers are (absolutely) central aspects of basic keyboard technique. If you remember these two golden rules, you won't go too far wrong:

RULE 1
WHEN YOU ARE ASCENDING WITH THE RIGHT HAND, YOU MUST <u>TUCK</u> THE THUMB; WHEN YOU ARE DESCENDING WITH THE RIGHT HAND, YOU MUST <u>CROSS</u> THE FINGERS.

RULE 2
WHEN YOU ARE ASCENDING WITH THE LEFT HAND, YOU MUST <u>CROSS</u> THE FINGERS; WHEN YOU ARE DESCENDING WITH THE LEFT HAND, YOU MUST <u>TUCK</u> THE THUMB.

ASCENDING AND DESCENDING SEQUENCES BETWEEN C AND A

To emphasise the point beyond all reasonable doubt (did we mention it is pretty important stuff?), here are two step-by-step examples of the fingering required to play ascending and descending sequences of notes between C and the next occurrence of A above C. Learn them thoroughly before you move on any further in the book.

PLAYING THE ASCENDING SEQUENCE

1. Play C with the thumb.

2. Play D with the first finger.

3. Play E with the second finger.

4. Tuck the thumb behind the fingers to play F.

5. Pivot on the thumb and play G with the first finger.

6. Play A with the second finger.

PLAYING THE DESCENDING SEQUENCE

1. Play A with the fourth finger.

2. Play G with the third finger.

3. Play F with the second finger.

4. Play E with the first finger.

5. Play D with the thumb.

6. Cross the first finger over the thumb to play C.

SCALE OF C MAJOR

The staff at the foot of the page shows eight notes being played as a sequence. However, instead of using the third finger to play F, this time you bring the thumb underneath. This enables you to play the remaining four notes with the four fingers.

When you play this sequence of notes it will probably sound familiar to you. You might even have heard this range of notes sung as "Do-Re-Me-Fa-So-La-Ti-Do" (think of that song which begins "Doe, a deer…" from *The Sound Of Music*). This sequence of notes is called a MAJOR SCALE. Since this one begins on the the note C, it is known as "C MAJOR". We'll look at scales in more detail in Lesson Four (*pages 66–81*).

To play the sequence in reverse – as a DESCENDING SCALE – play C with the fourth finger, B with the third finger, A with the second finger, G with the first finger, and F with the thumb. Cross the second finger OVER the thumb to play E, pivot the hand on the second finger to play D with the first finger and C with the thumb.

EIGHT-NOTE SEQUENCE

Now we're going to extend the range of notes up to eight – from Middle C to the next occurrence of C on the keyboard. First let's discuss the important concept of the OCTAVE. If you play both C notes (that's Middle C and then the next occurrence of C at a higher pitch) one after the other, you will hear that they are the same note, even though one has a higher pitch than the other. THE INTERVAL BETWEEN THE TWO NOTES IS ONE OCTAVE, OR TWELVE SEMITONES. To see how this works, count every note (including the black ones) from Middle C until you reach the higher C. The interval between any two adjacent notes is a semitone, so your count should come to twelve.

Before you play the eight-note sequence at the foot of the page, take a look at the individual notes shown below. These three notes will be added to the five you already know so that you can play the sequence in full.

Try to play this sequence as smoothly as possible. Concentrate on spending the same amount of time sustaining each note. Try to get into the habit of applying equal pressure to each note. Don't forget that on a piano or decent electronic keyboard, the volume of the note will depend on how hard the key is pressed. Since your fingers will be of different strengths – the thumb and first finger will naturally be stronger than the fourth finger – it may take a while to master the art of consistent touch.

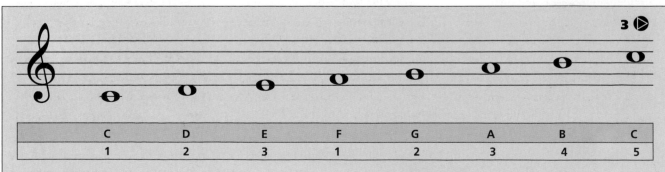

JOHANN SEBASTIAN BACH (1685–1750)

Throughout the book, we will periodically take time out to look at the lives of a number of composers who have had an impact on the development of piano music. Our first subject, Johann Sebastian Bach, is fascinating since none of his famed keyboard works were written for the piano. Indeed, during his lifetime the piano was barely even in its infancy.

Johann Sebastian Bach was born in 1685 in the northern German town of Eisenach. His family was already well known in the region, having produced notable musicians and composers since the 16th century. Orphaned at the age of ten, Bach was raised by his elder brothers, and underwent the same rigorous musical training that was by then a tradition among male members of the family.

At the age of 18, Bach was appointed organist at the Bonifacius-Kirche in Arnstadt. It was here that he began composing pieces to be played at Sunday services. In 1708 he became court organist at Weimar where his abilities as both a composer and musician began to spread.

In 1717, Bach took up residency at the court of Prince Leopold of Cöthen. After years spent struggling against unsympathetic employers – musicians at this time were largely viewed as servants – Bach finally found himself in an environment where he was able to enjoy a degree of peace and tranquillity. The six years spent at Cöthen were among his most enjoyable and productive. Bach's principal duties were to compose for and conduct the court orchestra. Here he created his six *Brandenburg Concertos* and the majority of his chamber music.

During this period Bach also wrote some of the most groundbreaking keyboard works of the 18th century. His employer had little interest in these compositions – Bach created them for his own amusement, and that of his family and pupils. His most notable keyboard work remains the 48 preludes and fugues of *The Well-tempered Clavier*. (The word "clavier" was at that time a generic term for any keyboard instrument.) It has remained a standard part of the keyboard repertoire ever since.

In 1723, following the earlier death of his wife, and his remarriage to Anna Magdalena, Bach moved to Leipzig, where he became Cantor of the noted Thomasschule. Bach remained there for the rest of his life.

By 1740, Bach's second son, Carl Philipp Emmanuel, began to emerge as an important figure in his own right, and secured a prestigious appointment at the court of the Prussian Emperor Frederick the Great. Through his son, Bach was able to extend his own reputation, which continued to grow after his death in 1750 from a stroke.

The hallmark of Bach's keyboard music is his remarkable use of polyphony. The term "fugue" refers to the interweaving of separate melody lines, one being played by each hand. The essence of a fugue is that the different lines are thematically related. At its simplest it works rather like a "round", where the melody begins, and then the same melody joins in at a different point, creating a harmonic effect. Johann Sebastian Bach remains the undisputed master of the form.

JESU, JOY OF MAN'S DESIRING: JOHANN SEBASTIAN BACH

Now we're really getting down to some serious business. We're going to use the techniques shown on the previous few pages to play the opening part of the melody line from Johann Sebastian Bach's famous composition "Jesu, Joy of Man's Desiring".

As with the previous examples, both the note names and finger positions are shown beneath the staff. Of course, if you wish, you can cover up the note names and try to work them out for yourself by reading the staves. Pay especially close attention to the fingering, though. It would be easy enough to play this melody using only the thumb and first two fingers (or even just your index finger!), but that won't be much use to you when playing more demanding pieces.

It should be emphasised, though, that the fingerings suggested below represent just one way of playing the music.

If you follow them carefully you will find that you can play the notes efficiently, and that your hands and fingers are always in an appropriate position ready to play the next note in the sequence. But there are many other possibilities.

Even as an experienced player, when you encounter a piece of written music for the first time, rather than attempting to play it straight away, you should spend a few moments studying the music. It's clearly important that you understand exactly what's going on. As you will see later, you will encounter situations where it may not be readily obvious which notes need to be played. Similarly, many pieces of music will be heavily adorned with PERFORMANCE MARKS – a variety of symbols that give instruction as to the way the music should be played. It will take some time to become familiar with these.

4 ▶

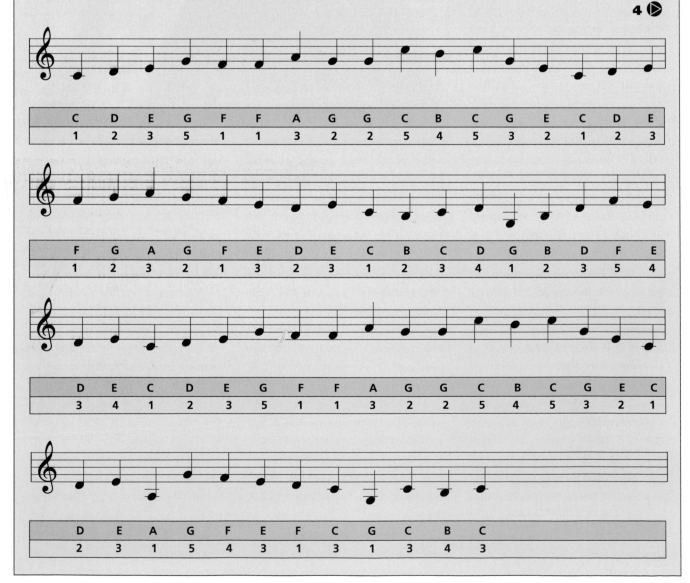

THE CHROMATIC SCALE

When you are using just the white notes on the piano keyboard, fingering practice is fairly straightforward to achieve efficiently. Things can start to become a little tricky with the introduction of the black notes (or ENHARMONIC notes, to give them their proper name). Because the black keys stand back from the white keys, the entire hand has to be moved back and forth as well as from side to side for them to be played. Once again, there are different ways of dealing with such sequences of notes, depending on whether the movements are ascending or descending in pitch.

Look at the example below. This is what is known as a CHROMATIC SCALE. It is a sequence of all 13 notes between C and octave C – every semitone interval is played.

1. Play C with the thumb.
2. Follow it up with the first finger on C♯.
3. Using the second finger to play D is a little awkward, especially if the sequence has to be played quickly, so use the thumb, passing it behind the first finger.
4. Repeat this movement between D and D♯.
5. Bring the thumb under the first finger once again, this time to play E.
6. Play F with the first finger.
7. Play F♯ with the second finger.
8. Since the third finger is not in a comfortable position to play G, you must again revert to the thumb.
9. The remaining five notes follow the same type of pattern: play G♯ using the first finger, A with the thumb, A♯ with the first finger, B with the thumb and C with the first finger.

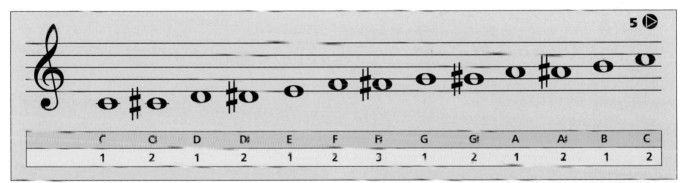

DESCENDING THE CHROMATIC SCALE

We can take a similar kind of approach when descending the chromatic scale, starting on the higher-pitched C. Descending can be a little trickier, involving some slightly awkward crossings of the fingers. You'll rarely be called upon to play a chromatic scale in full, but integrating black notes smoothly and efficiently is a basic necessity for playing the piano. Once again, such movements don't necessarily use adjacent fingers:

1. Play C with the third finger.
2. Play B with the thumb.
3. Cross over the second finger to play A♯.
4. Play A with the thumb.
5. Play G♯ with the second finger.
6. Play G with the thumb.
7. Play F♯ with the first finger.
8. Play F with the thumb.
9. Play E with the second finger.
10. Play D♯ with the first finger.
11. Play D with thumb.
12. Play C♯ with the first finger.
13. Play C with the thumb.

SHARPS OR FLATS?

The scale above shows the black notes as being made up of sharps (♯), meaning that each one takes the name of the adjacent white note to its left. These enharmonic notes could equally be labelled as their equivalent flats (♭). The staff below shows the same pitches with all of the enharmonic notes described as flats. In this instance, the second note of the sequence (D♭) is shown as D on the staff with the flat symbol alongside, indicating that it is a D which has been lowered by a semitone.

On that same staff, pay attention to the use of the NATURAL symbol (♮). Whenever a note is sharpened or flattened, the symbol only needs showing in the first instance. Thereafter, notes on the same line are assumed to remain at that pitch. The natural symbol returns a note to its "natural" state – thus the third note has to have a natural to be D – if it had no symbol it would still be D♭.

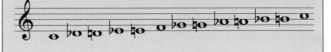

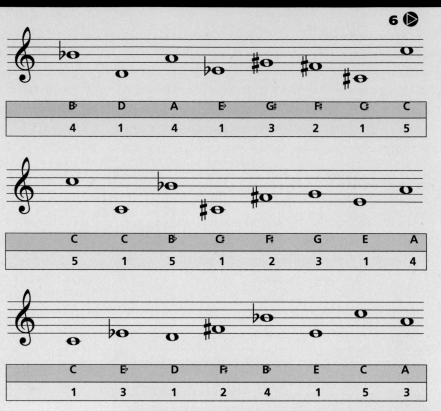

NOTES ON THE TREBLE STAFF #2

6

This final set of exercises features randomly selected notes within the range of the octave from Middle C. Exercises like these are useful for several reasons. Most significantly, they get your fingers moving around the keyboard. They will also familiarise you with the names of the notes as they appear on the staff.

Recognising this new language is at the very heart of acquiring sight-reading skills – the ability to see a piece of music and play it just as if you were reading a book.

Finally, hearing groups of notes played one after the other will help you to hear how these notes sound in relation to one another – this is fundamental to understanding the mechanics of music.

B♭	D	A	E♭	G♯	F♯	C♯	C
4	1	4	1	3	2	1	5

C	C	B♭	C♯	F♯	G	E	A
5	1	5	1	2	3	1	4

C	E♭	D	F♯	B♭	E	C	A
1	3	1	2	4	1	5	3

ACCIDENTALS

By now you will be familiar with the idea of sharps raising a pitch by a semitone, flats lowering a pitch by a semitone, and naturals, which revert a sharp or flat to its original pitch. These symbols are all examples of what are termed ACCIDENTALS.

In some situations, however, it also becomes necessary to sharpen a note that has already been sharpened, or flatten a note that has already been flattened. To achieve this you use either a DOUBLE FLAT or a DOUBLE SHARP symbol.

The double flat is shown in written music using the symbol "♭♭". This has the effect of reducing the pitch of the note by one tone. A note named B♭♭ has the same pitch value as the note A, although it would be wrong to call it A in this context.

Similarly, the double sharp – shown either as "x" or the symbol "𝄪" – has the effect of raising the pitch by a tone. The staff on the right illustrates a situation where this could occur. The sharps at the beginning of staff indicate that all the notes on those lines or spaces have to be played as sharps. The seventh note in the sequence is "F double sharp". Although it has the same pitch value as a G it wouldn't be correct to place it on the G "space" – we can tell from the start of the staff that all of the notes shown in that space have already been sharpened.

SUMMARY OF ACCIDENTALS

SHARP
Raises a note by a semitone.

♯

FLAT
Lowers a note by a semitone.

♭

DOUBLE FLAT
Lowers a note by a tone.

♭♭

DOUBLE SHARP
Raises a note by a tone.

𝄪

NATURAL
Returns a sharpened or flattened note to its previous value.

♮

G♯	A♯	B	C♯	D♯	E♯ (F)	F𝄪 (G)	G♯

TWO MORE TUNES

Here are two further simple melodies for you to practise. In each case, the note names and fingering are shown beneath the staves.

"ODE TO JOY"

This melody is part of the finale of Beethoven's *Ninth Symphony*. This time you'll notice some enharmonic notes have also been included. This highly simplified arrangement features only the first two lines of the piece, and also takes the liberty of altering the last three notes in each line so that all of the notes have exactly the same TIME VALUE (*see Lesson Two*). Since only five notes are used, it is possible to play the whole piece without moving the hand.

WALTZ IN A

To phrase this melody correctly, count from "one" to "three" in a repeating cycle, emphasising slightly the note played on the count of "one".

LESSON TWO
UNDERSTANDING TIME, TEMPO AND RHYTHM

This lesson is concerned with the essential elements of time, tempo and rhythm. Playing "in time" is a basic art that every musician has to develop. This means being able to play a piece of music (or accompany other musicians) at the right pace. For many beginners tempo and rhythm are among the hardest skills to master, although – like everything else related to playing a musical instrument – they are bound to improve the more often you practise.

THE ELEMENTS OF TIME

In all forms of music, time is made up of two distinct and essential elements: tempo and rhythm. The TEMPO is the speed at which a piece of music is played. It can be measured either in terms of a specific number of "beats" per minute (abbreviated as BPM) or a series of written instructions called "tempo marks". RHYTHM, on the other hand, refers to the way in which notes are played or accented.

FINDING THE PULSE

Irrespective of genre, if you listen to any piece of music you will hear a pulsing effect that seems to be "driving" the music along. This pulse is its rhythm. Try this experiment: take any piece music at random and start to clap along or tap your fingers in time. You will almost certainly find yourself naturally drawn to a consistent, pulsing beat. This is distinct from the tempo, because whatever the speed, the time elapsed between each beat will remain the same value.

A good proportion of the music played in the West can be counted out in cycles of four beats. This natural grouping of beats is known in written music as a BAR. The rhythm is created and defined by the length of the notes played within each bar. The simplest beat you will hear groups together four notes called CROTCHETS. Each one has a value of one beat. A rhythm that is made up of four beats in a bar is said to be in FOUR-FOUR TIME.

A note that has a value of four beats is called a SEMIBREVE. The value of any other note is fixed to its relationship to the

NOTE APPEARANCE

The pitch of a note is governed by the position of its HEAD on the staff. The time value of a note is also discerned from its appearance. A semibreve is indicated by an open circle; a minim, by an open circle with a STEM attached; a crotchet is a filled circle with a stem. Durations of less than a crotchet are shown as filled circles with stems and a system of so-called FLAGS. The complete set of note values is shown in the box at the foot of the page. When appearing in sequence, groups of quavers and lower) can be shown "joined" together, the flags being replaced by BEAMS (*see the diagram on the opposite page*).

semibreve. The semibreve can be subdivided four times to create the crotchet – the note value that forms the beat in most music. One way or another, every note can be viewed as being a multiple or division of a crotchet. This is an important point to grasp in understanding written music. Each of these multiples or subdivisions has its own name.

The length of time a note is played is named after its value in beats. These are shown using a number of different symbols. For example, the crotchet note is shown as a filled circle with stem. (The direction of the stem above or below the head depends on its position on the staff.)

The different types of note are shown in the diagram on the right, along with their European names, American names (shown underneath in brackets) and value in beats.

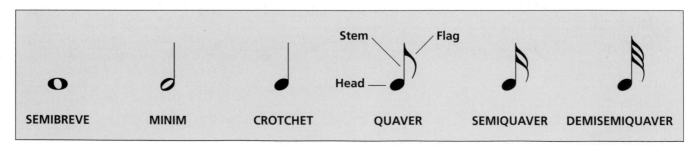

| SEMIBREVE | MINIM | CROTCHET | QUAVER | SEMIQUAVER | DEMISEMIQUAVER |

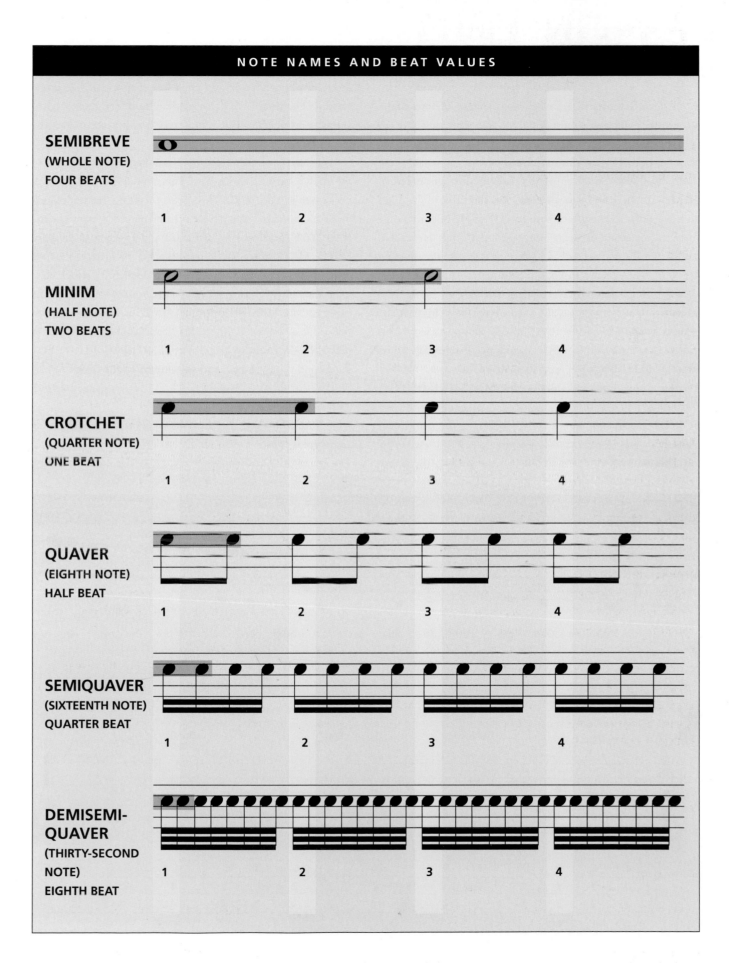

CREATING RHYTHM BY MIXING NOTE VALUES

If the music we listened to was always made up of notes of the same time value, it would soon become very dull indeed. Rhythm is created from the manner in which the notes are grouped or accented within each bar. To create more interesting rhythms, notes of different time values are brought together. However, they must be arranged so that the value of the notes in a bar remains consistent with the TIME SIGNATURE.

Music is made up from notes grouped into bars: these appear on the manuscript as a series of vertical lines dividing the staff. The specific number of beats in any bar of music is defined by its time signature. This is indicated by the two numbers that you see on the staff at the beginning of the music. You already know that four crotchet beats in a bar is called "four-four time" – this is an example of a time signature. What it means in practice is that any bar of four-four, whatever the beat value of the individual notes, MUST ADD UP TO A TOTAL OF FOUR BEATS.

Look at the two staves shown below – the traditional American folk tune "Yankee Doodle". In contrast to the notated music you encountered in Lesson One, the staves

below are divided into eight bars. The two numbers at the start of the staff tell us that it is four-four time: if you add up the value of the notes in any single bar, they will always come to four. The double bar line at the end of the eighth bar – showing a thickened line – indicates that it is the end of the piece of music.

As before, the note names (*blue*) and finger positions (*green*) are shown beneath the staves. This time, however, you will notice a third line (*pink*). This shows the beat – the underlined numbers indicate when a note is to be played. Count out the beats in the bar (from one to four), and play one note on every beat for the first three bars. You will notice that two of the bars differ from the others in that they include minims, which have a duration of two beats. When you get to Bar 4, play C on the count of "one", sustain it through "two", before playing B on the count of "three", and "G on "four". Likewise, in Bar 8, play C on the count of "one", sustain it through "two", play the second C on "three", and sustain it through "four".

THREE-FOUR TIME

After four-four time, the next most commonly heard time signature is "three-four", which has three beats in every bar. The piece of music across the page is the famous lullaby

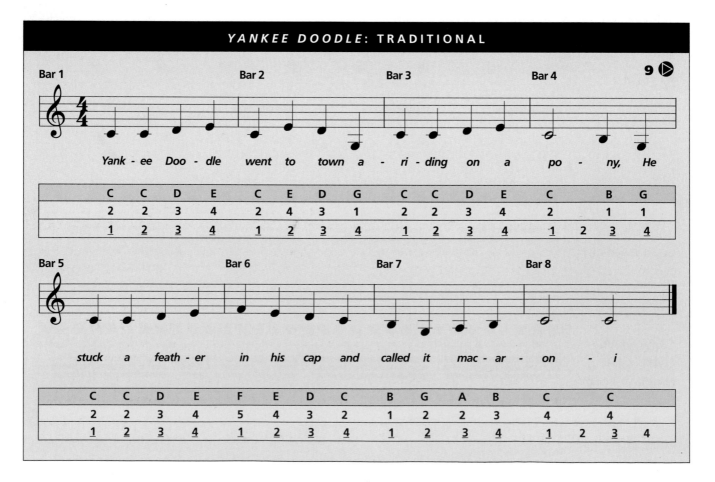

"Lullaby" ("*Wiegenlied*") by Johannes Brahms. This is written in three-four time (also known as "waltz time"). There are a greater variety of note values on display here, including a number of quavers, each with a value of half a beat.

To count out three-four time, you need to repeat cycles of three beats. The easiest way to count out quavers is to insert the word "and" between each beat. Start off by counting "one— two—three…" and then split the beat: "one—and—two—and— three—and…" Let's try this out in Bar 2. Play G (minim) on the count of "one", let it sustain through "and—two—and", play E (quaver) on the count of "three", and finally the second E (quaver) on "and".

Now work through the entire piece, counting out the beats as you play.

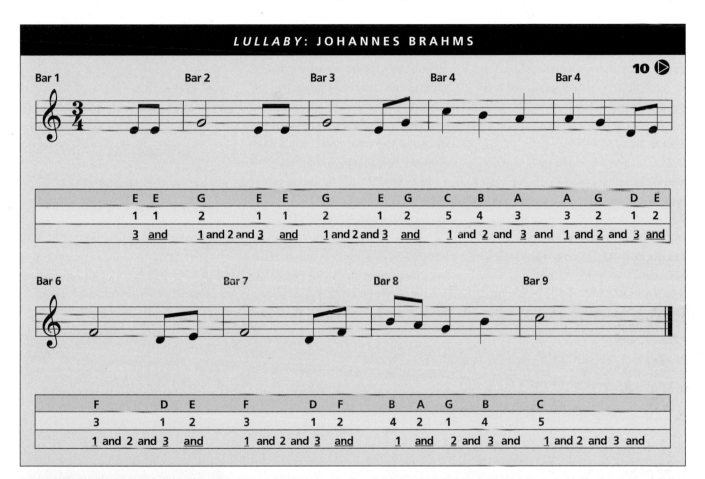

HOLD ON A MINUTE…

… didn't we say that the note values in every bar had to add up to the number of beats specified by the time signature? So what's the deal with the first and last bars? Why does the first one add up to one, and the last one add up to two, when they should both total three? This happens because the music doesn't actually start on the first beat of Bar 1 – the first quaver is played on the third beat. This discrepancy is picked up on the final bar, which uses a minim that sustains for two beats. If you add the value of the two bars together you'll find that it comes to the correct total of three beats.

For a one-time sequence of music, it would be possible to fill the blank spaces with RESTS (you'll encounter these later in this lesson). If, however, you think of it as being a repeating musical sequence the logic becomes clearer: if the final bar were to take its full count of three, and then return to the beginning of first bar – including the first two "empty" beats – there would be a silence of three beats, which would sound incorrect. The implication of the music as it's written above is that as far as this repetition is concerned, Bar 1 and Bar 9 ARE the same bar, it's merely that one of the beats is in the former, and the other two are in the latter.

EXTENDING NOTE VALUES

All of the notes we've seen used so far have been based around the idea of continually halving semibreves and their subdivisions. As useful as this is, it does actually provide a fairly limited palette from which to draw. What, for example, do you do if you want to play a single note that lasts for THREE beats? Or if you want to play a note on the last beat of a bar that sustains across the first beat of the following bar? The answer is to use DOTS and TIES.

USING TIES

A tie is a curved line that links together two notes, creating the effect of a single note with the value of the two notes combined. Look at the first two bars below. The two minims either side of the bar line are linked by a tie. This gives the first minim an effective value of four beats. In this case, the first minim is played on the third beat of the first bar

TIED VALUES

The logic behind the use of ties is very straightforward indeed. You simply add the values of the two notes together, and then sustain the FIRST note for the combined duration.

The only way to sustain notes across a bar line is to use a tie. However, ties can be used within a bar to produce note values that can't easily be created by other means. They can also be used to aid interpretation.

Ties always join the notes at the head. If the stem points downward the tie curves above the head; if it points upward, the tie curves below the note.

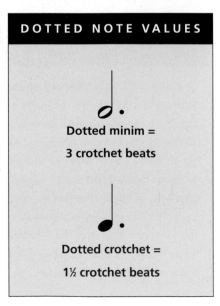

and sustains into the first two beats of the following bar. THE SECOND MINIM IS NOT PLAYED – the second note in a tied pair is NEVER played, its value is merely added to that of the first tied note. Play the four bars below, paying special attention to the value of the notes shown beneath the staff.

DOTS

By adding a dot to any note type, it becomes possible to increase its value by half. For example, a minim followed by a dot has a value of three crotchet beats. This is referred to as a DOTTED MINIM. Using the same principle, a DOTTED CROTCHET has a value of one-and-a-half crotchet beats.

Take a look at the first bar in the example at the top of the opposite page – the one that begins with two dotted crotchets. The first dotted crotchet plays on the first beat; the second comes in halfway between the second and third

beats; the final crotchet plays on the fourth beat. Notice, however, that whatever alterations are made to any of the notes, the total value remains consistent with the four-four time signature: $1\frac{1}{2}$ beats + $1\frac{1}{2}$ beats + 1 beat = 4 beats.

The second bar comprises a dotted minim and a crotchet. The note C is played on the first beat and sustains for three beats; the crotchet is played on the fourth beat.

The third bar is a little trickier to follow in that it features dotted quavers and semiquavers. Although the two notes

DOTTED NOTE VALUES

Dotted minim =
3 crotchet beats

Dotted crotchet =
1½ crotchet beats

making up each pair have a different time value, they are easier to read if they are joined together, or BEAMED. To interpret such notes, remember that the number of beams equates directly to the number of flags on a single note. Thus, the first note has a single beam, making it a quaver (half a beat). HOWEVER, since the note is dotted it has a time value of three-quarters of a beat. The second note has a beam and a "broken" beam coming from the stem, meaning that it can be interpreted as having two flags, and is thus a semiquaver, with a value of a quarter of a beat.

Work through all four bars carefully counting out the note values as you play. You can hear them played on Track 12 of the CD.

WOLFGANG AMADEUS MOZART (1756–1791)

The most celebrated child prodigy of them all, by the age of four, Wolfgang Amadeus Mozart had already made clear his potential. As his sister, Anna Maria, related: "He learned a piece in an hour, a minuet in half an hour, so that he could play it faultlessly and with the greatest delicacy, and keeping exactly in time. He made such progress that by the age of five he was already composing little pieces".

Witnessing the birth of such an extraordinary talent, his father, Leopold, set out to exploit it as fully as possible. By Mozart's tenth birthday he had astonished audiences at the courts of Europe with his precocious keyboard skills.

During the seven years that followed, having been employed as Konzertmeister by the Prince-Archbishop Colloredo of Salzburg, Mozart composed prodigiously; his works during this period include masses, symphonies, all his violin concertos, six piano sonatas, several serenades and divertimentos and his first great piano concerto.

After periods spent in Paris and Munich, Mozart was recalled to the Salzburg court. However, increasingly unable to accept the ignominy of being treated as little more than a musical servant, in May 1781 he moved to Vienna. Here he would embark upon a perilous freelance career, forging a living by teaching, performing or by composing operas to commission. In 1782 Mozart embarked on a series of piano concertos; within four years he had written 15 of them. They represent, perhaps, the greatest of his considerable achievements.

In 1786 Mozart wrote the first of his great operatic works: *The Marriage of Figaro*. This was followed by *Don Giovanni* (1787), *Cosi Fan Tutte* (1790) and *The Magic Flute* (1791). They are now among the most popular of the standard operatic repertoire.

Although he continued to travel, Mozart based himself in Vienna for the rest of his life. But however celebrated he had been as a musician and composer, his final years were beset by poverty and distress. A lavish lifestyle, poor management of dwindling funds, and the cost of medical fees for his ailing wife, Constanze, left him in dire straits.

Mozart died following a fever on December 5, 1791. He was buried in an unmarked grave in the churchyard of St Mark's, Vienna. His passing aroused little interest, and within a few years the exact location of his grave was lost.

GROUPING NOTES

As you've already seen, time values of a quaver and lower can have their "flag" joined together in what is called a BEAM.

There is a certain protocol for grouping notes in this way. The three examples below are essentially the same. In practice, the bar of single quavers would not be used. However, in the second and third bars, there is an implication that the grouped notes are related in the way they are "phrased".

In the second bar, each pair of crotchets could be thought of as a separate entity; the third bar comprises two four-beat phrases.

Mixed Notes

The two bars below show how mixed values can be grouped. Notice how the beaming conforms to logical divisions of the bar, with each separate grouping taking place within a single beat.

RESTS

It may sound odd, but if you think about it, silence is a fundamental aspect of pretty well any piece of music: without it, all you would hear is continuous sound. It is these intervals of silence that create (or at least emphasise) the rhythm of any piece of music.

Standard musical notation has a specific set of instructions for indicating periods of silence. These are called RESTS. In fact, each of the standard note types that you've encountered has its own associated rest. All of these can be seen in the box below.

A rest is used in written music in exactly the same way as any other regular note. Let's consider, for example, a bar of music with a time signature of four-four. A note that starts on the first beat and is sustained for three beats, followed by silence on the fourth beat, would require a dotted minim and a crotchet rest. The total beat value of the notes AND the rests must be the same as that suggested by the time signature.

NOTE: Pay special attention to the difference between the semibreve and minim rests: the former hangs from the second staff line; the latter sits on the third staff line.

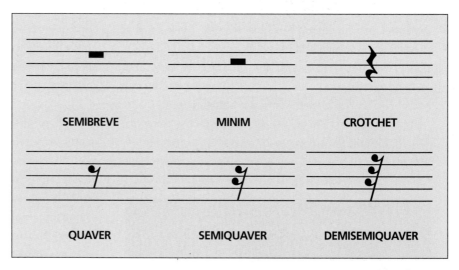

| SEMIBREVE | MINIM | CROTCHET |
| QUAVER | SEMIQUAVER | DEMISEMIQUAVER |

HEARING THE REST

Look at the four examples on the right. Each one is a single four-four bar. Count from one to four and then play each one. The note in the first bar sustains for all four beats; in the second bar, play the note for three beats and rest for one; in the third bar, play the note for two beats and rest for two; in the final bar, play the note for one beat and rest for three.

A rest can sometimes be difficult to perceive, especially below the value of a quaver, where the difference between a rest and the natural pause that occurs when moving from one note to another may be hard to discern.

A LITTLE BIT OF MOZART

The next exercise is the most demanding one you'll have tried so far. This is the melody of "Zerlina's Song", from Mozart's opera, *Don Giovanni*.

Make sure you read about playing staccato (*see right*) before attempting the piece – the eighth bar has a series of notes that must be played in this way.

Once again, the note names, fingering and count are shown beneath each staff. First try to work out the note for yourself.

STACCATO

The opposite of dotting a note is to play it STACCATO. Literally meaning "detached", staccato reduces the length of a note. It is most commonly indicated by the placement of a dot above or below the head of the note.

As a general rule, the staccato can be treated as halving the value of the note and replacing the second half with a rest, as shown below.

The staccato mark is a stylistic effect indicating more a manner of playing rather than imparting a precise measurement, but it is NOT an instruction to shorten the note as much as possible.

MORE ABOUT TIME SIGNATURES

As we've already seen, the time signature of any piece of music is defined by the two numbers at the beginning of the staff. The number at the top tells you how many beats there are in the bar. The number at the bottom indicates the time value of each of those beats. If the bottom number is two, the beat is shown as minims; if it is four, the beat is shown as crotchets; if it is eight, the beat is shown as quavers.

COMPOUND TIME SIGNATURES

Each of the three "simple" time signatures shown above has beats that are divisible by two. A different type of time signature is possible where the beats are divisible by three. This is known as COMPOUND TIME.

A two-beat bar in simple time will be played as two groups of quavers. In compound time, however, a two-beat bar with a time signature of SIX-EIGHT would be played as two groups of three quavers. Similarly, a three-beat bar can be played as three groups of quavers in a time signature of NINE-EIGHT, and a four-beat bar can be played as four

Indicates the number of beats in the bar.

Indicates the note value of each beat: "4" means that they are crotchets.

A four-four beat is the most commonly used time signature – so much so that it can be called COMMON TIME.

SIMPLE TIME

The three bars on the left are written in time signatures of two-four, three-four, and four-four respectively. These are examples of SIMPLE TIME. In each case, when counting through the beats, the natural emphasis always falls on the first beat, creating the mood of the music.

The distinction between two-four and four-four may need clarification, since it is possible to count two bars of two-four as a single bar of four-four. There is a clue in that most military marches are written in two-four time: imagine soldiers marching to the order "LEFT-RIGHT-LEFT-RIGHT." The emphasis is in groups of two, NOT groups of four.

groups of quavers in a time signature of TWELVE-EIGHT.

Play the three four-bar examples below – you will be able to hear the effect more clearly if you emphasise the first beat of each bar.

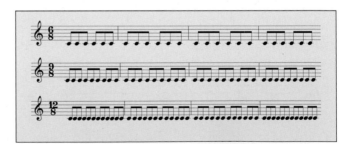

EXAMPLE IN SIMPLE TIME

To get you away from working exclusively in time signatures of four-four and three-four, here is a melody written in two-four time – the folk song "She'll Be Coming Round the Mountain".

It covers a number of important areas introduced earlier in this lesson, such as tied notes, dotted notes and rests.

Since the music makes extensive use of quavers, instead of counting out "one–two", try inserting "and" between each beat. As before, the beat count is shown beneath the staves.

EXAMPLE IN COMPOUND TIME

A time signature of six-eight is an equivalent of two-four in compound time. This effectively means that each bar of music has a value of six quavers.

The example below is the traditional tune "For He's a Jolly Good Fellow". As you play the tune, count out in cycles of six.

(NOTE: The symbol above the E in the seventh bar is a FERMATA. It is an instruction to pause after that note has been played – the extent of that pause is at the discretion of the player.)

LESSON THREE

SIMPLE POLYPHONY

So far you have just been playing single notes. But one of the reasons why the piano is such a great instrument is that if you use both hands it becomes possible to play up to ten notes simultaneously. This degree of polyphony – the effect of more than one note being played at the same time – allows for the creation of some extremely sophisticated music, the likes of which may simply not be possible with any other musical instrument. In this lesson, we'll be aiming to get your left hand working, accompanying right-hand melodies with some simple bass parts.

BASS-CLEF ISSUES

For most notated piano music, the left hand is used to play the bass notes. These can be found on a second staff beneath the treble notes. To indicate that they are lower in pitch, the staff containing the left-hand notes is headed by a BASS CLEF. You may remember from the introductory chapter that the names of the notes on the lines and spaces on a staff that uses a bass clef are not the same as for a treble clef. The lines are (from bottom-to-top) G, B, D, F, A (think of the phrase <u>G</u>ood <u>B</u>oys <u>D</u>eserve <u>F</u>un <u>A</u>lways); the spaces are A, C, E, G (or <u>A</u> <u>C</u>ow <u>E</u>ats <u>G</u>rass, if you like).

To show that the bass and treble staves are related to one another (and that they are to be played at the same time) they must be "joined" by a bracket at the beginning of the two staves.

THE LEFT HAND

For most novice pianists – especially those who are right-handed – getting the left hand working can be a demanding and frustrating experience. For most of us, the left hand gets much less use, and so is weaker and more difficult to control

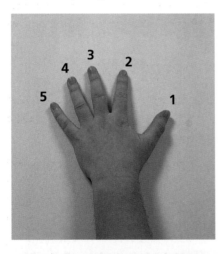

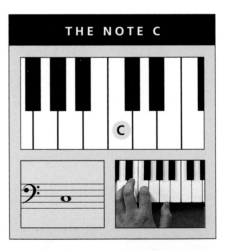

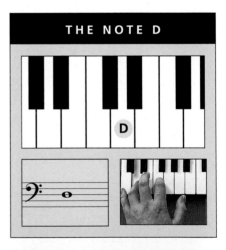

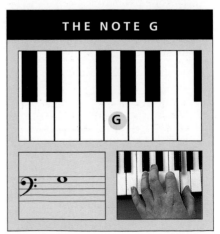

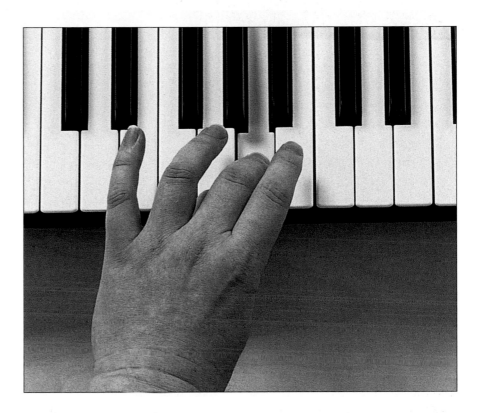

than the right. This is especially the case for movements between the third and fourth fingers.

SIMPLE EXERCISE

To begin with, we'll simply get the different fingers playing the five notes shown on the opposite page. Start by playing C with the fourth finger (5) as shown in the photograph. Pay special attention to the notation. Notice how the bass clef redefines the names of the notes so that, in this instance, C is represented on the second space of the staff. THIS IS NOT MIDDLE C, THOUGH: on the bass clef, Middle C would appear on the first ledger line above the staff, which means that the C you are playing is one octave below Middle C.

Continue the exercise, playing the contents of each new box as you go. This means that D is played by the third finger (4), E by the second finger (3), F by the first finger (2) and G by the thumb (1).

Once you've played the sequence in ascending order, play them in reverse, starting with the thumb on the note G and working back down to C with the fourth finger (5).

CROSSING THE FINGERS

You're already familiar with the idea of moving the fingers so that they can extend beyond the range of five notes by tucking the thumb beneath the fingers or crossing the first or second fingers over the thumb to move beyond the range. The same principle applies to the left

hand, although – since the thumb and fingers of the left hand are mirror images of the right hand – they are used in reverse order. This means that when DESCENDING in pitch, the thumb is tucked beneath the fingers to extend the range of notes; when ASCENDING in pitch, the first or second fingers can be crossed over the thumb.

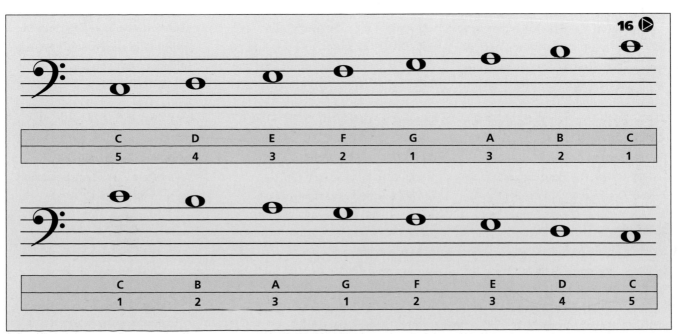

IDENTIFYING THE BASS NOTES

17 ▶

Here are four simple exercises aimed at helping you get acquainted with the notes on the bass clef. Beneath each staff you'll see both the note name and the finger with which you should play. Don't forget that numbers given to the thumb and four fingers are the same as they are for the right hand – the thumb is "1", and the first, second, third, and fourth fingers are "2", "3", "4", and "5" respectively.

When learning any new musical instrument, it's always tough getting the fourth and fifth fingers working smoothly. In our everyday lives we rarely have to exercise these muscles. And the problem is multiplied on your "weak" hand. Getting those two fingers to move independently (there's a tendency for one to follow the other automatically) requires them to be strengthened. This will come with practice.

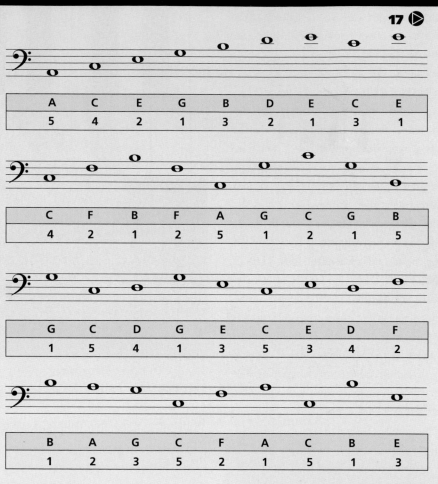

A	C	E	G	B	D	E	C	E
5	4	2	1	3	2	1	3	1

C	F	B	F	A	G	C	G	B
4	2	1	2	5	1	2	1	5

G	C	D	G	E	C	E	D	F
1	5	4	1	3	5	3	4	2

B	A	G	C	F	A	C	B	E
1	2	3	5	2	1	5	1	3

ASCENDING AND DESCENDING A SCALE

The two staves at the foot of the previous page show a sequence of notes between C and C played on the bass clef. The first staff is an ascending scale, the second is a descending scale. These notes are an octave lower than the similar sequences you played on the treble clef with the right hand.

If you pay careful attention, you will see that the fingering for the ASCENDING C major scale played with the left hand is identical to the DESCENDING C major scale when played with the right hand. The full fingering is listed below.

ASCENDING SEQUENCE

1. Play C with the fourth finger (5).
2. Play D with the third finger (4).
3. Play E with the second finger (3).
4. Play F with the first finger (2).
5. Play G with the thumb (1).
6. Cross the second finger over the thumb to play A (3).
7. Play B with the first finger (2).
8. Play C with the thumb (1).

DESCENDING SEQUENCE

1. Play C with the thumb (1).
2. Play B with the first finger (2).
3. Play A with the second finger (3).
4. Tuck the thumb beneath the fingers to play G (1).
5. Play F with the first finger (2).
6. Play E with the second finger (3).
7. Play D with the third finger (4).
8. Play C with the thumb (1).

EXERCISING

You don't actually have to be seated at your piano to carry out useful finger exercises. Here is a selection that you can do at the dinner table, at your work or study desk, or while riding on a train. Simply press your fingers down on any solid surface as if it were the keys of a piano.

Try these exercises (the numbers refer to the fingers):

1—2—3—4—5—4—3—2—1
5—4—3—2—1—2—3—4—5
1—5—4—2—3—1—2
1—3—2—4—3—5—2—4—1
5—3—4—2—3—1—2—5

LEFT-HANDED MELODIES

In most cases, the melody line appears on the treble clef and is played by the right hand. Here are two simple melodies for you to try with your left hand.

The tune shown in the first box below is the old folk tune "John Brown's Body", which later came to be known as the "Battle Hymn of the Republic". Pay attention to the fingering on the second line below each staff. Notice also that in Bar 7 the four crotchets are played staccato – it can be easy to muddle them up with other "dotted" notes.

The second box shows the traditional English melody, "Oh Dear! What Can The Matter Be?" Notice this has a time signature of six-eight.

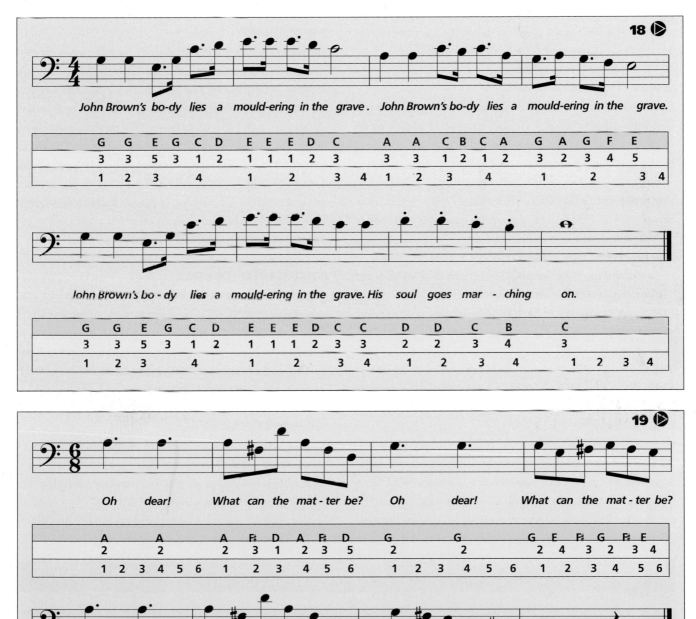

YOUR FIRST TWO-HANDER

Although getting the left hand working may be tricky for most novices, you should now be ready to take on your first piece of "two-handed" music.

The piece shown across the page is a simplified arrangement taken from the overture from *Light Cavalry* by Franz Suppé (1820–1895). The suggested fingering for treble notes is shown in the blue panel above the staff; the fingering for the bass notes is shown directly beneath the staff.

WHERE TO START

First, consider the time signature: the piece is written in six-eight time. This means that each bar has a value of six quavers or three beats. Your beat count should therefore also be in threes – although since we are dealing with quavers, cycles of six should make your task a little easier.

Another factor you need to think about is the tempo. How fast or slow should you be playing the music? If you look at the treble staff above the time signature, you will notice the word *allegretto*. This is an example of a TEMPO MARK. It tells you the speed of the piece and it can also indicate the "character" of the music. *Allegretto* could be translated literally as "fairly fast". We'll discuss tempo marks in more depth later in the book.

THE RIGHT HAND

Since this is your first attempt at a piece written over both staves, begin by working out the right-hand part and playing it in isolation.

First, notice the beaming of the quavers in Bars 2, 3 and 4. Although there is a sequence of four quavers, only the latter three are beamed; the first one is shown as a single note. Since the music is written in a time signature of six-eight, notes with a value of a half beat or less can be grouped in twos or threes. The fact that this example uses beamed groups of three tells us

a little about the way the notes should be played. Had there been two pairs of quavers, there would have been a subtle emphasis on the first note of each pair; grouping them in threes shifts that emphasis to the first note of the group of three.

In Bars 5, 9 and 13, pay special attention to the quaver rest, making sure that you don't sustain the crotchet for three beats – which is easy to do by accident.

THE LEFT HAND

Once you are happy with the melody, you can move on to the bass part. In this example, the music on the bass staff is just about as simple as you can get. Since each bar has a value of six quavers (defined by the time signature of six-eight), the duration of each bar is three beats. This extremely simple bass line consists largely of single dotted minims played on the first beat and sustained for the entire bar. Where this differs (Bars 5, 8, 13, and 16), a dotted crotchet is played on the first beat, and a second dotted crotchet is played halfway between the second and third beats. If you are counting in multiples of six, this means that the notes fall on "one" and "four".

PUTTING THEM TOGETHER

Once you are happy with the music on both the treble and bass staves, you are ready to attempt to play both parts at the same time. Try to play through the piece as smoothly as you can. Although the music should ultimately be played quite quickly, take it at a pace that makes you feel comfortable while you're learning. Don't worry if you make the odd mistake – that's inevitable at this stage. Try to carry on until you reach the end of the music.

Your first attempts are bound to sound rough, so don't be disheartened if it doesn't go as well as you would like: the old saying "Practice makes perfect" is quite apt here. The more you play, the better you will be.

You can hear this piece of music played in full on Track 20 of the CD.

NOT SO TOUGH...

If your reaction to the piece of music across the page is one of mild panic – and that's not uncommon among novice sight-readers – just try to relax. If you study the music carefully you will realise that it consists of a series of repeated themes and rhythms.

For a start, the first half of the piece of music (Bars 1–8) is quite similar to the second half (Bars 9–17). This means that once you've worked out the first eight bars, the rest

should come quite easily. And even within each half there is still plenty of repetition: if you look at Bars 2, 3 and 4, you will notice that they are identical.

A lot of music is based on repetition, so always look out for patterns when you are studying the staves. Even if the pitches are not the same, you may still notice repeating rhythmic patterns, which might well make the learning process much more straightforward.

TECHNICAL ROUTINES

Having worked through a "real" piece of music, you should feel quite pleased with yourself, and motivated toward your next success. But before you do that, take a look at a set of exercises that are not intended to sound particularly nice, but which should play an extremely important part in your development as a pianist.

Since time immemorial, one word has struck terror in the hearts of music students everywhere. It's the dreaded "P-word" – PRACTICE. And there's no way around it. Quite simply, you have no chance of becoming a decent musician without putting in some hard work.

There are two distinct types of practice. REPERTOIRE practice refers to working on pieces of music that you want to be able to perform; TECHNICAL practice takes the form of a

series of exercises that are aimed at improving your playing technique and increasing your musical understanding. Your regular daily sessions should include both types of practice.

BROKEN CHORDS

Each of the staves below (and across the page) consist of a series of ten-note sequences. These are called BROKEN CHORDS. The pattern of notes ascends in the first staff and descends in the second; the third and fourth staves are repeats of the first two for the left hand. They are played one octave lower. When you play these sequences you really MUST follow the fingering exactly.

Working through exercises like this has multiple benefits. Principally, though, it is as a critical aid to keyboard mobility. With time and practice, deciding which fingers to use when playing a piece of music will become instinctive.

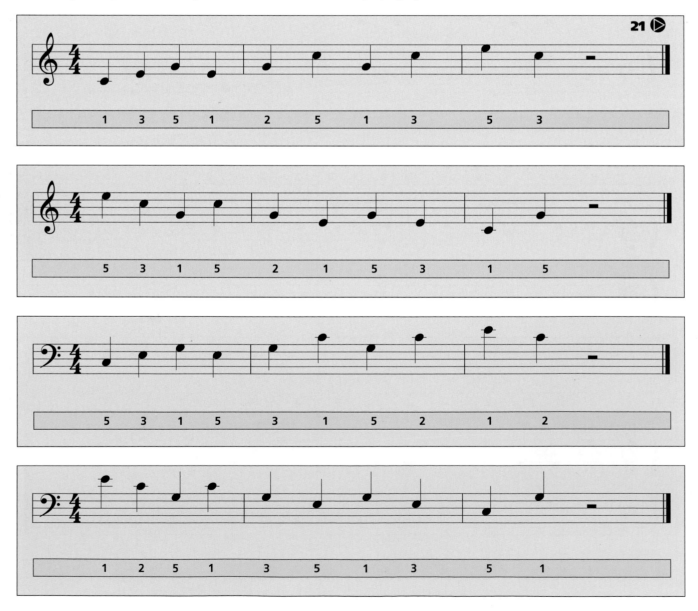

PRACTISE TIPS

Here are some pointers that should help make your practice sessions more effective and enjoyable.

1. Set aside a regular time for practice. Try to practise for about one hour a day, five days a week. As you become more experienced, increase your daily practice.

2. Relax. Practise slowly.

3. Begin your sessions with a technical warm-up, such as the exercises shown here. You will learn more of these technical exercises in the coming lessons. You should eventually think about spending up to a quarter of your practise time in this way.

4. Create a set of measurable and manageable goals before each session. After playing a piece, assess your performance and how it could be improved it – then repeat the piece.

5. Concentrate when practising. If you can't concentrate, stop: continue at another time.

6. Vary your practice sessions. Don't always play the same pieces in the same order.

7. Practise difficult passages before playing an entire piece.

8. Try to play along with a metronome (or other time-keeping device) for at least a quarter of your time.

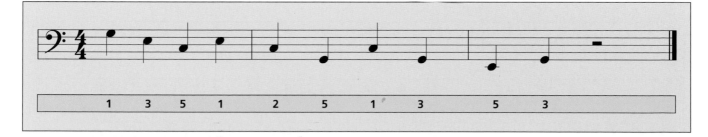

CONTINUITY ACROSS THE STAVES

This next technical exercise takes the form of a little tune that crosses between the staves and then ends with both hands playing at the same time. As your fingers get used to moving across the keyboard you will find it increasingly easy to play notes in time.

In this exercise, you may find it easy to lose time on the crossover between the first two bars, where the left hand stops playing and the right hand begins.   **22** ▶

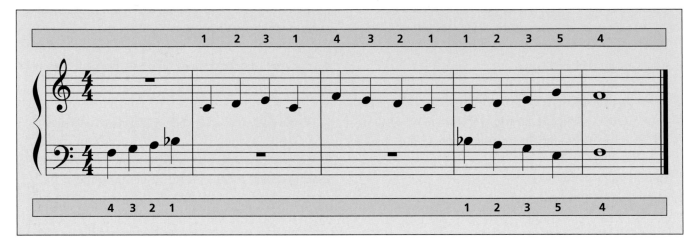

BROKEN CHORD PATTERN

This exercise takes a basic broken-chord pattern, but raises the pitch following each bar. The bass part uses notes from the treble staff, but played one octave lower.

To master the exercise, first play with the right hand in isolation, and then repeat using the left hand – these are both useful exercises in their own right. When you are satisfied with the individual parts, play both staves together.   **23** ▶

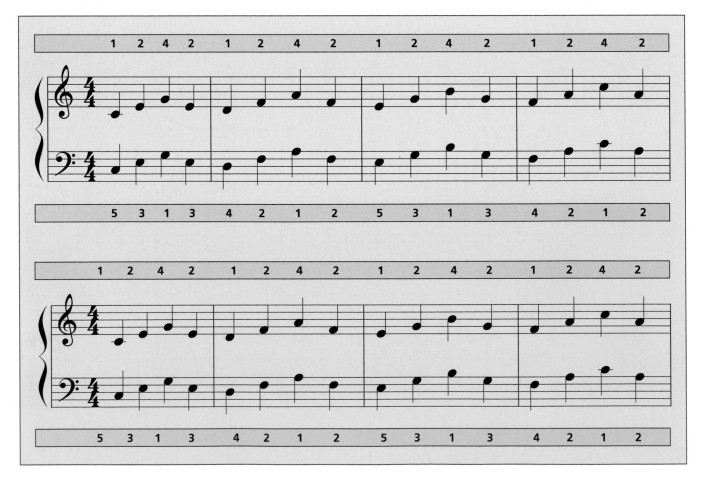

THREE MORE TWO-HANDED EXERCISES

Finally, here are three variations on the last exercise. The first one is essentially the same as the first four bars only the notes are played in a descending sequence.

The two remaining pieces differ slightly in that the right and left hands are no longer playing the same notes in different registers. This time, the hands must play with a degree of independence. The bottom example is especially tricky in that the fingers are not moving in a complementary manner. The previous sequences have all been either ascending or descending in pitch – this one requires the hands to work the fingers out of sequence. **24** ▶

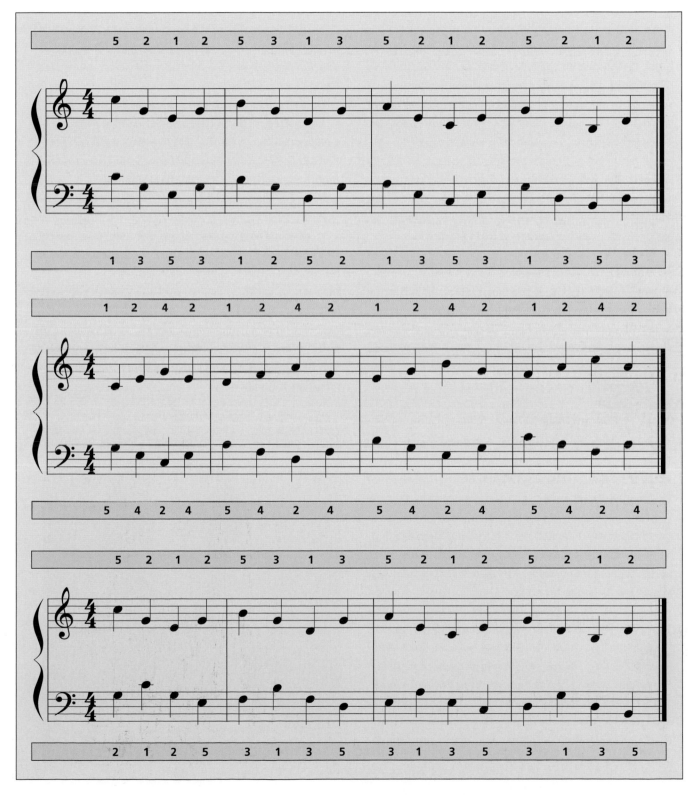

FELIX MENDELSSOHN (1809–1847)

Born into a wealthy banking family, Felix Mendelssohn-Bartholdy enjoyed an upbringing of considerable privilege. A liberal education introduced him to music and other cultural pursuits from a very early age.

Although he was fortunate enough to have benefited from the best teachers money could hire, his prodigious gifts at the piano were immediately obvious. By the age of eight Mendelssohn had learned all of Beethoven's symphonies and was able to play them brilliantly from memory. By the age of 14 he had memorised every one of Johann Sebastian Bach's known keyboard works. His first compositions were penned in 1820 – at the age of 11.

At the heart of Berlin's intellectual society, the family mixed in elite circles. From the age of 12, Mendelssohn began an extraordinary correspondence with the poet Goethe. Not long after, he began to widen his circle of acquaintances by giving Sunday morning recitals at his family home.

His first composition to be recognised as a work of prodigious genius was the *Octet*, written in 1825 and now widely revered as one of the masterpieces of the string quartet repertoire. Mendelssohn was barely 16 years old, and had only learnt to play the violin a year earlier specifically to help him with his composition. The following year his arrival on the musical scene was confirmed with the astonishingly vivid and poetic overture to *A Midsummer Night's Dream*.

Among his other extraordinary achievements, he also single-handedly brought about the rehabilitation of Johann Sebastian Bach. Following half a century of near-obscurity, in 1829 Mendelssohn directed a pioneering performance of Bach's great choral work the *St Matthew Passion*. That the composer remains so popular to this day is largely down to the enthusiastic championing of the young Mendelssohn.

Completing his studies in philosophy at the University of Berlin, where he was tutored by Hegel, for the next four years Mendelssohn travelled widely, giving concert performances in England, Scotland, France and Italy. Important new works that were influenced by his journeys throughout this period included *The Hebrides*, the G Minor Piano Concerto, *Die erste Walpurgisnacht*, the *Italian Symphony,* and the first volume of *Songs Without Words*.

In 1935 he accepted the prestigious post of conductor and music director of the Leipzig Gewandhaus Orchestra. Here is demanding programmes were notable for championing both historical and modern works.

By now Mendelssohn's fame had spread throughout Europe. In England he was considered the leading composer of the day, and was a personal favourite of Queen Victoria and Prince Albert: his *Scottish Symphony* was later dedicated to the Queen.

In 1841, at the behest of Emperor Frederick William IV of Prussia, Mendelssohn accepted the demanding post of *Kapellmeister* of Berlin. A major task in its own right, Mendelssohn, still only 32 years old, took it on willingly while maintaining his obligations in Leipzig.

Composing mostly in the summer holidays, he produced among other things the *Ruy Blas* overture, the now famous *Violin Concerto* and music for performances of *A Midsummer Night's Dream*. He was also much sought after as a festival organiser, premiering *Elijah* at the 1946 Birmingham Music Festival.

A ruthlessly hard worker from an early age, Mendelssohn was now close to exhaustion. Devastated by the death of his beloved sister, Fanny, in May 1847, six months later, following a series of severe strokes, Felix Mendelssohn died. He was just 38 years old.

Unlike many composers, whose fame came only posthumously, Mendelssohn enjoyed enormous popularity and the greatest respect from his peers. His death was mourned internationally.

MUSIC THEORY WEBSITES

Here is a list of some online locations where you can find further information on music theory.

EMusicTheory
www.emusictheory.com

Center for the History of Music Theory and Literature
www.chmtl.indiana.edu

The Canons and Fugues of J.S. Bach
http://jan.ucc.nau.edu/~tas3/bachindex.html

Tonal Soft
http://tonalsoft.com/enc/default.aspx

Learn-Theory-Music
www.learn-theory-music.com

Music Theory Online
www.societymusictheory.org/mto/

Music Theory On Line
http://music-theory.com

Music Theory
http://library.thinkquest.org/15413/theory/theory.htm

The Society for Music Theory
www.societymusictheory.org

IRCAM
www.ircam.fr/index1-e.html

Nicci Adams' MusicTheory.net
www.musictheory.net

Music Theory for Songwriters
http://chordmaps.com

ChordWizard
www.chordwizard.com/theory.html

A Beginner's Guide to Modal Harmony
www.standingstones.com/modeharm.html

Chord Naming
www.standingstones.com/chordname.html

Music Theory Online by Dr Brian Blood
www.dolmetsch.com/theoryintro.htm

O FOR THE WINGS OF A DOVE

On pages 64 and 65 you'll find a simple arrangement for Felix Mendelssohn's perennially popular choirboy's solo "O For the Wings of a Dove". This piece has been designed as a special challenge for you, since it is the first example of music in the book to be stripped of the note names and finger positions. You will have to figure these out for yourself.

THE READ-THROUGH

Before you attempt to play, read through the music carefully. Go through it note by note, making sure that you know all of their names. Pay special attention to the enharmonic notes. It may help if you write down the note names on both staves of the music (use a pencil if you don't want to mark the book permanently). The fact that you will have worked the notes out for yourself will, of course, have been a useful learning exercise in its own right.

RHYTHMS

Next, concentrate on the note values and rhythm of the piece. You will find that there is nothing too complicated in the music, although there are a number of pairs of quavers which you'll need to count out carefully. Since "O For the Wings of a Dove" has a time signature of four-four, you should count out "one—

and—two—and—three—and—four—and…" throughout every bar. In this way you will be able to place the quavers precisely.

To reinforce this point, let's look at the top line of the first bar. The notes will be played according to this count:

1	A	Crotchet
and		
2	G	Quaver
and	F	Quaver
3	B♭	Crotchet
and		
4	A	Quaver
and	G	Quaver

FINGERING

When working out the fingering, always remember that the finger you select to play a note has to be chosen with the successive notes in mind. Since the melody begins with three descending notes, it wouldn't be very sensible to play the first note (A) with the thumb – there are no free fingers to play the notes that follow. If you use the third finger you are in position to play the complete sequence without having to move the hand, cross over the fingers, or tuck under the thumb.

O FOR THE WINGS OF A DOVE: FELIX MENDELSSOHN

LESSON FOUR
INTERVALS AND MAJOR SCALES

An appreciation of the concept of INTERVALS is fundamental to gaining an understanding of even the most basic music theory. An interval is the distance in pitch between any two individual notes. It can be measured in either tones or semitones. Every single interval can be given a unique name that reflects this measurement. The two notes that make up an interval can either be played at the same time or one after the other. A SCALE is a strict sequence of pitches that begins with a starting note called a TONIC and ends with that same note played one octave higher in pitch. It is the intervals between the tonic and the octave note that define the nature of the scale (NOT the tonic itself). There are a number of different types of scales that are widely used in Western melody and harmony. The most common are the MAJOR and MINOR series.

INTRODUCING SCALES

The vast majority of the melodies and harmonies in Western music are based around the use of a limited range of notes taken from the two most widely used types of scales: the MAJOR and MINOR series. Each of these scales is built from eight different pitches between the tonic (the starting point) and the octave (the end point). This means that each scale consists of seven different notes (the tonic and octave being essentially the same). These scales are the most frequently used of what are also known as the DIATONIC series. They can also be described as HEPTATONIC.

There are, in fact, numerous other scale variations used in different forms of music, or by different musical cultures – not all them are built from just seven notes within the octave: PENTATONIC scales consist of five different notes; the AUGMENTED scale uses six different notes; the DIMINISHED scale is made up from eight different notes; and the CHROMATIC scale uses all twelve notes.

Since the major and minor series are by far the most useful, in this book we will concentrate only on the major scale and the three minor scales (natural minor, harmonic minor and melodic minor). First, though, we should take a more detailed look at the way in which intervals work.

INTRODUCING THE MAJOR SCALE

It was during the very first lesson, on page 36, that we first referred to the major scale by name: this was when you played all of the white notes within the octave starting on Middle C: that was the sequence of notes C—D—E—F—G—A—B—C. You may not have understood the concept or point of a scale at that stage, but you will certainly have been familiar with the sound produced by that sequence of notes.

In this lesson we are going to take a more detailed look at the idea of the major scale – or, more precisely, the intervals that define a set of notes as a major scale. Let's start by looking at the intervals between each of the seven notes in terms of tones and semitones. Each note of the scale is also known as a DEGREE. The pattern of intervals between each of the notes that make up the scale are as follows:

I	C	to	D	Tone
II	D	to	E	Tone
II	E	to	F	Semitone
IV	F	to	G	Tone
V	G	to	A	Tone
VII	A	to	B	Tone
VII	B	to	C	Semitone

The fundamental point that you must understand here is that it is NOT the notes themselves that define this sequence as being a C major scale, but the intervals BETWEEN each note. From any tonic position, any scale that does not have those exact intervals between each of the degrees CANNOT be called a major scale.

A scale can be played in ascending or descending order, but the intervals between the notes always stay the same.

THE IMPORTANCE OF INTERVALS

If the two notes of the interval are played separately it is called a MELODIC INTERVAL. If the second note rises in pitch, it becomes an ASCENDING MELODIC INTERVAL; if the pitch falls it is a DESCENDING MELODIC INTERVAL. The two top staves in the box on the right shows both of these intervals using the notes C and G. The top staff shows an ascending melodic interval; the middle staff shows a descending melodic interval. For reasons which will become clear over the next few pages, an interval of seven semitones such as this is called a PERFECT FIFTH. Play the two notes both as ascending and descending intervals. Get used to the sound this makes – you will hear it used frequently in all forms of music.

Any pair of notes played at the same time can be referred to as a HARMONIC INTERVAL. The bottom staff in the box shows the notes C and G played at the same time. Play the two notes and contrast the sound it makes to the two notes when played one after the other.

Sometimes you may well hear harmonic intervals referred to as a CHORD. Although harmonic intervals can be used to create chordal effects, technically a chord requires three different pitches – we'll be looking at these in detail later, beginning on page 82.

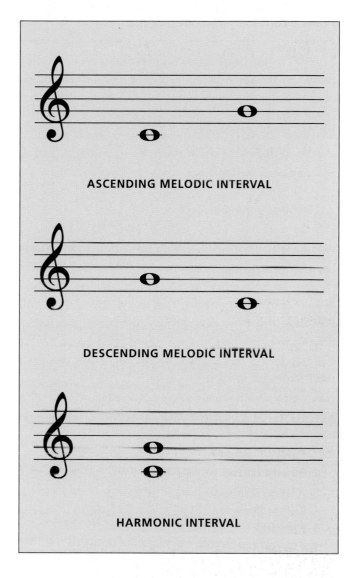

ASCENDING MELODIC INTERVAL

DESCENDING MELODIC INTERVAL

HARMONIC INTERVAL

CONSONANCE AND DISSONANCE

If you sit at the piano and randomly play two notes at the same time you will notice that some harmonic intervals sound naturally more pleasant than others. The musical terms to describe this effect are CONCORD and DISCORD. Although these words are sometimes used very loosely (and usually incorrectly) to describe whether a piece of music is pleasing to the ears, they also have very specific musical meanings relating to pitch intervals.

Every interval can be described in terms of being either CONSONANT or DISSONANT. There are two distinct categories of consonance. PERFECT concords are the so-called "perfect" intervals: unison (two notes of the same pitch played together); perfect 4th (an interval of five semitones); perfect 5th (an interval of seven semitones); and octave. The IMPERFECT concords are the minor 3rd (three semitones) and minor 6th (nine semitones) intervals. All other intervals are deemed to be dissonant. On the right you will see all the semitone intervals within an octave of C.

Note that the interval between C and F can be both consonant or dissonant in certain circumstances, and that C to F♯/G♭ is deemed to be neutral in this respect.

C-C	**OPEN CONSONANCE**
C-D♭	**SHARP CONSONANCE**
C-D	**MILD DISSONANCE**
C-E♭	**SOFT CONSONANCE**
C-E	**SOFT CONSONANCE**
C-F	**CONSONANCE OR DISSONANCE**
C-F♯/G♭	**NEUTRAL OR "RESTLESS"**
C-G	**OPEN CONSONANCE**
C-G♯/A♭	**SOFT CONSONANCE**
C-A	**SOFT CONSONANCE**
C-B♭	**MILD DISSONANCE**
C-B	**SHARP CONSONANCE**
C-C	**OPEN CONSONANCE**

PLAYING THE MAJOR SCALE

Now let's return to looking at the intervals that define the major scale. The staff at the foot of the page shows you the sequence of notes that makes up the C major scale. Pay special attention to the coloured panels that divide each pair of notes; those in blue show intervals of a tone; those in green show intervals of a semitone. Beneath the staff you will see the scale degree, the note name and the fingering.

ASCENDING C MAJOR

Play the ascending C major scale. To play C, D and E, use the thumb and first two fingers respectively; bring the thumb under the two fingers to play F; and then use the four fingers to play the notes G, A, B and C. For this exercise, also count out beats as you play, making sure that each new note is played on the beat. This kind of exercise will help to improve your skills in keeping time.

DESCENDING C MAJOR

Now try playing the same notes in a descending sequence. This will require you to alter your fingering.

1. C (fourth finger)
2. B (third finger)
3. A (second finger)
4. G (first finger)
5. F (thumb)
6. E (second finger – crossed over the thumb)
7. D (first finger)
8. C (thumb)

Each of the notes of the major scale can be given a name and a Roman numeral "degree" based on its position within the scale. They are:

First degree (I)	TONIC
Second degree (II)	SUPERTONIC
Third degree (III)	MEDIANT
Fourth degree (IV)	SUB-DOMINANT
Fifth degree (V)	DOMINANT
Sixth degree (VI)	SUB-MEDIANT
Seventh degree (VII)	LEADING NOTE
First degree (I)	TONIC

The intervals between the tonic note and any of the other degrees of the major scale can also be given a unique name:

TONIC to TONIC	Unison
TONIC to SUPERTONIC	Major 2nd
TONIC to MEDIANT	Major 3rd
TONIC to SUBDOMINANT	Perfect 4th
TONIC to DOMINANT	Perfect 5th
TONIC to SUBMEDIANT	Major 6th
TONIC to LEADING NOTE	Major 7th
TONIC to TONIC	Octave

These relationships are summarised in the keyboard diagram shown across the page.

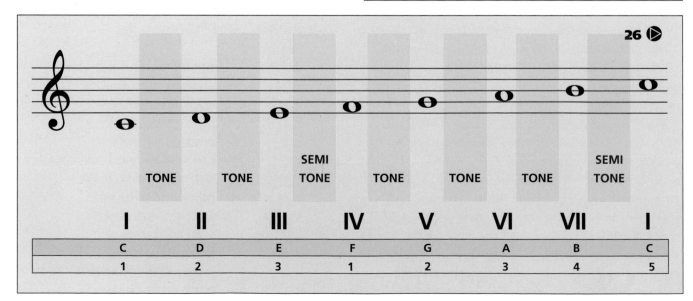

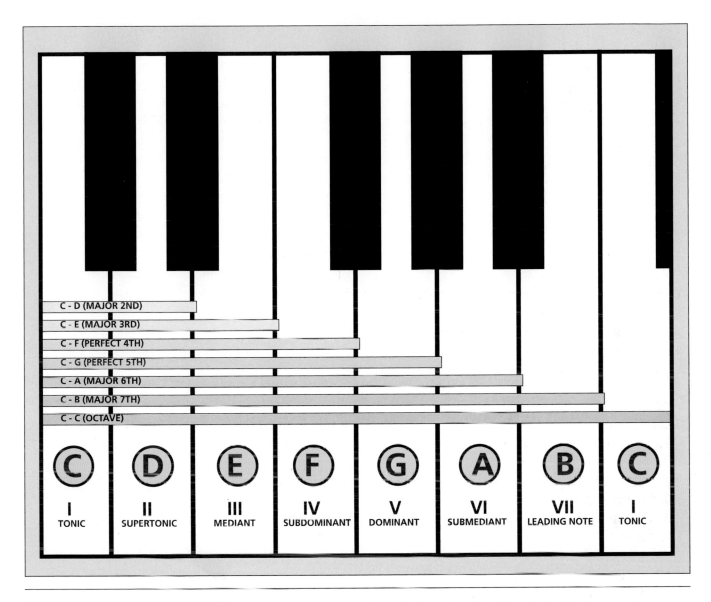

C - D (MAJOR 2ND)
C - E (MAJOR 3RD)
C - F (PERFECT 4TH)
C - G (PERFECT 5TH)
C - A (MAJOR 6TH)
C - B (MAJOR 7TH)
C - C (OCTAVE)

C	D	E	F	G	A	B	C
I	II	III	IV	V	VI	VII	I
TONIC	SUPERTONIC	MEDIANT	SUBDOMINANT	DOMINANT	SUBMEDIANT	LEADING NOTE	TONIC

NAMING AND NUMBERING THE INTERVALS

It's not only the intervals between the degrees of a major scale that we can name. ANY note can be named in relation to any other note. In a scale, these intervals can be given an identifying number by counting from the lowest-pitched note through each degree of the scale until you reach the highest-pitched note.

Here is a practical example: the interval between the notes C and D is known as a SECOND, because D is the second degree of the C major scale. Similarly, the interval between C and E is a THIRD, and so on.

However, labelling intervals numerically doesn't necessarily create a unique description. For example, the notes that make up an interval of a 3rd in a C major scale are C and E, but (as you will see in Lesson Five) in a C minor scale they are C and E♭. The situation can be clarified unequivocally by adding a prefix to

describe the QUALITY of the relationship between the notes.

In a major scale, because of their open consonance, the term PERFECT is used to describe the tonic and the 4th and 5th degrees of the scale; the other degrees are prefixed with MAJOR. Thus, C to F is a described as a perfect 4th, whereas C to A is a major 6th.

In a minor scale (see page 84), the notes that have been flattened to distinguish them from the major scale are referred to as MINOR intervals. In this way, the interval between C and E♭ is a minor 3rd – the interval between C and B♭ is a minor 7th.

All intervals that are not part of the major or minor series of scales can be termed CHROMATIC. For example, the notes D♭ and F♯ do not form part of a major or minor scale in the key of C. In the first instance, since the interval between C and D is a major 2nd, the effect of flattening the D creates an interval that can be called a MINOR 2ND.

LISTENING TO THE MELODIC INTERVALS ON THE MAJOR SCALE

To help you appreciate the way the different intervals within a major scale sound in their own right, the staff below illustrates all of the notes of the C major scale presented as a series of ascending melodic intervals from the tonic. For example, the first pair ascends from C to D, the second from C to E, and so forth throughout the entire C major scale.

Play through each pair of intervals and listen out for the unique characteristics of each one.

As an experiment, try playing each of the pairs as a DESCENDING melodic interval (D—C—E—C—F—C—G—C—A—C—B—C). What ever order you play the notes, the fundamental characteristics of the interval remain in tact.

After you have played the C major series you may find it interesting to play the full list of semitone intervals shown across the page in the same way. This

will help to place the idea of consonance and dissonance in a practical context. In particular, listen out for the way in which the intervals of the perfect 4th (C to F) and perfect 5th (C to G) sound compared to the others when played both as melodic and harmonic intervals. These are openly consonant and create an effect that sounds pleasing to the ear. As your experience increases, the importance of the relationship between the tonic and these two notes will become increasingly apparent.

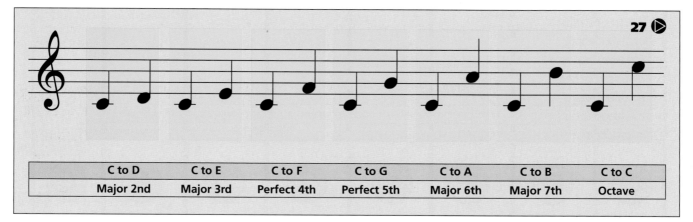

C to D	C to E	C to F	C to G	C to A	C to B	C to C
Major 2nd	Major 3rd	Perfect 4th	Perfect 5th	Major 6th	Major 7th	Octave

HEARING THE HARMONIC INTERVALS ON THE MAJOR SCALE

The next exercise is essentially a repeat of the one above, only this time each degree of the C major scale is played AT THE SAME TIME as the tonic, C.

Play through all of the intervals on the staff, beginning with the note C on its own. Contrast the effect of hearing the the intervals played as pairs of notes rather than single notes – play them both as harmonic and melodic intervals.

Being able to pick out intervals, however they are played, will be useful

when you are dealing with more advanced concepts such as chords. This facility will help to enable you to distinguish three or more notes when played together. For this reason, understanding and recognising intervals is absolutely fundamental to the art of composing and arranging music.

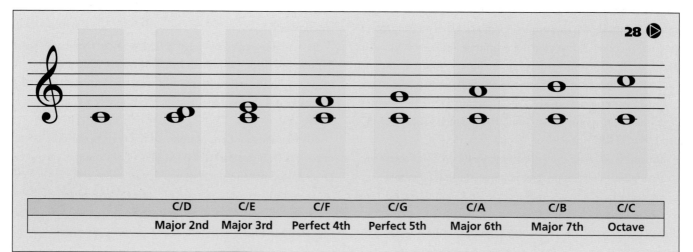

C/D	C/E	C/F	C/G	C/A	C/B	C/C
Major 2nd	Major 3rd	Perfect 4th	Perfect 5th	Major 6th	Major 7th	Octave

ENHARMONIC INTERVALS

Since enharmonic notes can have either of two names, it follows that an interval name may depend on whether the note is a sharp or flat. Let's begin by looking at the difference between C♯ and D♭ with a tonic of C.

AUGMENTED INTERVALS

To see how the numbering works we first need to look at the relationship between two identical notes. Rather than calling the interval between C and C a "1st", it is instead referred to as a UNISON. So although the the intervals between C and D♭, and C and C♯ sound identical in pitch, they take two different names depending on their use, You've already seen that the interval between C and D♭ is a MINOR SECOND.

When a note is raised by a semitone, it is said to be AUGMENTED. This means that an interval between C and

C♯ is an AUGMENTED UNISON. It is possible for any interval to be augmented in this way.

DIMINISHED INTERVALS

The opposite effect of an augmented note is one that is DIMINISHED. This flattens the upper note, lowering it in pitch by a semitone. Like its augmented counterpart, any interval can be diminished.

THE FIVE QUALITIES

We now have the full set of "qualities" used to describe intervals between any two degrees of any type of scale. They are: perfect, major, minor, augmented and diminished.

Intervals with a numeric value of a 2nd, 3rd, 6th and 7th can be diminished, minor, major or augmented; intervals of a unison, 4th, 5th and octave can only be diminished, perfect or augmented.

THE FULL SET OF INTERVALS

A full set of the intervals from a tonic of C are shown in the chart below. Notice that when perfect intervals are flattened, the results are always diminished intervals. However, where major intervals are flattened, the result is always a minor interval; a diminished major interval has to be "double-flattened" – meaning it is reduced in pitch by two semitones (or a tone, if you like).

All of these possible intervals can also be notated in shorthand using a variety of different symbols.

A major or perfect interval can be shown as upper-case roman numerals – for example, a major 7th can be notated as "VII". Minor equivalents are always shown in lower-case Roman numerals. In this way, a minor 2nd can be notated as "ii".

Augmented intervals are indicated with a "plus" sign and diminished intervals with a "degree" symbol. Thus, "V+" signifies an augmented 5th and "V°" denotes a diminished 5th.

RANGE	ABBREVIATION	INTERVAL	RANGE	ABBREVIATION	INTERVAL
C-C♭	I°	DIMINISHED UNISON	C-G♭	V°	DIMINISHED 5TH
C-C	I	UNISON	C-G	V	PERFECT 5TH
C-C♯	I+	AUGMENTED UNISON	C-G♯	V+	AUGMENTED 5TH
C-D♭♭	II°	DIMINISHED 2ND	C-A♭♭	VI°	DIMINISHED 6TH
C-D♭	ii	MINOR 2ND	C-A♭	vi	MINOR 6TH
C-D	II	MAJOR 2ND	C-A	VI	MAJOR 6TH
C-D♯	II+	AUGMENTED 2ND	C-A♯	VI+	AUGMENTED 6TH
C-E♭♭	III°	DIMINISHED 3RD	C-B♭♭	VII°	DIMINISHED 7TH
C-E♭	iii	MINOR 3RD	C-B♭	vii	MINOR 7TH
C-E	III	MAJOR 3RD	C-B	VII	MAJOR 7TH
C-E♯	III+	AUGMENTED 3RD	C-B♯	VII+	AUGMENTED 7TH
C-F♭	IV°	DIMINISHED 4TH	C-C♭	VIII°	DIMINISHED OCTAVE
C-F	IV	PERFECT 4TH	C-C	VIII	OCTAVE
C-F♯	IV+	AUGMENTED 4TH	C-C♯	VIII+	AUGMENTED OCTAVE

OTHER MAJOR SCALES

If you use both the black and white keys, there are twelve different notes within an octave. It is possible to create major scales using any of these notes as the tonic, but using the same intervals between each degree.

G MAJOR SCALE

If the tonic is moved from C up to the note G, the same set of intervals will produce a G major scale. As you can see from the staff immediately below, the interval between the sixth and seventh degrees means that we must use a black note to make the correct scale: if the note were left as F, the interval between the sixth and seventh degrees would only be a semitone, and thus the scale would not be correct. In the key of G, the black note has to be named F♯, even though it has the same pitch as G♭. This is so that a note appears on every line or space in the sequence of the scale. In this case, if the note were to be called G♭ there would be two Gs on the staff, meaning that every occurrence of G♭, which would be common in a piece of music in the key of G major, would have to indicated with a flat symbol.

Play the G major scale using the fingering shown beneath the note names.

It is the same fingering as you used to play C major.

F MAJOR SCALE

Moving the entire C major scale up in pitch by a perfect 4th creates the scale of F major. As you can see from the diagram at the foot of the page, the intervals have remained the same. This time, the major scale incorporates a flattened note (B♭).

You will notice that fingering for this scale is slightly different from C major and G major. This is because of the position of the black note in the sequence.

You can hear both scales being played on Track 29 of the CD. **29** ▶

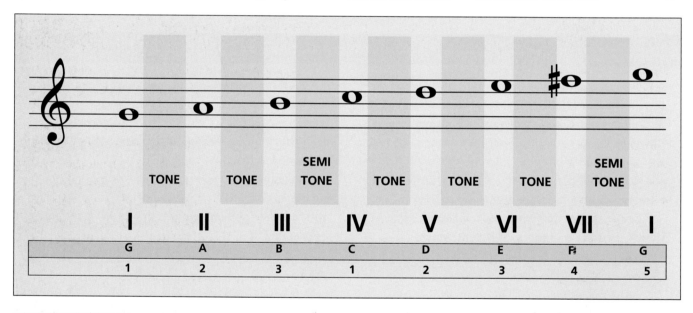

	TONE		SEMI TONE		TONE		TONE		TONE		SEMI TONE	
I		II		III		IV		V		VI		VII	I
G		A		B		C		D		E		F♯	G
1		2		3		1		2		3		4	5

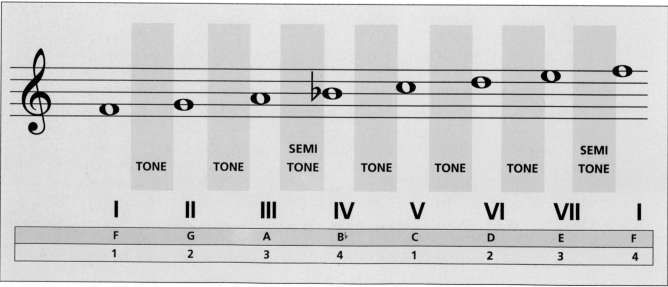

	TONE		SEMI TONE		TONE		TONE		TONE		SEMI TONE	
I		II		III		IV		V		VI		VII	I
F		G		A		B♭		C		D		E	F
1		2		3		4		1		2		3	4

INTERVAL EXERCISE

In the unlikely event that you haven't yet got the message, here it is one more time: comprehending intervals goes right to the heart of understanding the way every kind of music works. An instinctive interpretation of intervals will tell you which combinations of notes sound better than others, and how they can be used to create specific effects.

On the right you will see 28 different ranges of notes. Your task is to play the notes on the piano as melodic and harmonic intervals, and then work out the name of each one. This will test your understanding both of scales and of intervals. Watch out for the enharmonic notes, remembering that they take different names depending on their use. You can find the answers on page 191.

1.	G TO A	2	B TO F#
3.	F# TO A	4.	B♭ TO G♭
5.	D♭ TO C	6.	G TO D#
7.	D♭ TO A	8.	F TO G♭♭
9.	C TO A♭	10.	A♭ TO D♭
11.	D♭ TO A♭	12.	G♭ TO C
13.	C TO G#	14.	B♭ TO D♭
15.	E♭ TO C	16.	A TO B
17.	D TO F	18.	B TO F
19.	F TO B	20.	A TO A♭
21.	B TO A♭	22.	A♭ TO D
23.	F TO C	24.	B♭ TO F#
25.	E♭ TO A♭	26.	E TO G#
27.	D TO F#	28.	B♭♭ TO A

DYNAMIC MARKS

Dynamic marks can be used to set the the mood of a piece of music, and are often used in conjunction with foot pedals on a piano. These marks are shown in their abbreviated forms. They can also be used in conjunction with the crescendo and diminuendo "hairpin" marks (*see page 94*).

Like much formal musical terminology, the instructions are based on abbreviations of Italian words. The two most basic terms are *forte*, meaning loud, and *piano*, meaning soft. They are denoted using a stylised "*f*" and "*p*" symbols respectively. These two basic terms can be modified by prefixing with the word *mezzo*, literally meaning "half", but taken to mean "medium". They can also be exaggerated: if *f* is loud, *ff* is very loud, and *fff* is extremely loud.

Some composers have taken this approach to unusual extremes, adding a lot of additional letters – Tchaikovsky famously marked a bassoon solo in the first movement of his 6th Symphony as *pppppp*! But like tempo marks, dynamic marks are not a precise instruction of the volume. They are generally used in relation to other dynamic marks – *mf* (*mezzo-forte*) in the middle of a piece of music tells the player to play louder than the preceding music. The exact interpretation is largely down to the player.

ITALIAN NAME	INSTRUCTION	ABBREVIATION
FORTE	Loud	*f*
PIANO	Soft	*p*
MEZZO-FORTE	Medium loud	*mf*
MEZZO-PIANO	Medium soft	*mp*
FORTISSIMO	Very loud	*ff*
FORTISSISSIMO	Extremely loud	*fff*
PIANISSIMO	Very soft	*pp*
PIANISSISSIMO	Extremely soft	*ppp*
FORTE PIANO	Loud then immediately soft	*fp*
POCO FORTE	Slightly loud	*pf*
SFORZATO/SFORZANDO	Played with force	*sf*
RINFORZATO/RINFORZANDO	Becoming stronger	*rf*
SMORZANDO	Gradually fading	*smorz*
CALANDO	Slower with decreasing volume	*cal*

KEY SIGNATURES

So far, you have seen the major scales built from the tonics C, G and F. These notes represent the KEY SIGNATURES for each of those scales. The key signature is indicated at the start of a piece of music by a series of sharps or flats that can be seen between the clef and time signature. This doesn't happen in the key of C major, which uses no sharps or flats. For all the other major keys, however, the sharps or flats are positioned on the staff in accordance with their use within that scale. To see how this works, let's look at an example with a key signature of G major.

The G major scale consists of the notes G, A, B, C, D, E and F♯. Since music in the key of G major is far more likely to use the note F♯ than F, the staff is shown with a sharp symbol on the top line of the staff, directly following the treble clef.

In practice, this means that, unless otherwise shown by the use of the "natural" symbol (♮), the note names given to each space and letter on the staff are to be used throughout the piece. Thus, in G major, each time a note appears on the top line of the staff it must be played as F♯ rather than F – this is because F♯ is not a part of the G major scale.

The G major scale with the key signature correctly in place is shown below.

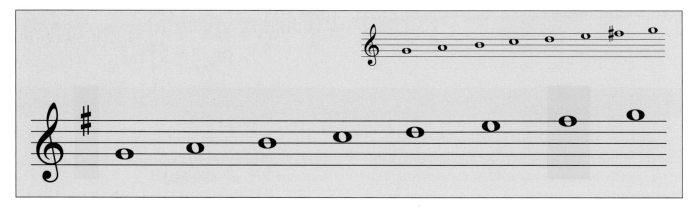

ENHARMONIC POINTS

Although a little confusing at first, eventually you will immediately know that any piece of music with one sharp after the clef has a key signature of G, and that all references to F should be played as F♯. This is the reason why the note MUST be called F♯ rather than G♭: if it were not, the staff would have no Fs, but two Gs (G and G♭), which could only be distinguished if every single occurrence of G was either marked as a flat or a natural. This would make the written music terribly confusing.

SCALE BUILDING

Like G major and F major, all the major scales can be recognised from the number of sharps or flats shown at the beginning of the staff. The number and position of sharps and flats on each new scale follows a very specific simple mathematical pattern. F is the fourth degree of the C major scale. Building a new major scale from the fourth degree creates the F major scale, which is recognisable by the fact that it features a single flat – the note B♭. If you continue this process, building new scales from the fourth degree, an interesting mathematical pattern emerges.

Projecting the same pattern of intervals from B♭ (which is the fourth degree of the F major scale) creates a B♭ major scale. This comprises the notes B♭, C, D, E♭, F, G and A. This has TWO flats. If we take it to the next stage, you will see the pattern emerge: the fourth degree of B♭ major is E♭. If we build a major scale with this note as the root, it comprises the notes E♭, F, G, A♭, B♭, C and D – THREE flats. Thus, building a new major scale from the fourth degree of an existing major scale, the new scale will always require the use of one extra flat.

A similar principle can be applied to those key signatures that use sharps. If you build a scale from the FIFTH degree of an existing major scale, the resultant scale always adds a sharp to the seventh degree.

ONE SHARP AND ONE FLAT

Music written in the key of G major has a KEY SIGNATURE of G major. This is shown with a sharp on the top line of the treble staff, indicating that unless otherwise shown by the use of a "natural" symbol, the note should be played as F♯

Music written with a key signature of F Major should always be shown with a flat symbol on the hird line of the treble staff.

CIRCLE OF FIFTHS

We can summarise the relationship between the key signatures using a diagram called the CIRCLE OF FIFTHS AND FOURTHS (commonly abbreviated as the circle of fifths). First created in 1728 by German musician Johann David Heinichen, the twelve segments of the circle are laid out so that moving clockwise, the notes change by a perfect 5th. (This also represents scales built on the fifth degree of the previous major scale.)

Starting with the key of C at the top of the circle, each step you count clockwise adds a sharp to the key signature of that note. Moreover, the additional sharp is ALWAYS ON THE SEVENTH DEGREE of the new scale. The principle also works for additional flats if you move in an counter-clockwise direction, where each subsequent key signature is a perfect 4th DOWN from the root note of the previous scale. In practice, this makes the root for each new scale the same as the fourth degree of the previous scale. Thus by starting at the top of the circle, each step you move counter-clockwise adds a FLAT to the key signature for that note.

The circle of fifths is useful in memorising the patterns that create key signatures. It's worth taking some time out to learn these key signatures by heart – and an absolute necessity if you want your sight-reading to reach a high standard.

CIRCLE OF FIFTHS

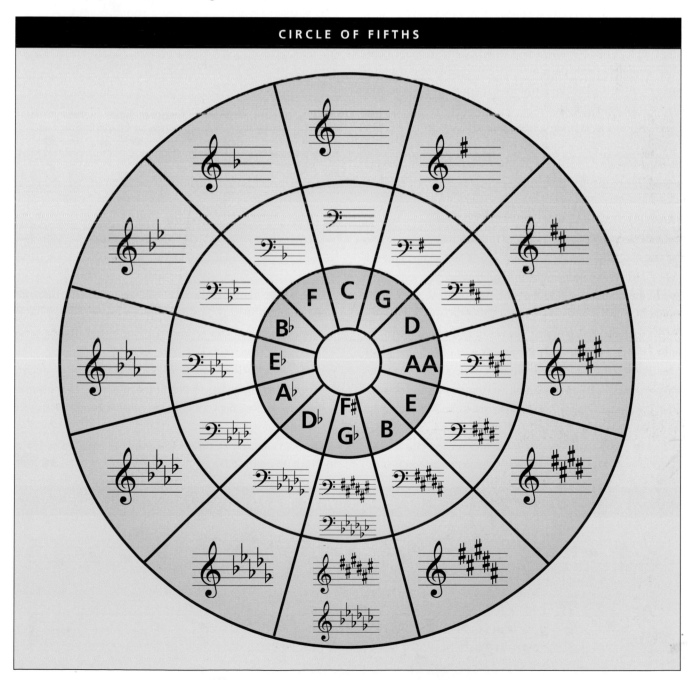

TRANSPOSING A TUNE

The process of taking a piece of music and altering the pitches so that it has a different key signature is called TRANSPOSITION. You've already seen two of the most basic examples of transposition in practice earlier in the lesson. We started with a C major scale, and then took the same pattern of intervals and shifted them up by a perfect 5th, creating a G major scale. We then did the same with an interval of a perfect 4th, creating a major scale in the key of F.

Any sequence of notes can be moved in this way. By transposing the scale from C major to G major, EACH OF THE NOTES HAD ITS PITCH RAISED BY AN INTERVAL OF A PERFECT 5TH – that's the exact interval between C and G. By applying that rule consistently, the intervals between the notes always remain exactly the same – the only difference is that they are in a different key. It guarantees, if you like, that the tune always remains the same.

Transposition is a very important concept in music. For example, if you have a song in a specific key that happens to be outside a vocalist's range, the ability to transpose allows you to rework the music in a different key.

TRANSPOSITION IN PRACTICE

Look at the three bars of music on the right. The top bar is in the key of C. The interval between the first and second note is a minor 2nd (one semitone); the interval between the second and third note is a major 2nd (one tone); the interval between the third and fourth notes is also a major 2nd. The notes are C—B—A—B. To transpose that bar to the key of F (the middle bar), we must take all the pitches up by a perfect 4th (or, as we know from the "circle of fifths", down by a perfect 5th). The notes then become F—E—D—E. If you play both bars, one after the after, it is clear that the tune is exactly the same. Finally, we can transpose the key of F major to E♭ major, by increasing all the pitches by a major 7th. The new range of notes becomes E♭—D—C—D. The melody, however, remains exactly the same.

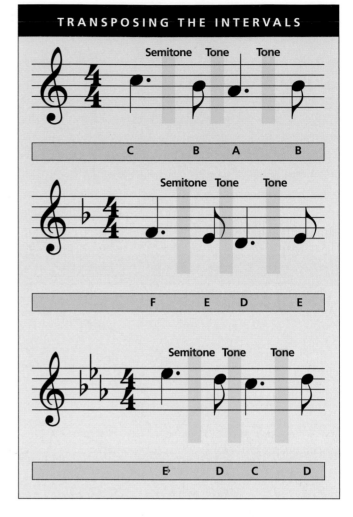

TRANSPOSING THE INTERVALS

The music above is, in fact, the opening bar from the traditional Welsh march, *Rhyfelgyrch Gwyr Harlech* (well known in English as *Men of Harlech*). The melody for the verse section is shown in full below in the key of C major. Across the page the same melody can be seen in F major and E♭ major. Notice the key signatures shown at the beginning of the music – no sharps or flats denotes C major; one flat denotes F major; three flats denotes E♭ major.

You can compare all three versions of the piece if you listen to Track 30 on the CD. **30** ▶

MEN OF HARLECH (C MAJOR)

MEN OF HARLECH (F MAJOR)

MEN OF HARLECH (E FLAT MAJOR)

MUSICAL PHRASES

Just as the way we speak can be broken into self-contained paragraphs and sentences, so too can a piece of music. The musical equivalent of a sentence is referred to as a PHRASE. A musical phrase can be shown formally using a symbol called a SLUR. This is a curve that can be placed around a phrase of any length.

A defining characteristic of a musical phrase is that it has a natural pause at its end – again, rather like the spoken word. A slur placed around a phrase has the practical effect of shortening the final note within its boundary, thus emphasising the self-contained nature of the group.

Implicit within the boundaries of a slur is the need for the notes to be played in a smooth and flowing manner, creating a cohesion that once again emphasises the "togetherness" of the phrase. Playing in this way is known as "LEGATO". The most important factor when playing legato is that all of the notes within the slur are played without any breaks – rather as if they were the result of single movement or gesture.

Take a look at the staff below. In Bars 2 and 3, you will see two identical groups of beamed quavers. The slurs tell us that they form two independent musical phrases. This is the flowing bass line from our arrangement of Brahms' *Lullaby*, shown on the next page.

In the hands of a good musician the interpretation of the slur is subtle and cannot be defined in any precise way. The term "feel" is probably as good as any to describe a process aimed at making the music sound as natural as possible.

BRAHMS REVISITED

This is the same Brahms piece that you first played on page 45. At that stage we were not concerned with key signatures: to keep things as simple as possible, it was written in C major. This time you will play a full version of the tune in the key of G major.

This is also the first piece of music you will have encountered that incorporates ARTICULATION MARKS, of which slurs are the most common example. As you've just seen, each bar of the bass line should be played in a single flowing movement, pausing only at the end of the phrase. Also pay attention to the phrasing on the treble staff.

Notice that at the end of Bar 3, rather than linking the two quavers together, the slur seems to curve off into the distance. This is to indicate that the slur continues on to the next line of music; if you look at Bar 4, you will see that the slur begins well in front of the note head, indicating that it is a continuation from the pervious line. The phrase in question begins with the last two notes of Bar 3, and ends with the second note of Bar 5.

Finally, you will notice the tiny numbers that suddenly seem to have appeared above and below the staves. These are fingering instructions that appear on sheet music when the composer or arranger wants to suggest the most appropriate positions. When more than one note is played, the numbers are stacked in the same order as the notes on the staff.

LULLABY: JOHANNES BRAHMS

ROBERT SCHUMANN (1810–1856)

Robert Schumann was one of the key composers of the Romantic era. Born in 1810, in Zwickau, Germany, Schumann initially studied law. While at university, however, he devoted himself almost entirely to the pursuit of literature and music.

At the age of 20 he decided to focus his attention on becoming a piano virtuoso. This ambition was quickly thwarted when he severely injured his right hand. Instead he turned to composition. The piano music he composed during his twenties was not immediately popular, being viewed as rather unconventional. Although Schumann's modern-day reputation is that of a "musician's musician", such works as *Carnaval*, the *Davidsbündlertänze*, and *Fantasy in C* remain standards of piano repertory.

In 1834, Schumann embarked on a significant secondary career, founding and editing the *Neue Zeitschrift für Musik* (*New Journal of Music*). Not only influential in championing the work of radical new composers such as Chopin and Berlioz, it became a forum for his frequent attacks on what he saw as an encroaching philistinism. Schumann became the best-known music critic of his day.

His marriage in 1840 to Clara Wieck was a turning point in his life. Already well-known as a leading pianist, Clara was responsible for introducing many of her husband's works to concert audiences. Although most of his compositions had previously been for the piano, Clara encouraged him to take on more ambitious projects for which he may not have been best suited. Although he produced some highly rated orchestral and chamber works, it is for his early compositions that he is best remembered.

Schumann's final years were overshadowed by illness. After a failed suicide attempt in 1854, he was committed to an asylum, where he died two-and-a-half years later.

REPEATING WHOLE SECTIONS OF MUSIC

Most music is based on repetition. Rather than write out music in full, we can be economical by inserting instructions within the staves that indicate that some sections must be repeated in full.

There are some very sophisticated ways in which this can be done – you'll encounter some of these in Lesson 7 – but for now let's look at the simplest way of repeating a section of music, by placing dots inside a double-bar line. The dots within the double-bar line indicate that preceding bars should be repeated: if any of those bars have double-bar lines with dots at the start, then you repeat from that bar, otherwise you repeat from the beginning of the music.

In the example below, you first play Bars 1 and 2; then you repeat Bars 1 and 2; play Bars 3, 4, and 5; then repeat Bars 4 and 5; finally, you end on Bar 6.

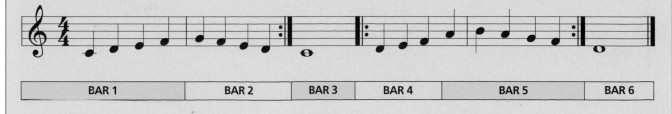

| BAR 1 | BAR 2 | BAR 3 | BAR 4 | BAR 5 | BAR 6 |

SCHUMANN'S *CHORALE*

Before you attempt this next piece, there are a number of factors that you must first consider.

Let's start with the key signature. The existence of the sharp on the fifth line of the treble staff, and the fourth line of the bass staff tells us that the music is in the "one-sharp" key, G major. This means that every note on the "F" line must be played as F sharp, unless the note has a natural symbol attached.

Where is the time signature? Instead of the usual two numbers, the stylised "C" symbol denotes that it is written in common time, which is the same as four-four time.

The repeat symbol at the end of Bar 8 tells you that the preceding bars must be repeated. Since there is no "start repeat" bar, you must repeat from the beginning of the music.

Watch out for the multiple voices that first appear during Bar 7. The panel on the right tells you all about interpreting music written in this way.

The tempo mark (*moderato*) tells you to play the music at a moderate speed.

The *mp* symbol at the start of Bar 9 indicates that the remainder of the piece is played *mezzo-piano* or "medium soft".

Look at the treble line in Bar 7 (*also shown above*): there seems to be something strange going on during beats three and four. These multiple VOICES occur when two notes with different time values are played at the same time. In this example, on the third beat, the minim (A) is sustained for the remaining two beats of the bar. At the same time, a crotchet (D) is also played. But this note only sustains for a single beat. While A is still being sustained, a crotchet (C) is played on the fourth beat. It's quite simple, really.

CHORALE: ROBERT SCHUMANN

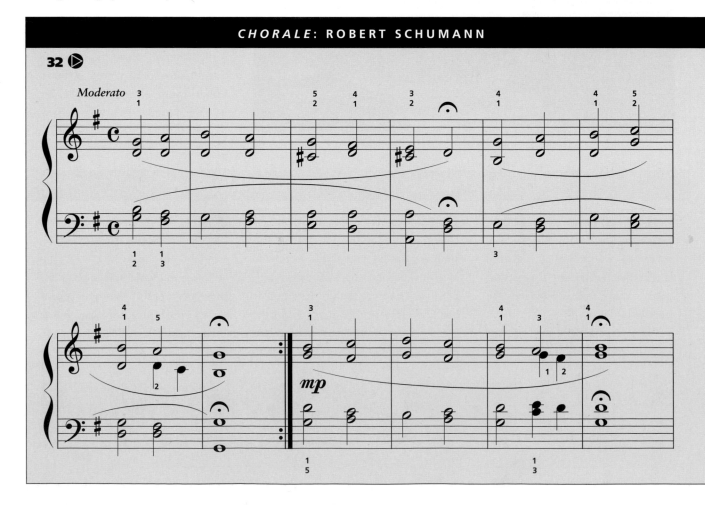

SIGHT-READING

Much of the content of this lesson has been aimed at developing or improving sight-reading skills. Although many non-classical keyboard players cannot read music well, it is a useful skill to develop, especially when playing with other musicians.

SIGHT-READING CHECKLIST

Here is a brief list of useful pointers that will help you gain sight-reading skills:

- Get used to reading unfamiliar music. Go to a music library and take out examples of written music. If you spend just five minutes a day working out time signatures, key signatures, note names and rhythms, within a year you should easily be able to comprehend even the most complex pieces of written music.

- When you tackle a new piece of music, begin by checking out the time signature. Remember that the top number tells you how many beats in the bar; the bottom number tells you what kind of beats they are.

- Study the key signature. Look at how many sharps or flats there are at the beginning of the staff – these tell you the sharp or flat notes you have to play.

- Look out for unfamiliar notes or symbols. In particular watch out for "accidentals" – sharps, flats and naturals – and their effect.

- A lot of written music revolves around repeating patterns of notes or rhythms. Look out for where these occur since this will make your task easier.

- When playing a new piece of music, begin with a steady tempo. Give yourself a one-bar count-in before you start, but keep counting the beats out in your head while playing.

LESSON FIVE
TRIADS AND MINOR SCALES

During this lesson we will formally introduce the idea of CHORDS. This is the effect of three or more notes being played at the same time. We've touched on the subject previously, but this time we will be discussing them in more detail – in particular, the importance of the three-note TRIAD chords. A good understanding of these chords is essential as they form the basis of more complex chord structures . As you will see, there is a natural link between chords and scales. To this end, we'll finally introduce the three different types of MINOR SCALE. We'll begin, though, with another look at the important issue of tempo – the speed at which you play a piece of music.

TEMPO MARKS

You've already briefly come into contact with the idea of TEMPO on page 42. Literally meaning "time", it is a measurement of the period elapsed between each beat, and is usually measured in BEATS PER MINUTE (BPM). It is sometimes shown at the top of a piece of music as a note-type followed by a number. The example below literally means that one hundred quaver beats are played every minute.

 = **100**

It is possible to measure this figure in a number of different ways. Traditionally, musicians and composers have used a pyramid-shaped mechanical device called a METRONOME. This can be set manually so that it provides an audible click at a specific tempo.

Invented in around 1812 by a Dutchman named Dietrich Winkler, the idea of the metronome was copied, modified and patented in 1815 by Johann Maelzel who, although later sued by Winkler, became the name most commonly associated with the device. So much so, in fact, that it became widely known as the "Maelzel Metronome". To the present day, some written music can be seen to show the letters "M.M." alongside the time value.

M. M. = **100**

A BRIEF HISTORY OF SCALES

What's so special about the major scale and the minor scale? To understand why things have turned out this way, let's look at some history.

The earliest musical scales were attributed to the ancient Greeks. The scales were composed of eight notes, the last being an octave higher in pitch than the starting note. The church adopted them in the Middle Ages and renamed them MODES. These scales were built around what would then have been the equivalents to the "white" notes on the piano keyboard. (The enharmonic notes were not used at this time.)

There were seven modes, each one starting on a different note. Each was built using a different set of intervals and produced different characteristic qualities. Modes were known by their original ancient Greek names. They were:

1. IONIAN (C—D—E—F—G—A—B)
2. DORIAN (D—E—F—G—A—B—C)
3. PHRYGIAN (E—F—G—A—B—C—D)
4. LYDIAN (F—G—A—B—C—D—E)
5. MIXOLYDIAN (G—A—B—C—D—E—F)
6. AEOLIAN (A—B—C—D—E—F—G)
7. LOCRIAN (B—C—D—E—F—G—A).

This arrangement survived until the 16th century when increasingly complex polyphonic composition began to outgrow the modal system. By the next century a new harmonic order evolved, based around keys and tonality. The idea of a tonic or home-key was developed and the intervals of the scale were fixed by their distance from it. This allowed key signatures that identified the tonic and ordered the scale and melody with reference to it.

In recent times, many modern musicians have turned to the electronic drum machine or MIDI sequencer to produce the same effect. As such, the terminology "B.P.M." used by such equipment has become more widely used. Indeed the growth of "DJ culture" and the widespread popularity of electronic dance music has brought the term into popular vocabulary.

While this figure is extremely precise, in practice it is often used as a general guide rather than a fixed value. Although most classical compositions would show such a figure in the music, it is fair to say that few musicians or conductors have such perfect timing skills as to know these values instinctively. Some compositions acknowledge these vagaries by prefixing the beat value with the Italian word *circa*, meaning "about". This is usually shown as "*c*".

WATCHING THE NOTE TYPE

Most "metronome marks" – a name sometimes given to these beat-per-minute values – are shown as crotchets, but they can alter depending on the nature of the music. Pay careful attention to these note types: if you were to muddle them up, the music would sound very different. For example, one hundred minims per minute would mean an equivalent speed of two hundred crotchets per minute.

TEMPO MARKS

A lot of classical music is specified in terms of a general tempo. These instructions are usually shown in their original Italian names, which has meant that for several centuries musicians around the world have had to acquaint themselves with a modest vocabulary of foreign terms. The panel above shows the most important of these instructions, or TEMPO MARKS. Alongside the translation you will find an approximate range measured in beats per minute. A wider selection of similar terms is shown on pages 116–117.

TEMPO MARKS

When judging at what speed to play a piece of music, the player or conductor has considerable scope for his or her own interpretation. If you look at the list below you'll see that a piece played *andante* could be played anywhere between 75 BPM and 105 BPM. That could result in some extremely varied performances.

A further traditional use for tempo marks – and one which has caused a degree of confusion in the past – is that they are also sometimes used to indicate the character or mood in which it should be played.

Here is a small list of the most commonly found tempo marks:

TERM	TRANSLATION	B.P.M.
GRAVE	VERY SLOW	40
LENTO	SLOW	40–55
ADAGIO	SLOW	55–75
ANDANTE	WALKING SPEED	75–105
MODERATO	MODERATE SPEED	105–120
ALLEGRO	FAST (LITERALLY, "CHEERFUL")	120–150
VIVACE	LIVELY	150–170
PRESTO	VERY FAST	170–210
PRESTISSIMO	AS FAST AS POSSIBLE	ABOVE 210

PRACTICAL TIME-KEEPING

For many beginners, keeping time one of the most problematic issues. Although some people seem to have more "natural rhythm" than others, don't worry if you struggle at first. It *is* something that you can learn.

Practising tempo is simple, so long as you have some form of device that keeps strict time. At its most basic, a clock ticking every second or half-second would be better than nothing at all, but a metronome, drum machine or MIDI sequencing software – anything that allows you to set the beat yourself – would be far more useful.

Working through scales and broken chords with a metronome – and not always at the same tempo – is a standard element of most serious players' practice regimes.

Here is a more basic exercise:

1. Set the metronome tempo at 60 (one click per second).
2. Play Middle C on every beat for four bars.
3. Play Middle C on every halfbeat for four bars.
4. Play Middle C on every quarterbeat for four bars.

Ensure that you vary the fingers you use, and that you play these exercises with both hands.

THE THREE MINOR SCALES

As you have realised (hopefully) the major scale is constructed from a fixed pattern of seven intervals from the tonic to the octave. Although the major scale is the most common type of scale in use, it is by no means the only one. Also frequently used is the MINOR SCALE. Unlike the major scale, in which the pattern of intervals always remains the same, there are three principal types of minor scales, each of which has its own subtly different characteristics. Each can also be defined by a fixed set of seven intervals from the tonic to the octave. They are the NATURAL MINOR (sometimes known as the RELATIVE MINOR), the HARMONIC MINOR and the MELODIC MINOR. All three minor scales have one common difference from a major scale in that the third degree is always flattened by a semitone. The differences between the three minor scales revolve around movements of the sixth and seventh degrees.

THE NATURAL MINOR SCALE

The pattern of intervals between the notes that make up the natural minor scale are, in the key of C:

I	C	to	D	One tone
II	D	to	E♭	One semitone
III	E♭	to	F	One tone
IV	F	to	G	One tone
V	G	to	A♭	One semitone
VI	A♭	to	B♭	One tone
VII	B♭	TO	C	One tone

PLAYING AN ASCENDING NATURAL MINOR SCALE

To form a natural minor scale from a major scale, the third, sixth and seventh degrees are each lowered by a semitone.

The fingering for the ascending scale can be played in the following way. You'll probably find it particularly demanding spreading the second, third and fourth fingers to move between A♭, B♭ and C, but the more you practise movements such as these, the easier they'll become.

1. Play C with the thumb.
2. Play D with the first finger.
3. Play E♭ with the second finger.
4. Bring the thumb underneath the fingers to play F.
5. Play G with the first finger.
6. Play A♭ with the second finger.
7. Play B♭ with the third finger.
8. Play C with the fourth finger.

PLAYING A DESCENDING NATURAL MINOR SCALE

Once you've done that, try the fingering shown below for playing the C natural minor scale in descending sequence (C—B♭—A♭—G—F—E♭—D—C):

1. Play C to G using the fourth, third, second and first fingers.
2. Play F with the thumb.
3. Bring the second finger over the thumb to play E♭.
4. Play D with the first finger.
5. Play C with the thumb.

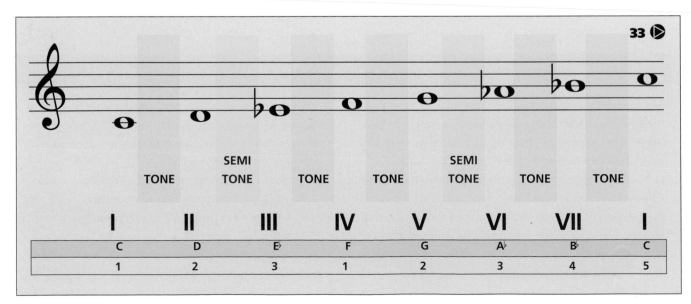

THE HARMONIC MINOR SCALE

The harmonic minor scale differs from the natural minor scale in that the seventh degree is sharpened – it is raised by a semitone. Thus, the pattern of intervals required to create the scale is:

I	C to D	One tone
II	D to E♭	One semitone
III	E♭ to F	One tone
IV	F to G	One tone
V	G to A♭	One semitone
VI	A♭ to B	One tone + one semitone
VII	B to C	One semitone

Notice that by sharpening the seventh degree, the interval between the sixth and seventh degrees is now three semitones.

PLAYING AN ASCENDING HARMONIC MINOR SCALE

Play the harmonic minor scale for the key of C shown. The fingering differs from the natural minor scale because of the rather awkward jump of three semitones between the sixth and seventh notes:

1. Play C with the thumb.
2. Play D with the first finger.
3. Play E♭ with the second finger.
4. Bring the thumb underneath the fingers to play F.
5. Play G with the first finger.
6. Play A♭ with the second finger.
7. Bring the thumb underneath to play B.
8. Play C with the first finger.

WHAT DOES MINOR MEAN?

As a piece of music written in a major key has an easily identifiable characteristic flavor, so too does music written in a minor key. As you should be able to discern from looking at and playing the natural minor scale, the most significant difference between the two is in the third note: the major scale uses an interval of a major 3rd to the tonic; the minor scale uses an interval of a minor 3rd—a half-step difference.

But what does the difference mean in practice? How does it affect the way in which we react to a piece of music? Although the comparison may be a little superficial, you can think of the difference between music written in major and minor keys as being rather like the difference between a sound that is happy and one that is sad. Generally speaking, music with a mournful or melancholic flavour will have been written in a minor key.

Perhaps a good symbolic example of this difference can be heard in the contrast between the joyful "Wedding March," which is played in a major key, and the mournful "Funeral March," which is played in a minor key.

PLAYING A DESCENDING HARMONIC MINOR SCALE

1. Play C to G using the fourth, third, second and first fingers.
2. Play F with the thumb.
3. Bring the second finger over the thumb to play E♭.
4. Play D with the first finger.
5. Play C with the thumb.

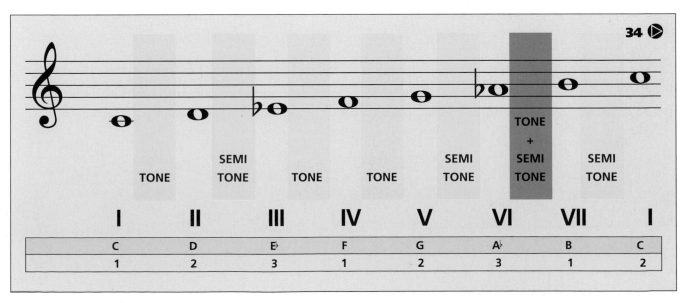

THE MELODIC MINOR SCALE

One of the problems of working with the harmonic minor scale is the "difficult" pitch interval of three semitones between the sixth and seventh degrees. To make this more musically palatable, the sub-mediant can be raised by a semitone to create the melodic minor scale.

Play the scale below to hear the effect of "sharpening" the sixth degree of the scale. You can use the following fingering:

1. Play C with the thumb.
2. Play D with the first finger.
3. Play E♭ with the second finger.
4. Bring the thumb underneath the fingers to play the note F.
5. Play G with the first finger.
6. Play A♭ with the second finger.
7. Play B with the third finger.
8. Play C with the fourth finger.

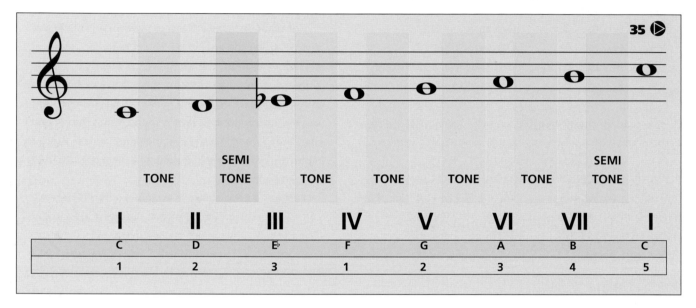

DESCENDING THE MELODIC MINOR SCALE

You can only use the intervals above for ASCENDING the melodic minor scale. When descending, the sharpened sixth and seventh notes sound awkward.

To resolve the problem, when descending the melodic minor scale you will find that playing the UNSHARPENED sixth and seventh notes will sound more pleasant. This means that when descending the melodic minor scale you revert to the notes of the NATURAL MINOR scale. It is extremely important that you understand the distinction between these two scales.

Play the fingering for the descending scale shown beneath the staff below.

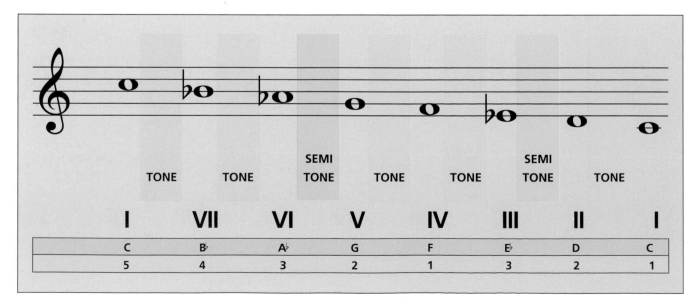

RELATIVE MAJOR AND MINOR

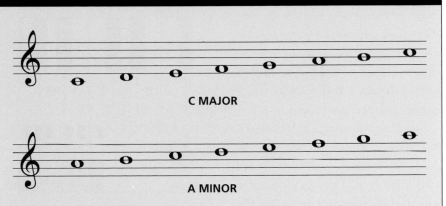

C MAJOR

A MINOR

If you build a natural minor scale from the sixth degree of a major scale, you should notice something interesting going on. Look at the two scales on the right. The top staff shows a C major scale; the bottom staff shows the natural minor scale in the key of A. (A is the sixth degree of the C major scale.)

The C major scale and the A natural minor scale use the same set of notes – albeit from different tonics. This significant relationship between the C major scale and the A natural minor scale can be described in two different ways. The A minor scale can be called the RELATIVE MINOR of the C major scale. Equally, the C major scale can be referred to as the RELATIVE MAJOR of the A minor scale.

The relationship between the two scales is important to understand. Since both are played without sharps or flats, the key signatures appear to be the same. You've already seen that it's possible to tell the key of a piece of music by counting the number of sharps and flats between the clef and the time signature. The relationship described above means that the same observations can also be made for music written in a minor key.

On the right you can see a list of the most common major key signatures along with their equivalent relative minor keys:

C MAJOR	=	A MINOR
G MAJOR	=	E MINOR (1 sharp)
D MAJOR	=	B MINOR (2 sharps)
A MAJOR	=	F♯ MINOR (3 sharps)
E MAJOR	=	C♯ MINOR (4 sharps)
B MAJOR	=	G♯ MINOR (5 sharps)
F♯ MAJOR	=	D♯ MINOR (6 sharps)
F MAJOR	=	D MINOR (1 flat)
B♭ MAJOR	=	G MINOR (2 flats)
E♭ MAJOR	=	C MINOR (3 flats)
A♭ MAJOR	=	F MINOR (4 flats)
D♭ MAJOR	=	B♭ MINOR (5 flats)
G♭ MAJOR	=	E♭ MINOR (6 flats)

NAME THAT KEY

Here is an exercise that will test your understanding of key signatures. There are three staves of music below. Each one is notated as is if it were in the key of C – this means that all occurrences of sharps or flats are shown within the bars of music, rather than by an identifiable key signature at the beginning of the staff. Your task is to play each piece of music and identify the key signature for each one. You can find the answers on page 191.

INTRODUCING THE TRIADS

When three or more notes are played at the same time, the resulting musical effect is called a CHORD. The simplest form of chord is called a TRIAD, which is made up from three notes.

Triads are built from a ROOT NOTE and follow a specific set of intervals. The three notes are always the root, the 3rd and the 5th. Since, however, there can be a number of different types of 3rd and 5th note, it follows that there are a number of different types of triad. There are, in fact, four different kinds of triad, each of which uses 3rds and 5ths of differing qualities: the MAJOR TRIAD, the MINOR TRIAD, the AUGMENTED TRIAD and the DIMINISHED triad.

If you play all four triads one after the other you will gain an appreciation the different sounds they create. You can hear them being played on Track 36 of the CD. **36** ▶

MAJOR TRIAD

The major triad consists of the root, major 3rd and perfect 5th. In the key of C, as shown above, the notes C, E and G are used. This combination of notes is commonly referred to as C MAJOR. Play the chord as shown above (*top left*),

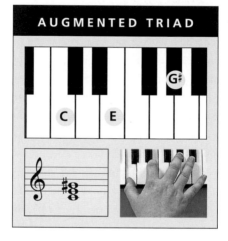

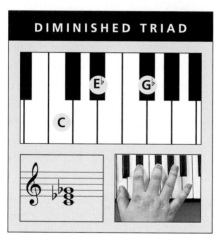

using the thumb, first and second fingers to play the three notes.

MINOR TRIAD

The minor triad consists of the root, minor 3rd and perfect 5th. In the key of

C it uses the notes C, E♭ and G. It differs from the major triad in that the 3rd is flattened. This chord is often known simply as C MINOR. Play the chord as shown, using the thumb, first and second fingers to play the three notes.

CHORDS ON SCALES

The relationship between scales and chords can be magnified by building a triad on each degree of the major scale. In fact, these chords can be named after the degrees on which they are constructed. The triad on the first degree of the scale, for example, can be referred to as the TONIC TRIAD; similarly, the chord on the second degree may be called the SUPERTONIC triad. You can name the chords in this way right up to the octave.

The idea has practical value in that the degrees themselves can also be used as a shorthand description. In the key of C major, for example, the DOMINANT TRIAD (G major) could also be called the "five" chord because it is built from the 5th degree. In such cases it would be written down as a "V" chord. As well as being used in music theory, this approach is also sometimes used within informal musical settings where chord charts may be used instead

of notated music. For example, a "one-four-five in G" would describe a chord sequence revolving around the chord progression G major ("I"), C major ("IV") and D major ("V").

As you will become increasingly aware, there is a special relationship between chords and notes built on the first, fourth and fifth degrees of a diatonic scale: indeed, the "I", "IV" and "V" triads are also known as the PRIMARY TRIADS.

AUGMENTED TRIAD

The augmented triad comprises the root, major 3rd and augmented 5th intervals. This chord differs from the major triad only in that the fifth note is sharpened – that's what augmented means. In the key of C the notes required are C, E and G♯.

DIMINISHED TRIAD

Finally, the diminished triad is made up from the root, minor 3rd and diminished 5th intervals. In the key of C the notes used are C, E♭ and G♭. This chord can be named C DIMINISHED.

CHORD RELATIONSHIPS

The most fundamentally significant aspect of harmonic theory is the way in which chords sound when played in relation to one another. This is, after all, the basis by which all musical structures must stand or fall.

You already know how the notes of a diatonic scales relate to one another, so the most effective way of showing similar relationships for chords is by building triads from the major and minor scales. The staff below shows triads built from the

scale of C major. It could be described as a HARMONIZED SCALE. If we build a triad from each note of the scale USING ONLY NOTES FOUND WITHIN THAT SCALE, we actually find that only the first, fourth and fifth chords are major triads: the second, third and sixth degrees create minor triads, and the seventh degree creates a diminished triad.

Play through this sequence. Listen to the natural manner in which they flow into one another—in particular how satisfactorily the B diminished triad RESOLVES back to C major.

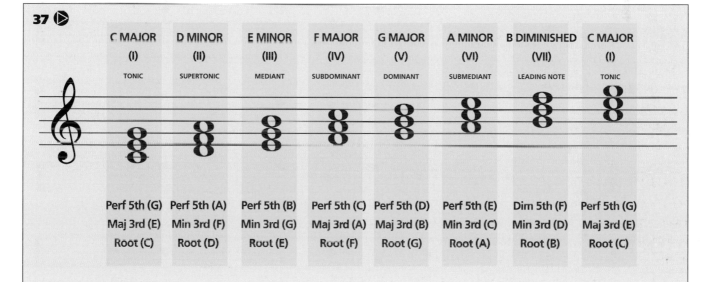

HARMONISED MINOR SCALE

It is also possible to build triads from each degree of the minor scale.

However, because the natural, melodic and harmonic minor scales all use slightly different notes, each scale generates three different triad sequences. The three scales are

shown below for the tonic of C. Play through each of the harmonised scales. You will hear that the differences in character between the three scales are now magnified.

C NATURAL MINOR

(I)	C Minor	(C, E♭, G)
(II)	D Diminished	(D, F, A♭)
(III)	E♭ Major	(E♭, G, B♭)
(IV)	F Minor	(F, A♭, C)
(V)	G Minor	(G, B♭, D)
(VI)	A♭ Major	(A♭, C, E♭)
(VII)	B♭ Major	(B♭, D, F)
(I)	C Minor	(C, E♭, G)

C HARMONIC MINOR

(I)	C Minor	(C, E♭, G)
(II)	D Diminished	(D, F, A♭)
(III)	E♭ Augmented	(E♭, G, B)
(IV)	F Minor	(F, A♭, C)
(V)	G Major	(G, B, D)
(VI)	A♭ Major	(A♭, C, E♭)
(VII)	B Diminished	(B, D, F)
(I)	C Minor	(C, E♭, G)

C MELODIC MINOR

(I)	C Minor	(C, E♭, G)
(II)	D Minor	(D, F, A)
(III)	E♭ Augmented	(E♭, G, B)
(IV)	F Major	(F, A, C)
(V)	G Major	(G, B, D)
(VI)	A Diminished	(A, C, E♭)
(VII)	B Diminished	(B, D, F)
(I)	C Minor	(C, E♭, G)

BROKEN CHORDS IN G MAJOR AND F MAJOR

We first introduced the idea of broken chords in Lesson 4. Here are two further sets for you to add to the technical aspects of practice sessions. Once again, follow the fingering carefully for both hands.

TRANSPOSING THE EXERCISES

Now that you understand the principles of transposition, you should be able to adapt these major-scale exercises for every other key, and for other types of scale. Since the exercises are based around the root (I), major 3rd (III) and perfect 5th (V) of each chord, adaptation is simple. The first exercise follows this pattern: I—III—V—III—V—I—V—I—III—I. To play the same exercise in the key of F♯ all you need to know is that the root is F♯, the major 3rd is A♯ and the perfect 5th is C♯, making the notes F♯—A♯—C♯—A♯—C♯—F♯—C♯—F♯—A♯—F♯.

Similarly, you can convert this kind of exercise to any of the minor scales. They will be the same as their major equivalents only with the major 3rd flattened to a minor 3rd. Thus the first exercise below in the key of C natural minor will be C—E♭—G—E♭—G—C—G—C—E♭—C. (Modify the fingering so that the top E♭ is played with the 4th finger, rather than the 5th.)

BROKEN CHORDS IN THE KEY OF G

38

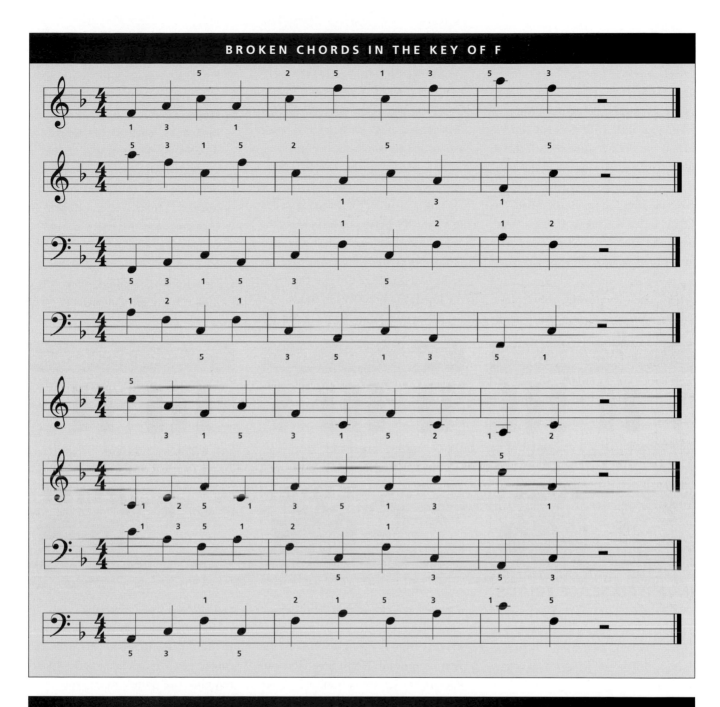

SYNTHETIC BASS LINES

If you listen to any pop, rock, jazz, blues or dance music, you will hear the overall sound underpinned by a line of low-pitched notes. This is the BASS LINE. Although this role has traditionally been carried out by a bass guitar, since the widespread use of the synthesizer, bass parts are increasingly generated on a keyboard. The modern keyboard

player is expected to have a good understanding of the way bass lines work within an arrangement.

A traditional approach to bass playing (which is effectively the mindset the keyboard player has to adopt in this role) is to write down the chords of the song and coincide the root note of the chord with each chord. Although this is a very safe

approach – it's impossible to do anything that sounds "wrong" when you play in this way – the results can sometimes be rather dull.

The best bass lines are approached from a melodic angle, creating an identifiable repeating sequence (or "riff") that underpins the sound, fits in with the harmonic structure of the song and helps to define the rhythm.

INVERTING THE TRIADS

The triads on page 88 all consisted of notes played in order of pitch from the root. That means the 1st, 3rd and 5th notes have all been successively higher in pitch. This need not always be the case.

In the three boxes below, there are three variations on the C major triad. The first chord is a familiar C major triad, using the notes C (root), E, (major 3rd) and G (perfect 5th). But what happens if we move the root ABOVE the 3rd and the 5th notes? If you name the notes from the bottom up, you can see that the

lowest pitch is now E. However, THIS DOES THIS MEAN THAT THE CHORD IS NOW IN THE KEY OF E.

Play the two triads. You will hear that they have a different balance to their sound, and yet somehow they still have a "sameness" to them. This is because they ARE the same chord. The process of altering the order of notes is called INVERSION. In fact, a triad in which the 3rd note is the lowest in pitch is called a FIRST INVERSION. That same triad can be further rearranged so that the 5th is the lowest in pitch. This is known as a SECOND INVERSION. **39** ▶

NAMING INVERSIONS

The abbreviated names given to the triads on the harmonized scales can be extended to cover inversions. Each of the Roman numeral degree positions can be suffixed with a lower-case letter denoting their construction. The letter "a" following the degree indicates that the chord should be played in its root position; "b" is used to indicate the first inversion of a chord; and "c" indicates a second inversion.

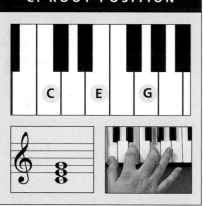

C: ROOT POSITION — C E G

C: FIRST INVERSION — E G C

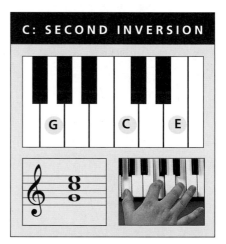

C: SECOND INVERSION — G C E

INVERTED SCALE TRIADS

The next two exercises teach you movement through the different inversions. Each of the eight bars

represents one of the chords on the harmonised major scale. Within each bar, triads are played as crotchets, moving from the root position to the first inversion, second inversion and back to the root position one octave

above the starting triad. Play the eight bars slowly, giving yourself sufficient time to change chords without making mistakes. Since the fingering for each chord always remains the same, every time you

40 ▶

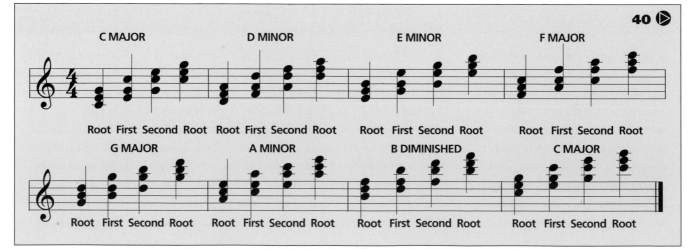

C MAJOR — Root First Second Root
D MINOR — Root First Second Root
E MINOR — Root First Second Root
F MAJOR — Root First Second Root
G MAJOR — Root First Second Root
A MINOR — Root First Second Root
B DIMINISHED — Root First Second Root
C MAJOR — Root First Second Root

play a new chord you need to move the entire right hand. The staff below is essentially the same exercise, only this time one octave lower on the bass clef, and played by the left hand.

When you've played each exercise through, try turning the triads into broken chords. This means playing each triad as a sequence of separate notes. To do this, you need to dispense with the time signature shown below, and instead play them as quavers within a bar of three-four time. Thus, the first four bars would play the notes C—E—G, E—G—C, G—C—E, and C—E—G.

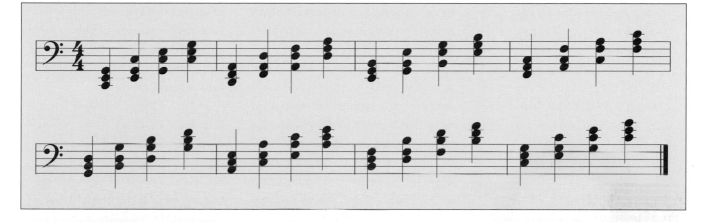

INVERSION IN MELODY

In those last two exercises all you were really doing was moving through inversions of the same chord one bar at a time. But you will have noticed how the tonal balance of a chord altered with each movement. This effect is used in music to create an "implied" melody. This works because when you change chords, the movement between the highest pitched notes creates a melodic effect.

To illustrate this, try out the piece of music on the right. As you will quickly begin to hear, it is not merely a set of chords, but creates the effect of playing a clearly defined melody – in this case, the song "Clementine".

If you study the make-up of each chord, you will see that the song is constructed from inversions from four different chords.

Before you play the piece in full, try this experiment. Work through each bar playing ONLY the highest pitch note in each chord. You should hear the

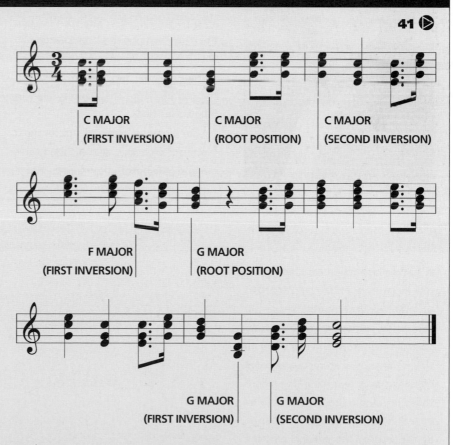

melody very clearly. Now play the full chordal version – the melody is still there.

You might find it easier playing this sequence if you use the thumb, first

and fourth fingers to play each chord. This will minimise the stretching that is necessary between some of the chords.

FREDERIC CHOPIN (1810–1849)

The son of a French schoolteacher working in Poland, Chopin grew up in Warsaw, entering the Conservatoire at the age of 16. By this time he had already performed in local salons and composed several rondos, polonaises and mazurkas.

With the harsh repression that followed the crushing of the Polish uprising in 1830, Chopin decided to abandon his homeland in favour of Paris. Here he first attempted a career as a concert pianist. Yet although he was indisputably a virtuoso musician, he was shocked to discover that his delicate playing style was not popular with either critics or audiences.

Chopin's circumstances were turned around following an introduction to the wealthy and influential Rothschild family. Putting aside a concert career (he gave little more than 30 formal concerts during his lifetime), he quickly became the toast of Parisian high society. With his courteous manner, sensitive playing and frail, attractive looks, he was able to live and work in considerable style, financed by lucrative engagements as a private teacher and salon performer. But as well known as Chopin became in Paris, he took almost no part in the "establishment" music world, preferring the company of artists and writers to fellow musicians.

Chopin never married, but his most famous liaison was with his long-term mistress, the notorious novelist George Sand. The period they spent together (1838–1847) coincided with perhaps his most productive creative period. Among his major compositions of the period were his Twenty-four Preludes, Fantasy in F minor, the Barcarolle, Scherzo in C sharp minor and the well-known Polonaise in C minor.

In 1847, Chopin and Sand had a turbulent break-up, and when revolution broke out in Paris a few months later, Chopin fled to England. However, by now his health – which had been frail at the best of times – began to deteriorate. He returned to Paris exhausted in November 1848, and eleven months later was dead. His funeral was attended by almost three thousand people.

No great composer ever devoted himself as exclusively to the piano as Chopin. He is admired above all for his great originality in exploiting the piano, and was a major influence on most of the great composers of the nineteenth century.

CRESCENDO AND DIMINUENDO

A further instruction for altering the playing is to use either CRESCENDO or DIMINUENDO marks. These are shown in notated music using "hairpin" symbols. The top stave on the right shows a crescendo mark stretched over two bars. This means that the volume should gradually be increased until it reaches a new level at the end of the second bar; the diminuendo shown in second staff does the reverse. They can be used in conjunction with dynamic marks (*see page 73*).

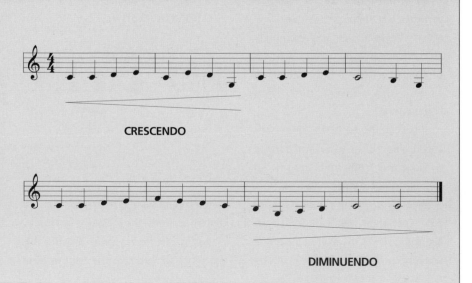

CRESCENDO

DIMINUENDO

PRELUDE OPUS 28 NO. 7: FREDERIC CHOPIN

Now it's time to put some of your newly acquired polyphonic skills to the test.

One of Frédéric Chopin's many preludes, this is among the most popular pieces of music ever written for the piano.

Let's have a brief look at any areas of note. We'll begin with the key: one sharp – as you ought to know by now – means that it is in the key of G major, and so all of the "F lines" on both staves are played as F♯.

The time signature is three-four, meaning there are three crotchets beats to each bar.

The tempo mark *Andantino* usually means that the piece should be played slightly faster than *andante* – which means literally "at walking pace".

Notice that in Bar 11 you must begin to play gradually louder until reaching a maximum volume (*forte* – "loud") in Bar 13. Pay attention to the diminuendo hairpins in Bars 14 and 16. The piece finishes on *piano* ("quiet").

NOCTURNE: FELIX MENDELSSOHN

A nocturne is a nineteenth-century instrumental piece, composed for piano, and characterised by an extended melody over a chordal accompaniment. Nocturnes are quiet, reflective pieces, written to be played at a slow tempo. Chopin is widely believed to be the finest exponent of the form. This nocturne, is taken from Felix Mendelssohn's music for William Shakespeare's *A Midsummer Night's Dream*.

One of the reasons we've selected this piece is that it was written in the key of E major, which is a tricky key for beginners. We can tell it's written in E major because there are four sharps at the beginning of the music. The E major scale goes: E—F♯—G♯—A—B—C♯—D♯—E. This means that unless otherwise shown by a natural symbol (as in Bar 3), F, G, C, and D must be interpreted as sharps.

The tempo mark tells us to play the piece *Andante tranquillo* – the two words literally mean "at a walking pace" and "calmly". Here is an example of a tempo mark not only being used as a guide to playing speed, but also to indicate the mood of the piece.

There is also further mood instruction before the performance mark. The *piano* symbol (p) is an instruction to play quietly, but it's also preceded by the word "dolce," meaning "sweetly" or "softly". The piece should be played this way until Bar 17, when the *mezzo-forte* ("medium-loud") instruction appears.

In Bar 20, there is an alternative *diminuendo* instruction, without the "hairpin". (It's also possible to show a *crescendo* as "*cresc*". This shows a gradual decrease in volume until *mezzo-forte* on the third beat of the following bar. The music remains at this level until the *piano* mark, after the fermata in Bar 27.

LESSON SIX

ADVANCED CHORDS

In addition to taking on a number of more demanding pieces of music, in this lesson, we'll also be examining some of the more complex chords – those which use more than three notes. The note most commonly attached to the four basic triads is the seventh note – major 7th, minor 7th or diminished 7th. These can be used to create an impressive array of interesting and harmonically rich sounds. It's also possible to add notes from beyond a scale's octave range. The distance between such notes and the tonic is called a COMPOUND INTERVAL. Chords using such notes are termed EXTENDED CHORDS.

BEYOND THE TRIADS

Moving around the notes of a triad can provide endless fascinating variations. However, why should we restrict ourselves to a harmonic palette of three notes when there are another nine different notes from which we can choose? There's no reason at all. In fact, if polyphony – the sound of more than one pitch being played at the same time – was restricted to three notes, hardly any of the music with which we are so familiar would be possible.

THE SEVENTH SERIES

Adding notes from outside the triad allows for the creation of a greater range of harmonic textures. Although there are many possible notes from which to choose, the most common addition is that of the leading note – the seventh. Adding a seventh to any type of triad creates a seventh chord.

WHICH SEVENTH?

As you've already seen, a seventh note does not in itself describe a strict pitch within a key. For example, in the key of C major, the minor 7th is B♭, the major 7th is B, the diminished 7th is B♭♭ (which has the same pitch as A) and the augmented 7th is B♯ (which has the same pitch as C). Thus, depending on the musical context, it is

possible to produce a number of different types of 7th chord.

The four most commonly used seventh chords are shown below. You can hear them played on Track 44 of the CD.

 44 ▶

DOMINANT SEVENTH

The first seventh chord we'll look at is the DOMINANT SEVENTH. It can be formed by adding a minor seventh to a

major triad. The C dominant seventh chord shown below uses the notes C, E, G and B♭. Dominant seventh chords are more often than not referred to simply as "sevenths".

MINOR SEVENTH

The MINOR SEVENTH chord is formed by adding a minor seventh to a minor triad. C minor seventh therefore

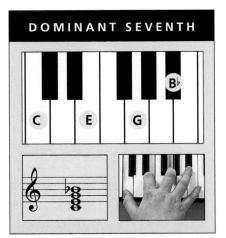

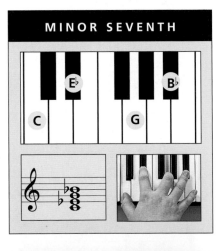

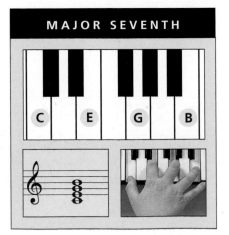

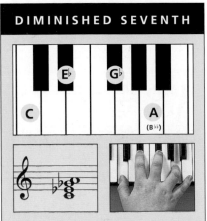

consists of the notes C (root), E♭ (minor 3rd), G (perfect 5th), and B♭ (minor 7th).

MAJOR SEVENTH

The next seventh chord we'll discuss is the MAJOR SEVENTH. This is a major triad with the addition of a major seventh note. Across the page (*bottom left*) you will find C major seventh, consisting of the notes C (root), E (major 3rd), G (perfect 5th) and B (major 7th).

DIMINISHED SEVENTH

This is a diminished triad with the addition of the diminished seventh. C diminished seventh is shown across the page (*bottom right*) and consists of the notes C, E♭, G♭ and B♭♭ (shown as A).

OTHER SEVENTHS

As you will discover when you look through the chord dictionary (*see pages 158–181*), there are many other kinds of seventh chords. For example, a

HALF-DIMINISHED SEVENTH adds a minor seventh to a diminished triad (C—E♭—G♭—B♭); a SEVENTH DIMINISHED FIFTH takes a major triad, flattens the perfect 5th and adds a minor 7th (C—E—G♭—B♭); a MAJOR SEVENTH DIMINISHED FIFTH takes a major triad, flattens the perfect 5th and adds a major 7th (C—E—G♭—B).

In each case, an understanding of intervals makes the naming of the chord quite straightforward.

HEARING THE SOUNDS OF THE SEVENTHS

The eight-bar sequence below puts together some of the seventh chords you've just seen. The chord name is shown immediately beneath the staff; in the mauve beneath that, you can see the SPELLING for each chord – this is the term used to

describe the notes and intervals that make up a chord.

As you play the sequence not only will you be able to contrast the way the different seventh chords sound, but the effect they create when played alongside one another will become obvious.

Some chords have also been shown in different inversions, allowing for an additional interesting contrast. These are shown in the green panel.

There are many other types of seventh chord. These vary in their musical obscurity and use.

45 ▶

C MAJOR	C 7	F MAJOR	F 7	C MINOR 7	C MINOR 7	C MAJOR 7	C MAJOR 7
						FIRST INVERSION	FIRST INVERSION
Root (C)	Min 7th (B♭)	Root (F)	Min 7th (E♭)	Min 7th (B♭)	Root (C)	Maj 7th (B)	Root (C)
Perf 5th (G)	Perf 5th (G)	Perf 5th (C)	Perf 5th (C)	Perf 5th (G)	Min 7th (B♭)	Perf 5th (G)	Maj 7th (B)
Maj 3rd (E)	Maj 3rd (E)	Maj 3rd (A)	Maj 3rd (A)	Min 3rd (E♭)	Perf 5th (G)	Maj 3rd (E)	Perf 5th (G)
Root (C)	Root (C)	Root (F)	Root (F)	Root (C)	Min 3rd (E♭)	Root (C)	Maj 3rd (E)

F 7	F 7	F MINOR 7	F MINOR 7	C DIM 7	C DIM 7	C DIM 7	C DIM 7
FIRST INVERSION		FIRST INVERSION		FIRST INVERSION		SECOND INVERSION	
Min 7th (E♭)	Root (F)	Min 7th (E♭)	Root (F)	Min 7th (A)	Root (C)	Min 3rd (E♭)	Min 7th (A)
Perf 5th (C)	Min 7th (E♭)	Perf 5th (C)	Min 7th (E♭)	Dim 5th (G♭)	Min 7th (A)	Root (C)	Dim 5th (G♭)
Maj 3rd (A)	Perf 5th (C)	Min 3rd (A♭)	Perf 5th (C)	Min 3rd (E♭)	Dim 5th (G♭)	Min 7th (A)	Min 3rd (E♭)
Root (F)	Maj 3rd (A)	Root (F)	Min 3rd (A♭)	Root (C)	Min 3rd (E♭)	Dim 5th (G♭)	Root (C)

SO WHAT ABOUT THE OTHER DEGREES?

So far we have created chords that use the first, third, fifth and seventh degrees of a diatonic scale. But what about the second, fourth and sixth degrees? Can these be turned into useful chords?

Adding the sixth degree to a major triad creates a chord which is generally referred to as a SIXTH. By adding the same note to a minor triad it's also possible to create a MINOR SIXTH.

Things are a little less straightforward for the second and fourth degrees. If you add these notes to major or minor triads the resulting dissonant intervals will create chords that have limited harmonic use. However, these notes can be used in what are termed SUSPENDED chords. This means taking a major triad and moving the major third up or down by a semitone to create either a SUSPENDED FOURTH or a SUSPENDED SECOND.

The suspended fourth chord consists of the root, perfect 4th and perfect 5th. So in the key of C, the suspended fourth chord is made up from the notes C, F and G. These chords are commonly used and are often referred to as "sus fours". The replacement of the major 3rd by the perfect 4th can also be used with seventh chords, creating a SEVENTH SUSPENDED FOURTH, or "seven sus four".

Suspended fourth chords are widely used in all forms of music. One particularly common movement sees the suspended fourth resolving to the major chord at the end of a piece of music in what is called a FULL CLOSE.

The SUSPENDED SECOND works in much the same way. This time, the major 3rd is replaced by the major 2nd. For example, C suspended second uses the notes C, D and G.

If you listen to Track 47 on the CD you will hear C sixth (usually called simply "C6"), C suspended fourth and C suspended second. **46** ▶

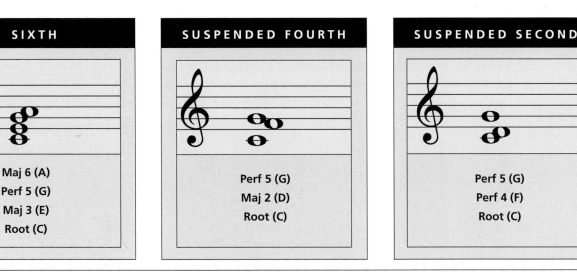

SIXTH	SUSPENDED FOURTH	SUSPENDED SECOND
Maj 6 (A)		
Perf 5 (G)	Perf 5 (G)	Perf 5 (G)
Maj 3 (E)	Maj 2 (D)	Perf 4 (F)
Root (C)	Root (C)	Root (C)

COMPOUND INTERVALS

Although the second, fourth and sixth degrees are the least useful degrees for chords, they come into their own when used beyond the octave. They can be used effectively where the interval is more than an octave from the tonic. Intervals stretching beyond the octave are called COMPOUND INTERVALS. The notes are named and numbered as continuations of the scale from the root.

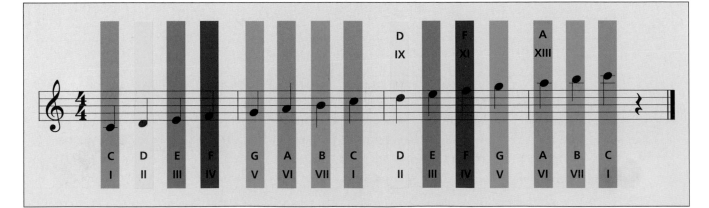

To see how this works, look at the diagram at the foot of the opposite page. It shows the C major scale played over two octaves. To work out the compound intervals, you simply count along degrees of the scale. If you think of the octave as the eighth degree, then one octave above the second degree can be called the ninth degree. Chords using these intervals are called EXTENDED CHORDS.

The common extended chords make use of three compound intervals: the NINTH, the ELEVENTH, and the THIRTEENTH. All compound intervals retain the "qualities" attributable to the same degrees within the scale. Thus, they become MAJOR NINTHS and MAJOR THIRTEENTHS, but PERFECT ELEVENTHS.

TESTING THE INTERVALS

Before we look at these chords, let's just ponder the intervals themselves. Start by playing a harmonic interval of a major second (C and D), and then play a harmonic interval of a major ninth (C and D). Although the "same" notes are being played, the effect created is very different. Repeat this exercise with perfect fourths and perfect elevenths (C and F), and major sixths and major thirteenths (C and A).

NINTH SERIES

The DOMINANT NINTH chord is created by adding a compound interval of a major 9th to a dominant seventh chord. In this way, the C dominant ninth chord (or "C9" as it's usually called) uses the notes C—E—G—Bb—D. MINOR and MAJOR NINTH chords can also be created by adding the major 9th to minor and major seventh chords respectively.

ELEVENTH AND THIRTEENTH SERIES

The DOMINANT ELEVENTH adds the perfect 11th to the dominant ninth chord. In the key of C it uses the notes C, E, G, Bb, D and F.

The dominant thirteenth adds the major 13th to the dominant eleventh chord. In the key of C it uses the notes C, E, G, Bb, D, F and A).

Minor and major equivalents of these chords can also be created.

TOO MANY NOTES?

Track 47 on the CD features all nine chords. However, if you listen to the thirteenth series you will become aware of a possible problem.

A full thirteenth chord requires you to play seven notes at the same time. But it doesn't actually sound that pleasant when you do play all of the notes. In practice, as long as the root, third, seventh and thirteenth notes are played, the essential character of the thirteenth chord will remain. The same kind of approach can be taken to elevenths and, to a lesser extent, ninths. **47** ▶

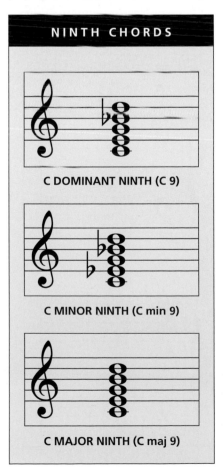

NINTH CHORDS

C DOMINANT NINTH (C 9)

C MINOR NINTH (C min 9)

C MAJOR NINTH (C maj 9)

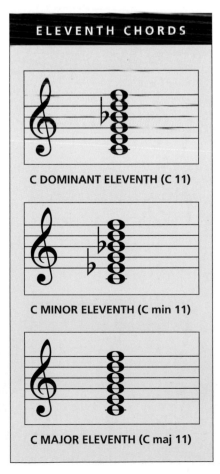

ELEVENTH CHORDS

C DOMINANT ELEVENTH (C 11)

C MINOR ELEVENTH (C min 11)

C MAJOR ELEVENTH (C maj 11)

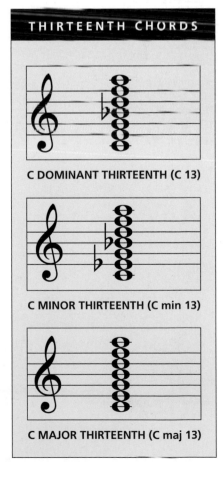

THIRTEENTH CHORDS

C DOMINANT THIRTEENTH (C 13)

C MINOR THIRTEENTH (C min 13)

C MAJOR THIRTEENTH (C maj 13)

CHORD DESCRIPTIONS

The naming system for the chords you have used so far is relatively self-evident once you have understood intervals and the way they are described. You know, for example, that by adding a minor 7th to a triad you can create a range of seventh chords, or by adding a major 7th, you can create major seventh chords. Or by adding extended notes from beyond the octave – the ninth, eleventh and thirteenth "degrees" – a further range of chords becomes available.

As you will discover when you come to *Informal Playing* (*see pages 154–181*), there are a great many other chord types – even the twenty-seven shown there for each key represents but a small proportion of the possibilities. All of these chords are logically named, based around the notes they contain. To name ANY chord – or work out the notes that are contained by any named chord – all you need is the root note and knowledge of the names of the notes in the chromatic scale for that note.

Let's look at an example of a chord made up from the notes C, E, G♭ and B♭. The interval names are: C (root); E (major 3rd); G♭ (diminished 5th); B♭ (minor 7th). The B♭ flat makes it a dominant seventh type of chord in the key of C, but the fifth note is flattened. Therefore, this makes the chord name C seventh diminished fifth, or "C seven flat five". It can be notated as C7-5.

So what are the notes of a chord called C maj 7+5 ("C major seven sharp five")? We can tell that it is a C major 7 chord: C (root), E (major 3rd), G (perfect 5th) and B (major 7th). However the "+5" tells us that the fifth note is sharpened and is thus played as an augmented 5th. This means that the notes that make up C maj 7+5 are C, E, G♯ and B.

INVERSION WITH BOTH HANDS

We've already seen how triads can be inverted – meaning that they use notes that don't appear in strict pitch sequence. This can yield some interesting results when applied to chords made up of four or more notes. In the box below there are six different ways of playing the C dominant ninth chord you encountered on the previous page. Only the first example (*top left*) is played in the root position. The others all have notes out of sequence. If you play them one after the other you will hear the difference clearly. **48** ▶

GERMAN DANCE: JOSEPH HAYDN

This arrangement of Haydn's waltz makes use of inverted chords split over the treble and bass staves.

To begin, notice that the tempo mark instructs you to play *allegretto*.

This means "quite quickly", although not as fast as *allegro*.

The dots above and below many of the notes throughout the piece indicate that they must be played *staccato*.

The *forte* mark in Bar 1 tells you that the piece should also be played quite loudly, before switching to *mezzo-forte* ("moderately loud") at the start of Bar 9.

49 ▶

MORE REPEAT SYMBOLS

The positioning of double-dot repeat symbols (*see page 79*) is the simplest way to indicate that a passage of music has to be repeated. There are several other more versatile methods of indicating similar types of repetition.

The DA CAPO marks (shown using the letters D.C.) literally means "from the head". This is a one-time instruction to return and play from the start of the music. Similarly, the DAL SEGNO mark (shown using the letters D.S.) literally means "from the sign". This is an instruction to repeat the music from a stylised "S" symbol called the SEGNO.

The FIRST ENDING and SECOND ENDING marks also allow for a lengthy passage of music to be repeated, but in a slightly altered form. For example, when you have played the first ending bar, you may return to the start of the music (or other predefined point) and play it through again. This time, however, when you get to the first ending bar, you skip over it and play the second ending bar. Any number of "ending" bars can be specified in a piece of music.

THE *DA CAPO* SYMBOL

THE *DAL SEGNO* SYMBOL

THE *SEGNO* SYMBOL

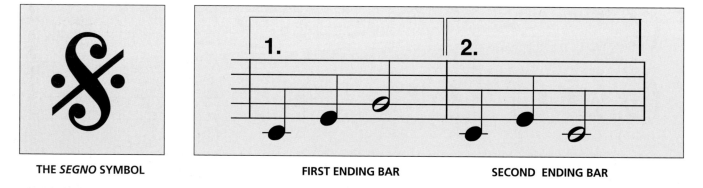

FIRST ENDING BAR   SECOND ENDING BAR

THE GREAT COMPOSERS

Throughout the book, we have highlighted some of the most significant composers, giving brief biographies detailing their lives and works, and then providing arrangements of some of their pieces for you to play. Of course, there have been many other great keyboard composers.

Since the majority of the most popular "classic" composers lived and worked between the seventeenth and nineteenth centuries, their works are now generally deemed to be in the public domain. This means that collections of piano music by the likes of Schumann, Mendelssohn, Schubert, Brahms, Mozart, Beethoven, Chopin and Haydn are widely available in music stores – often for less than the price of a compact disc. Any of these composers will provide even the most insatiable pianist

with enough of a musical challenge to last a lifetime. It's also interesting and worthwhile to hear professional recordings or performances of these great works, especially since their interpretations can differ so greatly.

Below is a list of some of the greatest composers of keyboard works from the sixteenth century onward.

William Byrd (1543–1623)
Giles Farnaby (c.1563–1640)
Girolamo Frescobaldi (1583–1643)
Jacques Champion de Chambonnieres (1601–1672)
François Couperon (1668–1733)
Johann Sebastian Bach (1685–1750)
Domenico Scarlatti (1685–1757)

REPEATS IN PRACTICE

You now should be familiar with all but the most obscure of repeat symbols used in written music. So here is an exercise to test out your understanding. Take a pen and paper and work through the music above, writing down the correct sequence of bars that must be played. The correct solution is shown below.

1. Play Bars A—B—C—D—E
2. The repeat at the end of Bar E sends you back to Bar A. Play Bars A—B—C—D—E.
3. This time, ignore the repeat at the end of Bar E. Play Bars F—G.
4. The repeat at the end of Bar G instructs you to look for the "repeat from" double dots – which is at the beginning of bar F. Play Bars F and G again.
5. This time, ignore the end repeat on bar G. Play bar H.
6. The *D.S.* (*Dal Segno*) at the end of Bar H tells you to return to the *Segno* symbol at the beginning of Bar B.
7. Play Bars B—C—D—E—F—G—H, ignoring the repeat symbols that have already been played.
8. Play BAR I. The *D.C.* (*Da Capo*) symbol at the end of the bar instructs you to return and start again from the beginning of the music.
9. Play bars A—B—C—D—E—F—G—H, ignoring the repeat symbols that have already been played.
10. The "first ending" tells you to skip bar I and move on to the "second ending" – which is Bar J.
11. Play Bar J.
12. The "*fine*" sign marks the end of the piece.

George Frideric Handel (1685–1759)

Jean-Philippe Rameau (1683–1764)

George Philipp Telemann (1681–1767)

Carl Philipp Emanuel (C.P.E.) Bach (1714–1788)

Franz Benda (1709–1786)

Padre Antonio Soler (1729–1783)

Jose Antonio Carlos de Seixas (1704–1791)

Wolfgang Amadeus Mozart (1756–1791)

Franz Joseph Haydn (1732–1809)

Ludwig van Beethoven (1770–1827)

Franz Schubert (1797–1828)

Muzio Clementi (1752–1832)

John Field (1782–1837)

Felix Mendelssohn (1809–1847)

Frédéric Chopin (1810–1849)

Robert Schumann (1810–1856)

Franz Liszt (1811–1886)

Johannes Brahms (1833–1897)

Antonin Dvorák (1841–1904)

Edvard Grieg (1843–1907)

Alexander Skriabin (1872–1915)

Enrique Granados (1867–1916)

Claude Debussy (1862–1918)

Gabriel Faure (1845–1924)

Erik Satie (1866–1925)

Maurice Ravel (1875–1937)

Sergei Rachmaninov (1873–1943)

Béla Bartók (1881–1945)

FRANZ SCHUBERT (1797–1828)

Born in Vienna, the son of a teacher, Schubert showed a remarkable aptitude for music as a child, studying the piano, violin, organ, and then composition with Antonio Salieri.

By 1814, at the age of 17, he had composed numerous piano pieces, string quartets, his first symphony, and a three-act opera. That same year, he created his first masterpiece, the song, "Gretchen am Spinnrade" ("Gretchen at the Spinning Wheel"), which he is purported to have written in a single day.

In 1820, following a brief period spent teaching at his father's school, he used aristocratic patronage to improve his standing in Viennese society. But that same year, what looked to be a major breakthrough turned to disaster when two of his operas, *Die Zwillingsbrüder* and *Die Zauberharfe*, were badly received by Viennese audiences. None of his theatrical works would be performed again during his lifetime.

In 1823 Schubert was struck down with syphilis. At that time there was no permanent cure for the disease, and it would almost certainly prove to be a major contributory cause of his premature death.

Throughout the remaining five years of his life, although musically perhaps his most productive, Schubert frequently lapsed into misery and despair. By the time of his death from typhoid at the age of 31, his reputation had spread well beyond Viennese circles and throughout Germany.

Schubert's fame was largely as a songwriter. During the fifty years after his death, he was almost forgotten. During his lifetime, the bulk of his vast output was never published, and some not even performed until the late nineteenth century. Yet, he is now recognised as being as significant a figure as the likes of Haydn, Mozart or Beethoven. In spite of being thought of as a songwriter, he clearly produced major instrumental masterpieces of intense lyrical depth, and among the most enduring are his final three piano sonatas.

SCHUBERT'S *WALTZ*

As well as putting into practice some of the more complicated repeat procedures, this piece also requires some rather complex hand positioning, so pay special attention to the finger numbering marked on the staves.

Before we go any further, however, you may have noticed an unusual marking, which first appears on the first crotchet of Bar 2. The note has a small horizontal stroke above the head (this can appear below the head when the stem is pointing in the other direction). This is called a TENUTO MARK. You can think of it as being the opposite of a staccato. Any note marked in this way should be played for its full value, and not shortened in any way under any circumstances. In some cases it may even imply a tiny, subtle lengthening of the note.

Let's now turn to the repeat symbols. The first repeat symbol appears at the end of Bar 8. This tells you to return to Bar 1 and play through from the beginning. HOWEVER, on the repeat, the "first ending" mark above Bar 8 tells you to SKIP that bar, and move on to the "second ending" bar – Bar 9.

In fact, if you look carefully, you'll see that the only reason that this repeat marking is really necessary is that the second part of the music (Bars 10–18) begins on the third beat of the preceding bar, so there has to be a way of distinguishing the ending of the first part when it has been played through a second time.

Now play through from Bars 10–18. The double dots at the end of Bar 18 indicate that you must repeat from the double dots at the start of Bar 10.

So here is a summary of the playing sequence:

Part 1:   1—2—3—4—5—6—7—8
Part 1 (repeat): 1—2—3—4—5—6—7—9
Part 2:   10—11—12—13—14—15—16—17—18
Part 2 (repeat): 10—11—12—13—14—15—16—17—18

The dynamic instructions are reasonably straightforward, but don't ignore the *crescendo* and *diminuendo* instructions in Bars 13–14.

The key signature is A major, meaning that the notes C, F and G are played as sharps.

WALTZ: FRANZ SCHUBERT

HANDEL'S MARCH FROM *SCIPIONE*

This next piece is the triumphal march the precedes the first act of George Frederic Handel's opera *Scipione* – the tale of the conquering Roman general. There are a few things you need to look out for in this piece.

First, study the slurs in the beamed groups – in Bar 4, for example. The instruction here is to play each group as a phrase in its own right. To play *legato*, punctuate the rhythm with a subtle pause at the very end of the phrase.

The only new idea to be introduced in this piece of music is the short pause. If you look carefully through the music, you will see that a comma symbol periodically appears above the top line of the treble staff. If you think of the role of a comma in everyday writing, it will give you a clue as to how it should

be interpreted in music. You've already encountered the fermata symbol in several previous pieces: this a distinct pause in the music. A comma, however, is much more subtle than that – more like a very brief break in the sound. Rather than altering the tempo, the comma is more likely to be interpreted as "eating" into the value of the preceding note.

The tempo mark *con moto* is difficult to describe. Literally, it means "with movement", implying a certain quickness. But it certainly shouldn't be as fast as *allegro*, for example.

Notice that there is a repeat symbol at the end of Bar 9: when you get to that point, the first nine bars must be repeated.

In Bars 21 and 26 look out for the tenuto marks. Remember that these notes must be played for their full value. And don't miss the staccato crotchets that crop up within Bars 8, 13 and 25.

MARCH FROM SCIPIONE: GEORGE FREDERIC HANDEL

OPERATIC WEBSITES

Opera Across The Internet
operanut.com/radio.htm
Web radio broadcasts of operas from across the globe.

Naxos Introduction To Opera
www.naxos.com/education/opera_intro.asp
Educational site set up by world's biggest budget classical label.

The Opera Critic
theoperacritic.com
News and reviews from around the world.

Metropolitan Opera – Synopses
www.metoperafamily.org/metopera/history/stories
Outlines of the best-known operas.

Royal Opera House
www.roh.org.uk
Excellent site for general information.

Operamania!
operamania.com/websites-e.htm
Good general resource, including signposts to other useful operatic websites.

LARGO: ANTONIN DVORAK

Largo literally means "slowly" – so the title of this piece also tells us the tempo it should be played at. The only unusual aspects of this arrangement are the instructions relating to hand movement in the final two bars.

Looking first at the penultimate bar (Bar 26), the first four quavers are played in the usual way with the right hand. The *L.H.* instruction that appears at the start of the 3rd beat of the bar is an instruction to play WITH THE LEFT HAND. On the first beat of the final bar, the *R.H.* instruction tells you to revert to playing with the right hand. This crossover technique enables the complete phrase to be played in a single flowing movement.

In the final bar, the appearance of the bass clef on the treble staff indicates that all subsequent notes on that staff should be altered in pitch accordingly. They should still be played with the right hand, though.

LESSON SEVEN

PERFORMANCE

Although you may not feel so confident, from a technical point of view you are already armed with the necessary knowledge – if not the actual playing technique – to take on most pieces of written music. Most, but not all. In this lesson we'll look at a number of other topics that will help to fill the gaps in your knowledge. This includes the subjects of ornamentation and triplet note divisions. The lesson concludes with two Beethoven pieces for you to learn.

ORNAMENTATION

There are a number of symbols or written instructions which may appear on a piece of music but which do not give absolutely precise instructions as to how it should be performed. You've already come across some covering such important matters as tempo and dynamics. As such, much is left to the skills and interpretive abilities of the performer to make the most appropriate decisions. However, those aspects of instruction are about the *manner* in which notes are played, rather than the note values themselves.

As strange as it might seem, though, there is a further category in which the notes themselves can be viewed differently depending on the performer. This is when they are faced with what are known as ORNAMENTATION marks.

Essentially, ornamentation means the modification of music. It can be used to to make a composition more attractive or, in some cases, allow the performer to demonstrate their playing abilities to the full.

Ornamentation usually takes the form of additional notes, the most common of which are grace notes – the acciaccatura and appoggiatura (*see page 113*), and the family of effects that come under the category of trills (*see page 115*).

Although there is some consensus regarding the way ornamentation should be used, it is by no means universal. The situation is further muddied when we discuss its use with works composed before the twentieth century. Much of our understanding comes from the "performance manuals" of the eighteenth and nineteenth centuries written by the likes of C. P. E. Bach (1714–1788) and J. N. Hummel (1778–1837). But with the modern preoccupation with the sanctity of the score – something that has only come about since the 20th century – considerable discussion continues, as music academics debate what the composer *really* had in mind.

THE IMPORTANCE OF ORNAMENTATION

Whatever form it may take, ornamentation plays an essential role in the interpretation of many pieces of music. When faced with ornamentation marks, the player has to ask one very simple and basic question: "What did the composer *really* mean by this?" That may sound like an absurd example of stating the obvious, until we realise that ornamentation protocol can vary greatly, often depending on when and where the piece of music was written. Consequently, like most other matters of interpretation (for example, tempo, rhythm, instrumentation and fingering) the final outcome is at the discretion of the performer.

Important clues to a composer's intention can also come from a good understanding of music history, the role of the musician and composer, and the way in which performances have changed over time.

For a classic view of ornamentation, here is a quote from C. P. E. Bach's *Versuch über die wahre Art das Clavier zu spielen* (Berlin, 1753). The son of Johann Sebastian Bach, "C.P.E." was the first important figure in the performance and teaching of music for the piano:

"It is not likely that anybody could question the necessity of ornaments. They are found everywhere in music, and are not only useful, but indispensable. They connect the notes; they give them life. They emphasise them, and besides giving accent and meaning they render them grateful; they illustrate the sentiments, be they sad or merry, and take an important part in the general effect. They give to the player an opportunity to show off his technical skill and powers of expression. A mediocre composition can be made attractive by their aid, and the best melody without them may seem obscure and meaningless."

GRACE NOTES

In some pieces of notated music you are likely to come across a note prefixed by a "smaller" note. This is known as a GRACE NOTE, and may appear either as a single stemmed note or a beamed group of notes. There are two types of grace note – the ACCICCATURA or the APPOGGIATURA. Both have their own distinct uses.

THE ACCIACCATURA

Taken from the Italian verb *acciaccare*, literally meaning "to crush", the acciaccatura is a very short note – it's sometimes even called a CRUSHED NOTE – which is usually written as a small quaver with a stroke through its stem. It is positioned in front of the principal note of a melody.

The acciaccatura can be interpreted in two different ways. It can be played on the beat but BARELY PERCEPTIBLY before the principle note comes in, or at the same time as the principle note but played as "short" as possible. Irrespective of how the acciaccatura is interpreted, however, its value is NEVER included as a part of the whole bar.

Two examples of the acciaccatura in use are shown below. The first example shows a "crushed" E played with a crotchet C. The second example uses a beamed group of semiquavers. The inference here is of a four-note phrase which has a value of a single beat, but with the first three notes played as quickly as possible.

THE APPOGGIATURA

The term appoggiatura comes from the Italian verb appoggiare – "to lean". Although it may be similar to the acciaccatura in appearance, this description provides a clue to the way in which it differs. The appoggiatura is ALWAYS played so that the principal note is on the beat. In other words, the appoggiatura literally does lean on the main note.

The musician faces two problems when dealing with the appoggiatura. The first is that it can appear to be the same as an acciaccatura (for which diagonal strokes through stem and flag are not used religiously). Second, although the appoggiatura is usually shown as a quaver, it does not necessarily mean that it "eats" a quaver out of the value of the principal note. An informal definition was created in the eighteenth century by C.P.E. Bach who stated that the appoggiatura was worth half the value of the principal note if it was divisible by two, and two-thirds if it was divisible by three. While this is a workable "rule" it cannot be applied rigidly – this generally remains a matter for the discretion of the performer.

The staff below shows an appoggiatura used within the context of a chord. In this example, the grace note is ONLY linked to the highest notes of each chord (G in both cases). This means that on the beat it is NOT just the grace note that is played, followed quickly by the chord, but the notes C, E and F. After half a beat (using the Bach formula) the F resolves to G while C and E are still being sustained. The second example shows the same chord played an octave higher.

EMPHASISING SINGLE NOTES

Think about of way we talk in conversation. To create impact we emphasise certain words or phrases by speaking at a higher volume. This enables us to communicate our views or feelings more accurately. This dynamic process is equally true of music.

You've already seen how the volume of segments of music (or a piece of music as a whole) can be altered by using dynamic marks or by the *crescendo* and *diminuendo* "hairpins". It's also possible to emphasise individual notes using ACCENT MARKS.

Accent marks take several different forms. The most common is the symbol "ʌ" positioned above the note (or "v" below the note). Another valid accent mark is the HORIZONTAL ACCENT ">" which can be placed either above or below the music. Although they are often used in an interchangeable fashion, there is a prevailing view that the horizontal symbol has a milder effect than "ʌ" or "v".

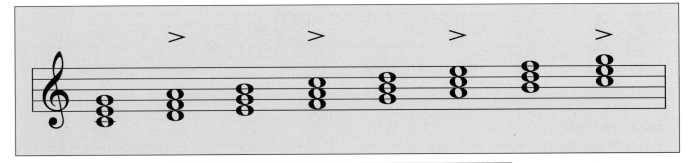

TREMOLO

The term TREMOLO refers to the fast repetition of a single note. On string instruments such as the violin or cello the effect can be created by the rapid up-and-down motion of the bow against the strings; on the guitar by swift plectrum picking; on the piano, however, it is produced by the very fast depression of the key.

To understand the tremolo, we must first look at notation for repeating individual notes. For this we use a diagonal stroke which passes through the stem of the note. The positioning of a single stroke through any of kind of note is an instruction to play the same number of quavers that make up the value of that note. For example, a crotchet with a single stroke either above or below means that two quavers of the same pitch are to be played. The addition of a second stroke means that the reiteration must be in sixteenth notes; a third stroke, as thirty-second strokes.

Above, on the right, you can see a crotchet (E) with three repeat strokes through the stem. This is the standard way in

which a tremolo effect is shown. In this instance, that single crotchet equates directly to the two groups of thirty-second notes shown below. The fact that they are shown within a slur tells us that the notes must be played in a single phrase.

TREMOLO

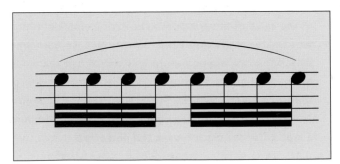

PHRASE SHOWN IN FULL

TRILLS, TURNS, AND MORDENTS

Sometimes also known as a "shake", a TRILL is a commonly used ornamental effect whereby a note is alternated at rapid speed with the next note above in the same key. Trills can be indicated either by placing the symbol "*tr*" above the note or a wavy line (some even show both methods). Below are three examples of a trill placed above a crotchet "C" (in the key of C) – together with the notes shown played in full.

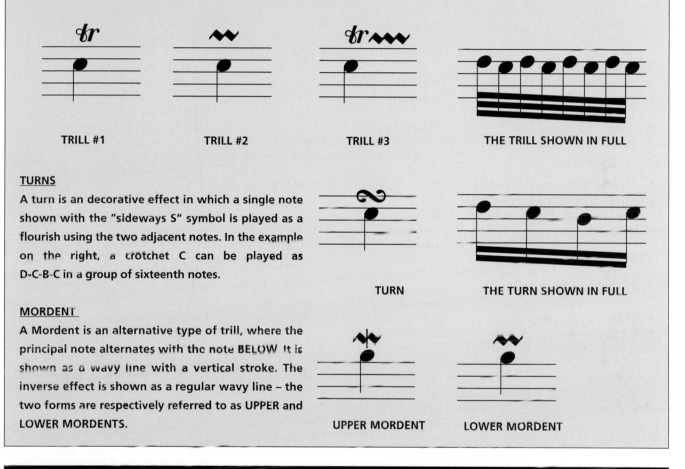

TRILL #1   TRILL #2   TRILL #3   THE TRILL SHOWN IN FULL

TURNS

A turn is an decorative effect in which a single note shown with the "sideways S" symbol is played as a flourish using the two adjacent notes. In the example on the right, a crotchet C can be played as D-C-B-C in a group of sixteenth notes.

TURN   THE TURN SHOWN IN FULL

MORDENT

A Mordent is an alternative type of trill, where the principal note alternates with the note BELOW It is shown as a wavy line with a vertical stroke. The inverse effect is shown as a regular wavy line – the two forms are respectively referred to as UPPER and LOWER MORDENTS.

UPPER MORDENT   LOWER MORDENT

VIBRATO AND TREMOLO

Throughout music history, the terms VIBRATO and TREMOLO have been used in an interchangeable fashion. This is quite wrong. They are in fact two very distinct ornamental effects.

Vibrato is used by most string instruments and by the human voice. The effect is created by a slight, though consistent, variation in pitch, which can create a full, rich sound, especially in an auditorium where the natural reverberation causes the pitches to blend.

Whether playing or singing, its use becomes almost subconscious, adding lustre to the tone of a voice or instrument. If the pitch change is small and the frequency of change quick enough, the ear no longer perceives a series of different notes, but only a change in timbre or tone-colour.

String players and guitarists can create vibrato by rocking the left hand back and forth from the wrist. Wind players achieve the same effect by the careful regulation of the flow of breath.

Vibrato cannot be achieved using instruments with a fixed pitch, such as the piano. However, this didn't prevent Liszt occasionally writing "vibrato" on his piano pieces. He claimed to believe that rocking the finger on the key – as a violinist rocks his or her finger on a string – will produce such an effect, even though the physical mechanism of the piano clearly made this impossible.

GLOSSARY OF "FOREIGN" MUSICAL TERMS

It will have become clear to you over the course of the previous six lessons that much of what we call "classical" music evolved and developed in Central Europe – most notably in Italy, Germany and Austria. Consequently, there is a considerable legacy of alien terminology of which the novice musician must be made aware. Here is a miniature glossary of the most useful non-English terms you are likely to encounter.

Accelerando
Becoming faster.

Acciaccatura
An ornamental effect sometimes called a "crushed note".

Accordare/accorder
To tune.

Adagio
Meaning "at ease". A slow tempo which is faster than *andante* but slower than *largo*. Its diminutive form is *adagietto*, which is slightly faster than *adagio*.

Adagissimo
Extremely slow – slower than *adagio*.

Addolorato
Performance mark literally meaning "pained" or "stricken".

Ad Libitum
Instruction that the performer may freely interpret or improvise a passage.

Affetuoso
Direction that a piece should be performed tenderly.

Agitato
Performance direction literally meaning "agitated".

Alla Breve
Played with a minim beat.

Alla marcia
In the style of a march.

Allegro
Played at a fast tempo, literally meaning "quickly".

Andante
Medium-paced tempo played "at walking pace".

Animando
Literally "becoming animated". An increase in tempo is also implied.

Appoggiatura
A grace note or "leaning" note.

Arpeggio
The notes of a chord played in quick succession rather than simultaneously. Commonly notated using a wavy line. Also known as a "broken chord".

A tempo
Literally meaning "in time", an instruction to return to the original tempo after deviations.

Bravura, con
An instruction that a composition or passage requires a virtuoso display by the performer.

Cadenza
An ornamental passage frequently performed over the penultimate notes or chord. In most cases this cadence signals the end of the movement and will resolve to the tonic.

Calando
Getting softer – dying away.

Calmato
Play in a calm, tranquil manner.

Capriccioso
Instruction to play capriciously or at the player's whim.

Celere/Celeremente
Instruction to play swiftly.

Coda
The concluding passage of a piece of music.

Comodo
Play at a comfortable speed.

Crescendo
Gradual increase in loudness.

Deciso/decisamente
Play decisively with resolve.

Delicato
Instruction to play delicately.

Diminuendo
Gradual decrease in loudness.

Doppio movimento
An instruction to perform a passage at double the tempo.

Duolo/Dolore
Instruction to play as if filled with sorrow or grief.

Empfindung, mit
Perform with feeling or emotion.

Espressivo
Instruction to play expressively.

Facile/facilmente
Play easily.

Flebile
Plaintive or mournful.

Forte/Fortissimo/Fortississimo
A set of instructions for the performer to play louder, of which *forte* is the quietest and *fortississimo* the loudest.

Forte-piano
An instruction to play loud then soft.

Forza/Forzando
Play with strength or force.

Glissando
A continuous sliding movement between two different pitches. On a piano keyboard, the effect of running the fingernails along the keys, creating a fast scale of discretely pitched notes.

Grazioso
Instruction to play with grace.

Joyeux
Play joyfully.

Lamentoso/lamentabile
Play with a mood of sadness.

Largo
Slow or stately.

Legato
Play with no separation between notes.

Lento
Instruction to play extremely slowly.

Licenza
Play freely with regard to tempo or rhythm.

Loco
Instruction to return to original pitch having been instructed to play at an alternative pitch.

Lugubre
To play mournfully.

Lunga
Prolonged pause or period of rest.

Maestoso
To play majestically.

Mancando
To create the illusion of fading away.

Marziale
Play in a military style.

M.D.
Mano destra, *main droit*, right hand.

Moderato
Play at a moderate speed.

M.S.
Mano sinistra, left hand.

Ossia
A term used to indicate an alternative version of a passage.

Ostinato
A short pattern that is repeated throughout a piece of music.

Parlato/parlando
Instruction to sing in a spoken style. Most commonly used in comic opera situations.

Perdendosi
Performance instruction to create the effect of the music fading away.

Piano/pianissimo/pianississimo
Instructions for the performer to play softer – *pianissimo* is the quietest.

Poco
Literally meaning "little". Derivatives include *poco a poco* ("little by little"), *fra poco* ("shortly"), *pochetto* or *pochettino* ("very little") and *pochimssimo* ("extremely little").

Presto
An instruction to play very fast – faster than *allegro*.

Prima/primo
The Italian word that translates literally as "first"; used in conjunction with other performance marks.

Restringendo
Literally meaning "becoming faster".

Retenu
Instruction to hold back and play more slowly.

Rigoroso
Strict.

Rinforzando
Accent notes.

Risoluto
Play boldly with energy.

Ritardando
Instruction to play gradually slower.

Ritenuto
An instruction to make a sudden reduction in tempo.

Rubato, tempo
Literally meaning "stolen time". An instruction that allows the performer to ignore the prevailing tempo and speed up or slow down according to his or her own preference.

Scherzo/scherzando
Literally meaning "joke", an instruction to perform a piece of music playfully.

Sempre
Literally meaning "always".

Sforzato/szforzando
Literally meaning "forced" but usually interpreted as "loud".

Simile
An instruction to continue playing as already marked; literally means "like".

Staccato
Literally meaning "detached," staccato notes or chords are reduced in length.

Stretto
An instruction to quicken the tempo; overlapping elements in a fugue.

Tenerezza/teramente
Instruction to play tenderly.

Tenuto
An instruction that a note or chord should be held for at least its full duration – and in some cases creating the effect of delaying the note that follows.

Tosto
Instruction to play swiftly or rapidly.

Tranquillo
Instruction to play in a calm manner.

Triste/Tristamente
An instruction for the performer to play with a mood of sadness.

Troppo, non
Literally meaning "not too much".

Vivace
An instruction to play in a lively or brisk manner.

Volante
Literally meaning "flying", an instruction to play fast.

Volti Subito (V.S.)
Instruction for the player to turn the sheet of music quickly.

NOTE DIVISIONS

All the note values you've used so far have been based on sub-dividing the notes by a factor of two – that is, they have been halved, quartered and so forth. However, a beat can also be divided into three equal parts. The beats that result are known as TRIPLETS. Every type of note can be divided in this way.

There are several methods for notating triplets. The options shown on the right are all equally legitimate, although NOT exclusive to those note values. Their use is largely down to personal taste.

The first example shows a semibreve along side three minim triplets: the three triplets must be played in the same time that it takes to play a semibreve. The second and third examples work in exactly the same way: crotchet triplets that must be played in the space of two beats; and quaver triplets that must be played within a single beat.

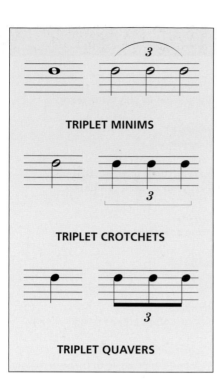

TRIPLET MINIMS

TRIPLET CROTCHETS

TRIPLET QUAVERS

TRIPLET GROUPINGS

Although the most common use of a triplet division is three notes of equal value, there are other variations. It is also possible to create groups of mixed triplets made up from notes and rests of different values. Four examples are shown below.

SIMPLE TIME OR COMPOUND TIME?

If a piece of music makes extensive use of triplet number "3" is sometimes dropped from the score. However, heavy use of triplets is relatively unusual within a simple time signature – it would be more usual for the piece to be written in the equivalent compound time signature. The example below shows the same bar notated in four-four time along with its compound equivalent – twelve-eight. Both bars sound the same when played.

TRIPLET QUAVERS IN SIMPLE TIME   **QUAVERS IN COMPOUND TIME**

IRREGULAR DIVISIONS

Note sub-divisions other than two and three are also possible.

The three examples on the right show how a crotchet can be divided into five (QUINTUPLETS), six (SEXTUPLETS), and seven (SEPTUPLETS). It is also possible to divide beyond seven, but rarely necessary in practice.

Pay special attention to the note values that are attributed to each group. As you can see from the examples above, divisions of three are treated as if they are divisions of two, and are therefore quavers; divisions of five, six and seven take the same note values as sub-divisions of four, and are thus semiquaver notes.

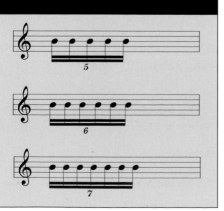

LUDWIG VAN BEETHOVEN (1770–1827)

Arguably the most admired and influential composer ever to have lived, Ludwig van Beethoven was born in Bonn, Germany, to a family with a rich if not particularly noted musical heritage.

Beethoven's musical education began in earnest in 1979 when he studied under Christian Gottlob Neefe, a teacher and musical director of a theatrical company. Although a precocious talent, Beethoven was certainly not a *wunderkind* in the manner of Mozart or Mendelssohn. Two years later, Neefe was appointed court organist, and within a year, before his twelfth birthday, Beethoven was acting as his assistant. The autumn of 1783 saw the publication of Beethoven's first significant compositions, three piano sonatas dedicated to the state elector, Maximilian Friedrich.

In 1795, Beethoven moved to Vienna, where he briefly studied under Haydn and Salieri. It was around 1800 that Beethoven's well-known deafness first began to manifest itself. By the age of 33 he had lost all sense of hearing, and was no longer able to perform in public. How a deaf man was able to compose some of the greatest and most popular music of the nineteenth century would seem to be beyond comprehension.

Beethoven's life and works are often described in terms of his "Three Periods": A first or formative period ending around 1802, a second lasting until around 1812 and a transcendent third period from 1813 to 1827. From a pianist's point of view, the heart of Beethoven's prolific output is his collection of thirty-two sonatas. Through these pieces, it becomes possible to "hear" clearly the three phases of his life: the "angry young man" of his youth; the crisis of his middle life when his deafness almost robbed him of his sanity; and the spirituality of the final phase.

The earliest of Beethoven's well-known piano sonatas is the so-called *Pathétique*. Composed in 1799, it uses Beethoven's favourite key signature – C minor. Two years later, he came up with perhaps his best-known piano work – *Opus 27 No. 2*, more commonly known as the "Moonlight" Sonata.

One of the hallmarks of Beethoven's piano works was a result of his reaction against the prevailing trend of the period, which saw the left hand relegated to the role of mere accompanist. In many of Beethoven's greatest compositions, the left hand fulfils a fundamentally melodic role. This is enhanced by the unusually wide separation of the hands, and also the registers he has chosen.

Beethoven evidently left a strong impression on those who encountered him. As a young man he was known to be difficult, impatient and mistrustful. Unlike many of the classical masters, Beethoven had virtually no formal education – indeed, he described himself as a man "who did everything badly except compose music". Yet he fascinated and endeared himself to those around him, who continued to value his friendship no matter how badly they may have been treated.

At the end of 1826, Beethoven fell ill with pneumonia and pleurisy. His condition was mishandled by his doctors and he died on March 26, 1827.

More than any other composer of his period, Beethoven's music has endured in popularity. His symphonies, overtures and piano sonatas made him a dominant force in the musical culture of the nineteenth century. Although his music was of its time, for modern-day concert audiences Beethoven remains by far the most popular pre-twentieth-century composer.

MINUET IN G: LUDWIG VAN BEETHOVEN

This next piece is a minuet composed by Beethoven. A dance that dates back to the seventeenth century, a minuet is characterised by being in a "triple" time – usually three-four; three-eight; or six-eight.

From a notation angle, the trickiest aspect of this piece is in the repeats used – most notably at the very end of the piece. When the final section of the music has played through twice, the second ending concludes with the

instruction *"D.S. al Fine"*. This means that you must return to the "segno" (the symbol sitting between Bars 1 and 2) and play through once again until you reach the "FINE" command at the end of Bar 19.

FUR ELISE: LUDWIG VAN BEETHOVEN

One of Beethoven's most popular pieces, "Fur Elise" is in three-four time with a key signature of D major.

As far as playing technique goes, this piece shouldn't be too taxing. However, you need to pay careful attention to the the fingering – since the composition makes heavy use of rolling quaver phrases, you must ensure that your fingers are in an appropriate position to play the subsequent notes in the sequence.

As with many of Beethoven's piano works, the left hand is especially notable. If you look at Bar 3, the three quavers that begin on the first beat could almost be seen as half of a complete phrase that continues on the treble line. For the rolling effect to work it's crucial that the third quaver on the bass staff is played as a quaver, and not sustained for longer – which may be a natural thing for the finger to do.

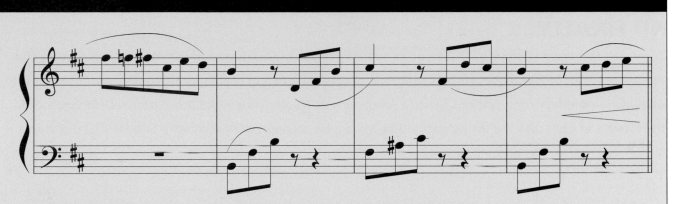

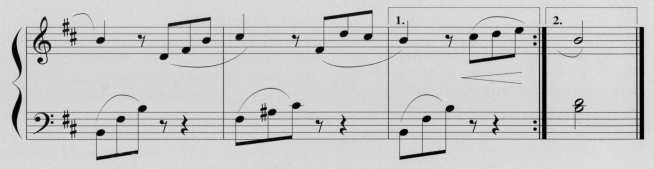

LESSON EIGHT

AND FINALLY...

This is the last lesson before we move on to some informal approaches to music. With the exception of a few extra issues of technique, such as using the pedals and playing chords as arpeggios, we'll concentrate on playing complete compositions by such composers as Tchaikovsky, J. S. Bach, Strauss, Offenbach and Beethoven. In each case the introductory text will advise on areas of special note or potential difficulty.

USING THE PEDALS

To understand how to use the piano's foot pedals you first need to know a little about how the piano works. As you've already learned at the beginning of the book, the piano produces its sounds when padded hammers linked to the keyboard strike the strings. For as long as the finger rests against the key, the string is free to vibrate; when the key is released, a damper mechanism prevents the note sounding any further. The lowest notes are produced by single strings; the middle notes have two strings tuned in unison; the highest notes have three strings tuned in unison.

THE SOFT PEDAL

One way in which the sound of the piano can be varied is by altering the way in which the hammers strike the strings. On a grand piano, the left pedal – usually known as the SOFT PEDAL – moves the keyboard and hammers very slightly to the right so that the hammers strike one less of the strings when sounding the note and the tone is therefore quieter. (For that reason it is also sometimes called the *una corda* pedal, literally meaning "one string".) The mechanism works slightly differently for domestic upright pianos. When the left pedal is depressed, the hammer mechanism is moved slightly closer to the strings, meaning that they are struck with less force.

In written music notation, *una corda* is the instruction to use this pedal on any type of piano. The pedal should not be released until you see the instruction *tre corde* ("three strings").

THE DAMPER PEDAL

On a grand piano, the right pedal is called the DAMPER PEDAL. It is also sometimes described as the "sustain" pedal or the "loud" pedal. On all types of piano, depressing the damper pedal causes the dampers for ALL the strings to be released. This means that when the key is pressed to sound the note, after it has been released, the string keeps on sustaining.

There is, however, more to the overall sound created by removing the dampers than simply sustaining the notes that have been played. Since all the dampers have been removed, strings from other notes will vibrate in "sympathy", which, depending on the quality of the piano, will create a richer tone.

The instruction to use the damper pedal can appear in a number of different ways. Some of the symbols used are shown in the box on the left. These cater for various levels of precision. The instruction *Con ped.* or *Col ped.* (both literally meaning "with the pedal") indicates (in the music) that the damper pedal should be used, but the way in which it is used is left to the discretion of the performer.

THE SOSTENUTO PEDAL

Concert grand pianos are equipped with a third pedal, which is located in between the other two. This SOSTENUTO PEDAL has the effect of sustaining notes that are being played while it is depressed, but not those played after it has been released. It is shown in written music either as *SP* or *P3*. (Note: Some upright pianos have a third pedal that effectively "muffles" the strings with a strip of felt. It has no real musical use, but acts as a very crude volume control.)

SYMBOLS FOR THE DAMPER PEDAL

The following symbols can be used to indicate that the damper pedal should be used. They are usually shown beneath the lower stave in piano music.

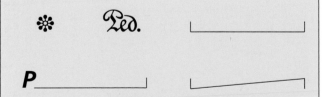

Also possible are instructions to press and release the dampers to allow specific notes or passages to be unaffected. This technique is known as "half-pedaling," and is indicated by breaks in the pedal line.

ARPEGGIATING CHORDS

If you look at the example directly below, you will see a C major chord played with both hands. However, alongside the chord you will notice a wavy line. This is an instruction to play the chord as an ARPEGGIO. When this occurs, instead of playing the notes simultaneously as you would when playing a regular chord they are instead played as a quick succession of sustained single notes. In fact, the term arpeggio only relates to the notes of the chord being played one at a time: the "broken chords" you encountered in earlier lessons are also examples of arpeggios.

The wavy line is an extremely useful piece of musical shorthand, since attributing accurate time values to each note would simply be confusing. Look at the example below once again (*left*). The bottom pair of staves shows an approximation of the effect if notated in full. The six notes are played from the lowest pitch to the highest pitch, one after the other, in the space of barely a semiquaver. Notice that the first five notes are shown as sixty-fourth note quintuplets! This would clearly be a nightmare for most players to interpret let alone play with any accuracy.

On the top pair of staves, although the "chord" is shown as having a value of a crotchet and playing on the first beat of the bar, it is only the lowest-pitched note that is actually played on that beat and has a value of a crotchet. But each successive note (when played) has to sustain FOR THE REMAINDER OF THAT BEAT. Even though all the notes are written out as crotchet, each subsequent note of the arpeggio has a shorter value.

The second example shown below (*right*) illustrates the same chord also with an arpeggio symbol. This time, however, there is a downward-pointing arrow alongside the wavy line. This means that the notes of the chord are to played in reverse sequence – from the highest pitch down to the lowest pitch.

In practice, arpeggios are used to create a kind of "rolling" effect: indeed, the technique takes its name from the Italian word for harp, which is frequently played in this manner. Like most other types of performance mark, arpeggios are not really precise in their instruction, but are largely a matter for the discretion of the player – although in many cases, this will be dictated by the context of the music. In the two examples shown below, some musicians may in fact choose to "roll" the notes as quickly as possible, at the other extreme, some may informally divide the six notes equally over the single beat.

PLAYING OUT OF THE STAFF RANGE

Up until now we have used the ledger lines to deal with notes that fall above or below the lines of the standard staff. However, given the extraordinary range of the piano, what are we to do if a piece of music uses large numbers of notes that are some way beyond the staff? We could still use ledger lines, but it would become increasingly difficult to interpret the notes with any degree of accuracy. Especially if the sequence continued for bar bar after bar. To overcome this problem we can use the *ottava* symbol.

8va---┐

DANCE OF THE SUGAR PLUM FAIRY: PETER ILYCH TCHAIKOVSKY (I)

This is an arrangement of Tchaikovsky's famous "Dance of the Sugar Plum Fairy" from *Casse Noisette* (*The Nutcracker Suite*).

There are three important aspects to this piece. First, notice the instruction "Staccato" in the first bar. This indicates that ALL of the notes over the entire piece of music should be played staccato – this an alternative to showing every note with a staccato dot.

Second, since much of treble line is played one octave higher, you need to pay special attention to the *ottava* instructions (*see above*).

Finally, turn to Bar 32 (you'll find it near the foot of page 128). Here you will see five bars containing arpeggiated chords. Standard practice here is to give all of the notes an equal value – the first four-note chord is effectively played as a sequence of semiquavers.

Andante non troppo

55 ▶

Ottava is the Italian word for octave and the symbol may be placed above or below any staff to increase or decrease a range of notes BY ONE OCTAVE in pitch. To work in practice, 8va is positioned directly above or below the note from which the pitch shift is to take effect; a line (which may be dotted or continuous) carries on for as long as the notes on the staff are to be altered. The notes only revert to the standard pitch when the line ends – this is shown with an upward- or downward-pointing marker.

Where the pitch alteration continues over more than one line of music, the standard practice is to begin each new staff line with 8va. An example of the use of the ottava symbol can be seen in the next playing example, Tchaikovsky's "Dance of the Sugar Plum Fairy".

DANCE OF THE SUGAR PLUM FAIRY: PETER ILYCH TCHAIKOVSKY (II)

A LITTLE BIT OF BACH

Here are two pieces composed by Johann Sebastian Bach.

"*Partita in E Minor*", shown below, has a symbol "𝄴" instead of a time signature. This tells you the piece is in two-two time – also known as *alla breva*. The key signature tells you that the piece is in E minor. Since E minor is the relative minor of G major, this means that it is the "one sharp" key. Consequently, F is played as F♯ throughout.

Across the page you will find one of Bach's minuets. This provides you with your first opportunity to interpret grace notes and trills for yourself. Let's begin with the lower mordent in Bar 3. Instead of playing this as a quaver C, try playing it as a demisemiquaver note C, followed by a demisemiquaver note B, followed by a semiquaver note C.

Bar 8 begins with an appoggiatura. Although the grace note appears as an quaver note, this doesn't mean that it "eats" that value out of the dotted minim.

PARTITA IN E MINOR: JOHANN SEBASTIAN BACH

MINUET IN G MAJOR: JOHANN SEBASTIAN BACH

TRITSCH-TRATSCH POLKA: JOHANN STRAUSS JNR (I)

The Viennese Strauss family – Johann, and his sons Johann Jnr, Josef and Eduard – exerted something of a stranglehold on nineteenth-century dance music. Although they all produced successful works, it is Johann Strauss Jnr whose works are best remembered. Among the many waltzes, polkas, quadrilles and marches he composed during a 55-year musical career, he is perhaps best remembered for the operetta *Die Fledermaus* (1874), the beautiful *Blue Danube Waltz* (1867), and – the piece shown here – the polka *Tritsch-Tratsch* (1858). Although the most famous dance composer of the nineteenth century, Strauss, famously claimed not to be able to dance.

Tritsch-Tratsch was composed for orchestra, but is in fact a simple piano arrangement. There is nothing too demanding in terms of notation, but be warned, the piece may prove deceptively tricky to play. This is due to the discipline needed to play the left-hand part smoothly and accurately.

Throughout some of this particular arrangement, the left hand is playing a broken chord. This motif is known as an *Alberti Bass*, named after an Italian composer of the eighteenth century. It is characterised by the notes of the chord being played in a strict 1st—5th—3rd—5th sequence. The most famous example of this left-hand line can be found in one of Mozart's piano sonatas (K.545). Playing the sequence smoothly is demanding, so follow the fingering shown in the first few bars with care. You may find the movements between the fourth and third fingers of the left hand especially troublesome.

Notice that at the end of Bar 17 the key signature alters in such a way that the B♭ of the F major scale is played as a B♮. This continues until the end of Bar 41, at the end of page 133. The positioning of the key signature at the end of the line warns in advance of changes taking place from the next line – in this case, across the page.

58 ▶

TRITSCH-TRATSCH POLKA: JOHANN STRAUSS JNR. (II)

SOME MORE TCHAIKOVSKY

We'll continue with piano arrangements of famous orchestral pieces with this version of the first movement of Tchaikovsky's sixth symphony – better known as "Pathétique". Although Tchaikovsky composed the piece in B minor, this arrangement transposes the theme to the slightly more demanding F♯ minor. (Remember that "three sharps" indicates a key of either D major or it's relative minor, F♯.)

As far as the notation is concerned, the only aspect you might not understand is the term *"rit".* in the penultimate bar. This is a tempo abbreviation of *ritenuto.* It is an instruction to slow down over a range of notes – usually signified by a dotted line.

The only minor playing difficulty you are likely to encounter is in Bar 8, where the right hand has to work through two sets of different "voices". Here is the fingering in full:

First Beat

You begin by playing E with the third finger (4), and A with the thumb (1). Sustain A for a full beat while playing C♯ with the first finger (2) on the half beat.

Second Beat

Play A on the second beat with the thumb (1) and C♯ on the half beat with the first finger (2).

Third Beat

On the third beat, play F♯ with fourth finger (5) and A♯ with the thumb (1). The F♯ sustains for one-and-a-half beats before you play E with the third finger (4); the A♯ sustains for one beat before you play B with the first finger (2).

ÓP. 74 "PATHETIQUE": PETER ILYCH TCHAIKOVSKY

MODULATION

The next piece of music for you to play is Offenbach's "The Celebrated Galop" from his operetta *Orpheus in the Underworld*. It's also known as "The Can-Can". We've used this piece to illustrate an idea with which you may not yet be familiar – MODULATION. This is where a piece of music changes key between movements. It is NOT the same thing as transposition, which is changing the pitches of the notes of a piece of music by the same interval so that that they are in a different key. Where modulation occurs it is fundamental to the structure of the music.

The music begins in the key of D major (the two sharps are on the notes C and F). However, after Bar 32, the piece MODULATES to the key of G major – we can tell this has happened because the key signature now has only one sharp. After Bar 64, the key signature reverts to D major once again.

This key change cleverly punctuates the music, making it clear in no uncertain terms that a new movement has begun.

Another point to consider before you begin playing is the nature of the notes themselves. This piece can be broken into a number of clearly defined sections.

The first 16-bar segment is quite self-contained, its character defined by the staccato quavers played by both hands.

The second group (Bars 17–32) alternate between delicate staccato (quavers) and dramatically accented crotchets.

The third movement (Bars 33–64) alternates between staccato and tenuto – once again, the contrast between the two techniques creating a feel of drama.

The final 18 bars see the first section reprised, with extended end bars.

This piece also provides a very clear illustration of the fundamental difference between two-four and four-four: the emphasis on every other beat creates a feeling of urgency.

THE CELEBRATED GALOP: JACQUES OFFENBACH (I)

THE PERIODS OF "CLASSICAL" MUSIC

Although the term "classical" is a widely used musical categorisation, it can be misleading, especially when you become aware that it has a much more specific meaning.

Musical works and their composers can be described as belonging to a specific era. There are six major periods of music which act as a kind of shorthand to describe the predominant style of pieces or music written during that era.

THE MIDDLE AGES era (450–1450) was predominantly based around Christian plainchant.

Guillaume du Fay and Claudio Montiverdi were leading composers of THE RENAISSANCE era (1450–1600). This period saw the emergence of melodies with clearly defined phrases, and greater polyphonic sophistication.

The BAROQUE period (1600–1750) saw the birth of new instrumental forms, such as the concerto and sonata. Significant composers were Henry Purcell, Antonio Vivaldi, and Johann Sebastian Bach.

Wolfgang Amadeus Mozart, Franz Josef Haydn, and Ludwig van Beethoven were the leading figures of the CLASSICAL era (1750–1825). This period saw the important emergence of the piano as a force in music.

Many of today's most popular composers – Schumann, Wagner, Verdi, Tchaikovsky to name but a few – hail from the ROMANTIC era (1825–1900).

The TWENTIETH CENTURY era is characterised by a view that any harmonic combination is possible. Composers have used extreme dissonance as well as microtonal intervals.

THE CELEBRATED GALOP: JACQUES OFFENBACH (II)

JESU, JOY OF MAN'S DESIRING: JOHANN SEBASTIAN BACH (I)

Although not originally composed for the piano – it had barely been invented at the time – many of Johann Sebastian Bach's keyboard pieces make for an ideal and enjoyable way of practising scales and broken chords. The next piece we have for you to play, "*Jesu, Joy of*

Man's Desiring", is one of Bach's most enduringly popular compositions.

Although this is one of the more demanding pieces in the book, once you get your head around the triplet quavers that form the basic rhythm (and get the right-hand fingering sorted) you should find it manageable.

This is the first example of triplet divisions used in practice. If you need a reminder of the theory turn back briefly to page 118.

If you look at the first bar you can see that each beat is broken down into triplet quavers. However, you'll notice that the number "3" beneath

the beam is only shown during the first bar; the word *"simile"* in the second bar tells you that this is the rule throughout the piece – it's a simple time-saving device that some music notators like to use.

To play these triplets, count out the beats in each bar as "<u>ONE</u>—two— three—<u>TWO</u>—two—three—<u>THREE</u>— two—three". The emphasised beats give you the basic three-four rhythm; the other beats provide you with the rhythm of the triplet quavers.

One of the trickiest aspects of this triplet rhythm can be found on the bass line. If you look at Bar 5, you will see a crotchet and a quaver "joined" by a number "3". This means that these two notes should be treated as triplet quavers, so in this case the crotchet note represents not "one" beat but two-thirds of a beat. The count is marked beneath the bar.

JESU, JOY OF MAN'S DESIRING: JOHANN SEBASTIAN BACH (II)

PIANO SONATA OP. 27 NO. 2 "MOONLIGHT": LUDWIG VAN BEETHOVEN (I)

This is the big one! It's the first movement of Ludwig van Beethoven's "Moonlight" sonata – arguably the most famous piece of piano music ever written. It was written in 1802, at around the time when his deafness was becoming acute. Some scholars also believe that he had previously just lost a lover, which could explain the profound sadness of the music.

Although something of a popular "showpiece", the sonata requires considerable finesse to play well. You should perhaps think of it as something to work toward, rather than master immediately.

Playing Tips

Let's begin with the key signature. Four sharps indicate that the piece is either in the key of E major or its relative minor key (C♯ minor) – you only have to play the first three notes to hear that it is in a minor key. This is a taxing key for novices. To begin with, from a sight-reading perspective it can be tricky to interpret: all occurrences of C, D, F and G are played as sharps (unless shown with the natural symbol). Second, the heavy use of enharmonic notes makes the fingering a little awkward.

If you look through the score, you will see a number of Italian phrases. Unfortunately, as you've already seen, there is a great deal of variation in the business of music notation. In many cases, when playing original pieces of music, performance instructions can depend on period and location, and sometimes the whim of the composer.

This is how the marks used can be interpreted:

Adagio (slow and leisurely) *Sostenuto* (sustained) – usually an instruction to hold back the tempo a little.

sempre (always) *e senza sordino* (and without muting) – thus, in the context of a piece of piano music, *sempre pp e senza sordino* means to play *pianissimo* (very quietly) without using the damper pedal).

marcato. ma sempre p – emphatically, but always piano (quietly).

il basso sempre ten – the bass notes are always "held" (played *tenuto*).

un poco slightly
subito suddenly
sempre legatissimo – always play as smoothly as possible.

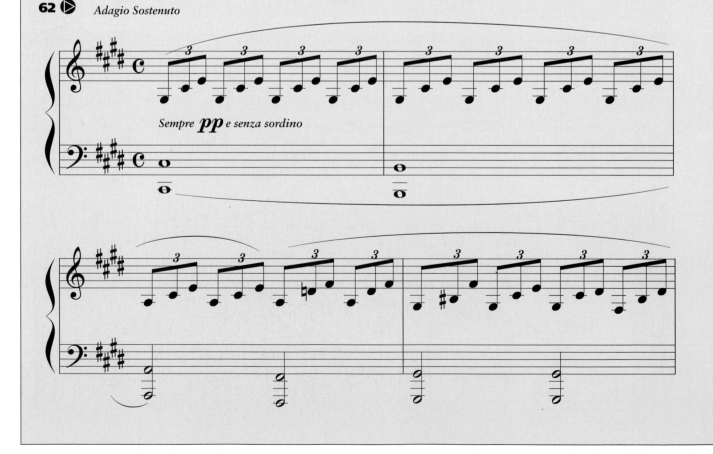

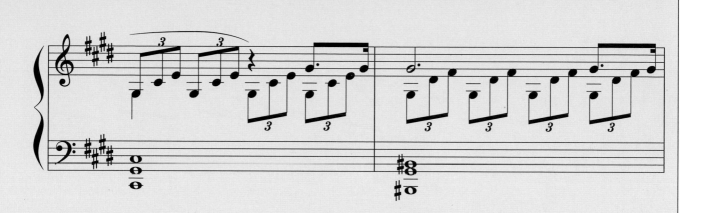

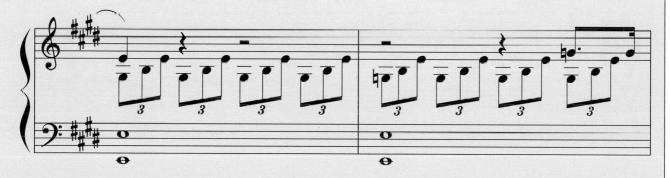

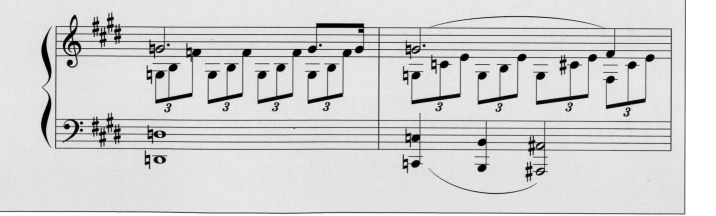

PIANO SONATA OP. 27 NO. 2 "MOONLIGHT": LUDWIG VAN BEETHOVEN (II)

PIANO SONATA OP. 27 NO. 2 "MOONLIGHT": LUDWIG VAN BEETHOVEN (III)

PIANO SONATA OP. 27 NO. 2 "MOONLIGHT": LUDWIG VAN BEETHOVEN (IV)

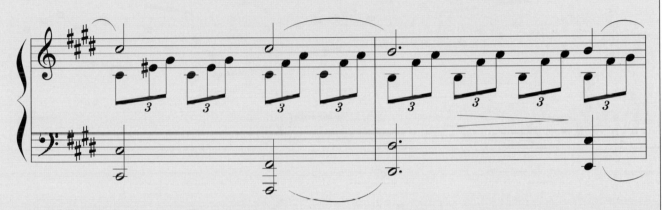

sempre legatissimo

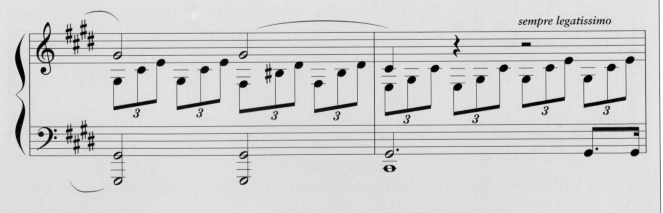

PIANO SONATA OP. 27 NO. 2 "MOONLIGHT": LUDWIG VAN BEETHOVEN (V)

attacca subito il seguente

WHERE DO YOU GO FROM HERE?

This is as far as we'll be taking our formal tuition. It's now up to you to decide the direction in which you want to go. Practice, both at playing and sight-reading, will enable you work through even the most demanding pieces of piano music. This is all well and good if you are playing for your own entertainment, but if you want to take the classical route to a much higher level, then you're going to need private specialised tuition. The same is likely to be true for jazz: since you know the fundamentals of playing the piano, you should be able to find many good, useful beginners' guides, but lessons with a jazz teacher should give better results.

For less formal types of music, such as rock, pop or country, your current level of technical skill should be enough for you to start working successfully in a band scenario. Although clearly an understanding of the roles of the keyboard, or the different possible sounds, is just as important as technique.

CHOOSING A TEACHER

Unless you have an unusual talent, there is only so far you can go by teaching yourself from a book. If you have followed the previous lessons carefully, you should have developed good playing habits that will stand you in good stead for future study. But whatever kind of music you want to play, the most effective learning is always likely to come from one-on-one private tuition. A good teacher should be someone who understands your aims and is able to motivate you. They should work to a methodology, and set and test measurable short-term goals. You could add to that list someone who contributes to your general musical education, introducing you to the work of interesting new composers and musicians.

Inevitably, finding a suitable piano teacher is much easier said than done. The wrong choice can result in a thoroughly miserable experience – in the worst cases, they can put you off playing for life. Don't just go with the first person you find: make an informed choice. Here are some pointers for you to consider when you interview prospective candidates:

1. The Right Personality

It's important that you get on with your teacher. This is not primary school – you no longer have to put up with teachers you don't like, or with whom you don't get on.

2. Are They Appropriate?

Not all teachers are the same. Some specialise in tutoring young children; others focus wholly on adults. Above all, though, they must be in tune with your current level of attainment and aims. If you can already play "*Jesu, Joy of Man's Desiring*", you won't want to be spending your time learning "Mary had a Little Lamb". Similarly, if you want to play keyboards in a rock band, then a purely classical tutor may not understand what you're looking to achieve; go for a specialist rock teacher – the results are bound to be more satisfactory.

3. Credentials

Is it more important to you that your prospective teacher has formal credentials (a degree in music or music education, for example), or that they have real-world experience as a player? Be warned, though: a good pianist doesn't necessarily make a good teacher. (Indeed, as most of us can attest, being a *qualified* teacher doesn't always guarantee being a *good* teacher.)

4. Recommendation

When selecting any kind of service, the best results are likely to come from personal recommendation. A good, successful teacher will be happy to give you references.

5. The Future

Your learning experience is likely to be more satisfactory if you are taught by someone who is already doing what you would like to do. If you seriously want to become a professional pianist or keyboard player, then you should try to find a teacher who is also a professional player. Not only will you get appropriate instruction, but also useful career advice. However good they may be as instructors, many qualified piano teachers have little or no experience of professional performance.

LISTENING

Finally, here is a brief mention of one of the best learning tools you have at your disposal: your ears. If you're serious about your playing, listen to as much music as you can. Most of the greatest musicians of the twentieth century have been captured in recordings. Study the way they play. Try to understand not only what they are doing, but *why* they are doing it.

PART 3
INFORMAL PLAYING

PLAYING WITHOUT MUSIC

There is little doubt that an understanding of formal music notation is a basic essential for any pianist intending to play "classical" styles of music to any reasonable standard. Some genres, however, are less formal in their demands. While many modern electronic keyboard players have graduated from the traditional route of classical piano tuition, they are likely to find that an ability to sight-read on demand is significantly less important than being able to come up with a coherent melodic or harmonic arrangement when faced with the barest of musical outlines – for example, a chord pattern or single-note melody. Even though there are many fine players who work with an intuitive talent, but have little or no understanding of formal music theory, those armed with a working knowledge of scales and chords should be better equipped to come up with a wider range of creative possibilities for any musical context.

"YOU HUM IT, I'LL PLAY IT"

It can be pretty impressive encountering a musician who is able to play "by ear", using no written music. There are undoubtedly some people who are imbued with an extraordinary facility for dealing with pitch and harmony. They may only need to hear a tune once or twice before they can give a reasonable rendition, or provide a useful accompaniment. But for most musicians this process need not be all that mysterious. If you devote enough time to learning scales, chords and simple, everyday practice, you will gradually gain an instinctive understanding of the way notes relate to one another. This is the key to playing melodies by ear.

PICKING OUT A TUNE

Every melody you have ever heard can be described in terms of a series of intervals between the composite notes. If you have a thorough knowledge of the intervals from any given root to any other note, any tune you hear should be straightforward enough to work out for yourself – even if you can't actually play it back immediately on the piano. This is one practical reason why the interval theory shown at the beginning of Lesson 4 (*see pages 66-70*) is so important.

Let's take a simple example – the song "When the Saints Go Marching In". Sing the first two notes ("Oh, when…") Starting with the first note, sing in ascending semitone intervals until you hit what sounds like the second note. The second note is four semitones above the first – that's an interval of a major 3rd. Do the same thing with the second and third notes – which have an interval of one semitone; the interval between the third and fourth notes is one tone. From any starting note you choose, you can now play the first four notes of the tune.

This is clearly a very laboured way of working out a tune. In practise, with experience you will come to know instinctively what those intervals are and how they are played back on the piano: some players are even able to "see" note intervals in terms of patterns on the keyboard.

CHORDS

When playing keyboards with less formal musical styles, many classically trained pianists face a particular problem: they will be more familiar with the idea of playing a "complete" piece of music, one where the melodic and harmonic content is integrated. When playing in a band or as an accompanist, keyboard parts generally concentrate on harmonic matters, leaving the singer or soloist to deal with the tune. Trained pianists, however, are not usually taught to think of music in terms of chords. Unfortunately for them, in practice it's much more common to be presented with a chord chart – a sheet of paper listing a series of chord names – than a full notated arrangement. The keyboard player's job is frequently to come up with an original musical part based around those chords.

WORKING OUT A SONG

If you're already well and truly bored with mention of the dreaded "P" word (that's PRACTICE, by the way) we make no apology. But while daily chord and scale workouts can admittedly become tiresome chores, there are plenty of ways of having fun and learning at the same time. If you want to gain the facility for playing by ear, there is no better way of doing this than sitting down at the piano and working out songs you already know for yourself.

This exercise is an example of what is known by music arrangers as "routining". Your task is to take a recording of a favourite song, identify its component parts, and work out the chords that are used. As with the melody exercise on the opposite page, this may seem a rather long-winded approach, but it makes for a good starting point – you'll quickly discover your own short cuts.

Begin with the song structure. Most modern songs are simple affairs, consisting of an introduction, repeated verses and choruses, and usually a one-off deviating segment that is usually described as a "middle-eight". When you've identified the structure, you can give each part a unique letter: (A) Introduction; (B) Verse; (C) Chorus; (D) Middle-eight; (E) Ending. You're now ready to work out the chords for each part.

Take a sheet of manuscript paper and divide it up into bars. (A sheet of plain paper with some horizontal bars ruled in will do the job just as nicely.) As you listen to your recording, count out the bars along with the music, making a mark on the paper every time there is a chord change.

Count along with the recording once again, but this time listen out for the TYPE of chord being played. (IMPORTANT CLUE: The vast majority of modern songs are made up from major, minor and seventh chords.)

All you have to do now is identify the root note of each of those chords. One way of doing this is to try to hum the lowest-pitched note that sounds "right", or play individual notes on the piano keyboard. (ANOTHER CLUE: When listening to a recording, pay special attention to the bass instrument – it will often be playing the root note.)

When it comes down to it, working out a song's structure is not all that tough. After all, most of the popular songs of the past century have drawn from a very limited musical spectrum. Indeed, if you play the chords built on the major scale (*see page 89*) there's a good chance that it will contain most of the chords found in the majority of songs written in that key.

The same can be said of harmonic progressions within songs. So many are based around simple movements between the TONIC TRIAD (the chord built on the first degree of the major scale), the SUBDOMINANT TRIAD (the chord built on the fourth degree) and the DOMINANT TRIAD (the chord built on the fifth degree). Indeed, these three chords are sometimes described as the PRIMARY TRIADS. As an experiment, play random sequences of chords built on the C major scale. You may be surprised how almost everything you play sounds "right" – the chords just seem to flow into one another very smoothly.

But before they can even think about that, they must reorient themselves, so that when asked to play a chord they don't first have to work out the notes in their head. For some players this is easier said than done.

PLAYING WITH CHORDS

When playing by ear, chords can be problematic: whereas a melody is a succession of single notes, a chord consists of three or more notes being played simultaneously. To isolate the notes, you have to be able to break down what may sometimes be complex harmonies into their component parts. Again, with time and experience this process can become almost automatic.

The first step is to become as familiar as you can with the different characteristics of the various chord types. It doesn't matter what the chord's root note is, every chord type is united by just one factor – the intervals between each of the notes in

the chord and its root. Although in a different key, C minor, G minor and B♭ minor all share that same "minorness" which comes from having a minor third three semitones above the root note, and a perfect fifth, seven semitones above the root note. As you can see, intervals are once again at the very heart of getting to grips with an important musical concept.

A good starting point is to become familiar with the sound of the four fundamental triads: major, minor, diminished and augmented. These form the basis of the vast majority of more complex chords, such as the sevenths, or those that use extended notes from beyond the octave, such as the ninth, eleventh, and thirteenth series. Practising playing the chord dictionary (*see pages 158–181*) will help to implant their unique sounds in your mind. (IMPORTANT POINT: Make sure that you pay attention to the chord names – recognising the sound of a chord is one thing; being able to identify it is considerably more use.)

THE CHORD DICTIONARY

Over the next 24 pages you will find detailed instructions for playing 324 different chords: that's 27 different chord types played over all 12 keys. This chord dictionary has three distinct functions: for reference; as an aid to theory; and as a useful practice tool.

REFERENCE

If you want to discover how to play a specific chord, or if you want to know the notes or "spellings" that define a chord, then the chord dictionary will provide you with most of the chords with which you are likely to come across.

LEARNING

You can also treat the chord dictionary as a series of learning exercises. By working methodically through all of the chords for each key, you will come across certain sounds that you might have heard used on familiar recordings, but not previously been able to name or play. You may find yourself newly acquainted with some of the more unusual or esoteric types of chord. Whatever type of music you want to perform, a broad vocabulary of chords will give your playing, composition or arrangements greater depth and versatility. And the more chord types that you recognise instinctively, the easier you will find it to work out and play songs for which you have no written music.

PRACTISE

Finally, you can treat the chord dictionary as a series of exercises that can be played alongside standard scale exercises. Some chord types are particularly demanding, so working through each key will help to keep your finger movements in good shape. One particularly useful playing exercise is to work out inversions for the chords listed. This is very straightforward for those chords that contain just three or four notes, but far more demanding for the ninth, eleventh and thirteenth series – here you may also be called upon to make decisions about leaving out certain notes.

USING THE CHORD DICTIONARY

Each set of chords is grouped according to their key. The 27 chords for each key are positioned across two pages – the name of the key is marked in the pale blue box in the top left-hand corner of the first page. Alongside the key identity, you'll see an additional box containing the notes of the major scale shown on the treble clef for that key. Each note is identified by its name and its scale degree. To make things clearer, each note also has a unique colour shading.

Each chord is shown in its own box. In the top left-hand corner of the box you will find the name of the chord. Directly beneath, you can see how the chord looks when written down on the staff. The main diagram shows an overhead view of a keyboard. The coloured dots on the keyboard represent the notes that have to be played. The colour equates directly to the degree on the scale, giving you an immediate visual key to the chord's "spelling".

Some of the lower-pitched notes are shown encircled. This occurs when the chord is impractical (or impossible) to play with just one hand. In these cases, the encircled notes should be played with the left hand; the remaining notes should be played with the right hand.

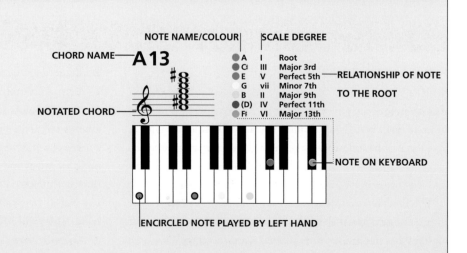

THE CHORD BOX

Each chord panel comprises six different elements – each one is labelled in the diagram on the right. Remember that the details in the top half of the diagram always refer to chords in the root position – they are to be played in ascending order of pitch from the root. The keyboard diagram in the lower half of the panel does NOT always indicate the same voicing; in the case of eleventh and thirteenth chords the most pleasant or commonly used inversions are shown.

NOTE NAME/COLOUR	SCALE DEGREE	
CHORD NAME — A13		
NOTATED CHORD —	A	I	Root
	C♯	III	Major 3rd
	E	V	Perfect 5th — RELATIONSHIP OF NOTE
	G	vii	Minor 7th TO THE ROOT
	B	II	Major 9th
	(D)	IV	Perfect 11th
	F♯	VI	Major 13th

NOTE ON KEYBOARD

ENCIRCLED NOTE PLAYED BY LEFT HAND

SCALE DEGREES

The eight degrees of the major scale from root to octave are shown at the top of the left-hand page for each of the 12 keys.

Pay special attention to the number of sharps or flats positioned alongside the treble clef. Don't forget that when you encounter these at the start of a piece of sheet music they tell you IMMEDIATELY the key in which the music has been written.

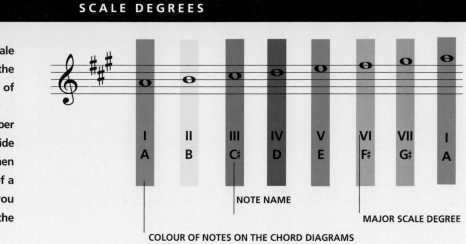

| I | II | III | IV | V | VI | VII | I |
| A | B | C# | D | E | F# | G# | A |

NOTE NAME

MAJOR SCALE DEGREE

COLOUR OF NOTES ON THE CHORD DIAGRAMS

There are no instructions as to which finger should be used to play a particular note, since most of the examples can be played by either hand. The finger positions should be easy enough to work out for yourself – play them in whatever way feels most comfortable. In practice, this is likely to mean that when using the right hand, the thumb will play the lowest note, and the little finger will play the highest note; when playing with the left hand, the thumb will play the highest note, and the little finger the lowest note.

In the top right-hand area of each box, you will also find the names of the notes that make up the chord (alongside the corresponding coloured dots). Any note shown surrounded by a bracket means that although it is an integral part of the chord's correct spelling, it is optional when playing.

Finally, alongside the note names you will see the description and abbreviated degree of each note's relationship to the root. For example, in the key of C, the note G is the perfect 5th, which can be abbreviated as the Roman numeral "V". It is these relationships that define each chord.

WHICH IS CORRECT?

In some cases you may notice that the notes on the fingerboard diagram don't tie up with the notes named or the music on the staff. There's a good reason for this. The note names and staff diagrams refer to each chord in its full root position. This means that the notes defining that chord will always appear in ascending pitch from the root. However, in the case of the eleventh and thirteenth series of chords, they don't always sound very pleasant when played in order from the root note. In these cases, the keyboard diagrams have been shown using more effective inversions.

As you've already seen, understanding inversion is crucial in all forms of music. When you practise chords, try inverting them in as many ways as possible. The easiest way to do this is to take the lowest-pitched note and replace it with one an octave above. For example, when playing a C dominant seventh chord, begin with C-E-G-B♭ (root position), then move to E-G-B♭-C (first inversion), then on to G-B♭-C-E (second inversion), before finishing with B♭-C-E-G (third inversion).

CHORDS ON THE CD

Track 63 of the CD contains a full set of chords for the key of C. These chords are all shown on pages 164–165. This may enable you to place certain chords or inversions that you might have heard, but have not been able to name or play. The chords are played in the following sequence:

1.	C major	2.	C minor
3.	C dominant seventh	4.	C minor seventh
5.	C major seventh	6.	C suspended fourth
7.	C suspended second	8.	C sixth
9.	C diminished seventh	10.	C minor sixth

11.	C augmented	12.	C seven flat fifth
13.	C seven augmented fifth	14.	C minor/major seven
15.	C major seven flat fifth	16.	C major augmented fifth
17.	C dominant ninth	18.	C minor ninth
19.	C major ninth	20.	C eleventh
21.	C minor eleventh	22.	C thirteenth
23.	C minor thirteenth	24.	C major 13th
25.	C seven flat five flat ninth		
26.	C seven flat five augmented ninth		
27.	C seven augmented fifth flat ninth		

63

A

I	II	III	IV	V	VI	VII	I
A	B	C#	D	E	F#	G#	A

A maj

● A	I	Root
● C#	III	Major 3rd
● E	V	Perfect 5th

A m

● A	I	Root
● C	iii	Minor 3rd
● E	V	Perfect 5th

A 7

● A	I	Root
● C#	III	Major 3rd
● E	V	Perfect 5th
○ G	vii	Minor 7th

A min 7

● A	I	Root
● C	iii	Minor 3rd
● E	V	Perfect 5th
○ G	vii	Minor 7th

A maj 7

● A	I	Root
● C#	III	Major 3rd
● E	V	Perfect 5th
● G#	VII	Major 7th

A sus 4

● A	I	Root
● D	IV	Perfect 4th
● E	V	Perfect 5th

A sus 2

● A	I	Root
● B	II	Major 2nd
● E	V	Perfect 5th

A 6

● A	I	Root
● C#	III	Major 3rd
● E	V	Perfect 5th
● F#	VI	Major 6th

A min 6

● A	I	Root
● C	iii	Minor 3rd
● E	V	Perfect 5th
● F#	VI	Major 6th

A aug

● A	I	Root
● C#	III	Major 3rd
● F	V+	Aug 5th

A dim 7

● A	I	Root
● C	iii	Minor 3rd
● E♭	V°	Dim 5th
● G♭	vii	Dim 7th

A 7-5

● A	I	Root
● C#	III	Major 3rd
● E♭	V°	Dim 5th
○ G	vii	Minor 7th

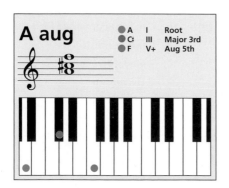
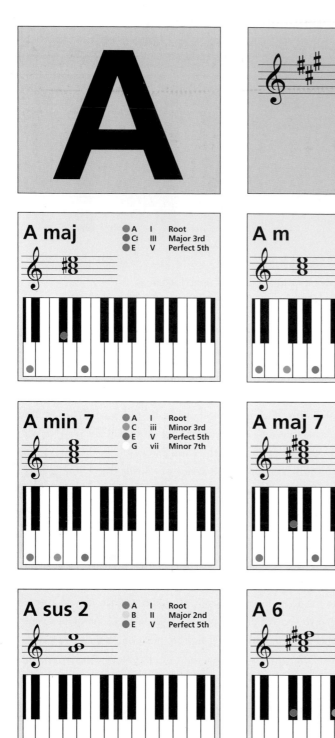

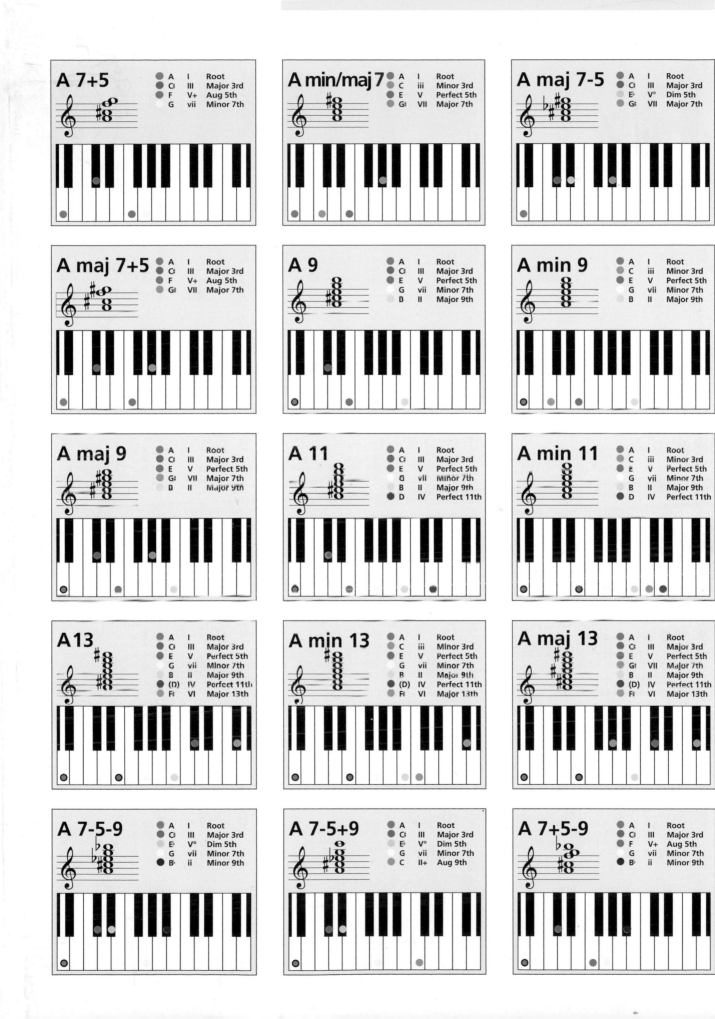

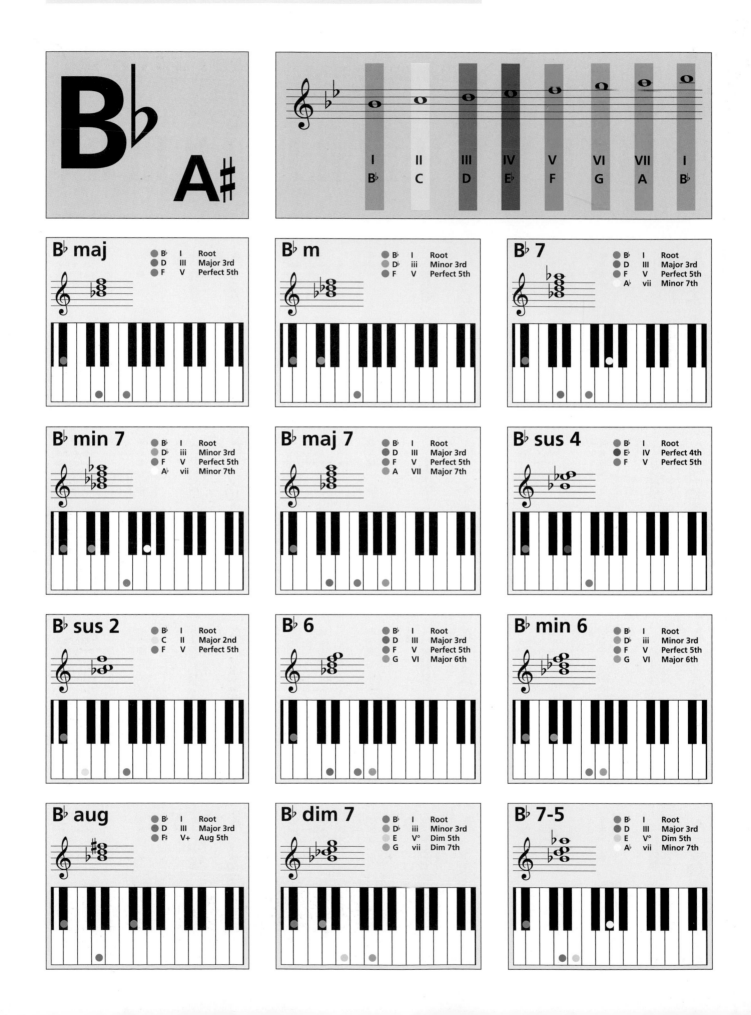

B♭ 7+5
B♭	I	Root
D	III	Major 3rd
F♯	V+	Aug 5th
A♭	vii	Minor 7th

B♭ min/maj7
B♭	I	Root
D♭	iii	Minor 3rd
F	V	Perfect 5th
A	VII	Major 7th

B♭ maj 7-5
B♭	I	Root
D	III	Major 3rd
E	V°	Dim 5th
A	VII	Major 7th

B♭ maj 7+5
B♭	I	Root
D	III	Major 3rd
F♯	V+	Aug 5th
A	VII	Major 7th

B♭ 9
B♭	I	Root
D	III	Major 3rd
F	V	Perfect 5th
A♭	vii	Minor 7th
C	II	Major 9th

B♭ min 9
B♭	I	Root
D♭	iii	Minor 3rd
F	V	Perfect 5th
A♭	vii	Minor 7th
C	II	Major 9th

B♭ maj 9
B♭	I	Root
D	III	Major 3rd
F	V	Perfect 5th
A	VII	Major 7th
C	II	Major 9th

B♭ 11
B♭	I	Root
D	III	Major 3rd
F	V	Perfect 5th
A♭	vii	Minor 7th
C	II	Major 9th
E♭	IV	Perfect 11th

B♭ min 11
B♭	I	Root
D♭	iii	Minor 3rd
F	V	Perfect 5th
A♭	vii	Minor 7th
C	II	Major 9th
E♭	IV	Perfect 11th

B♭ 13
B♭	I	Root
D	III	Major 3rd
F	V	Perfect 5th
A♭	vii	Minor 7th
C	II	Major 9th
(E♭)	IV	Perfect 11th
G	VI	Major 13th

B♭ min 13
B♭	I	Root
D♭	iii	Minor 3rd
F	V	Perfect 5th
A♭	vii	Minor 7th
C	II	Major 9th
(E♭)	IV	Perfect 11th
G	VI	Major 13th

B♭ maj 13
B♭	I	Root
D	III	Major 3rd
F	V	Perfect 5th
A	VII	Major 7th
C	II	Major 9th
(E♭)	IV	Perfect 11th
G	VI	Major 13th

B♭ 7-5-9
B♭	I	Root
D	III	Major 3rd
E	V°	Dim 5th
A♭	vii	Minor 7th
B	ii	Minor 9th

B♭ 7-5+9
B♭	I	Root
D	III	Major 3rd
E	V°	Dim 5th
A♭	vii	Minor 7th
C♯	II+	Aug 9th

B♭ 7+5-9
B♭	I	Root
D	III	Major 3rd
F♯	V+	Aug 5th
A♭	vii	Minor 7th
B	ii	Minor 9th

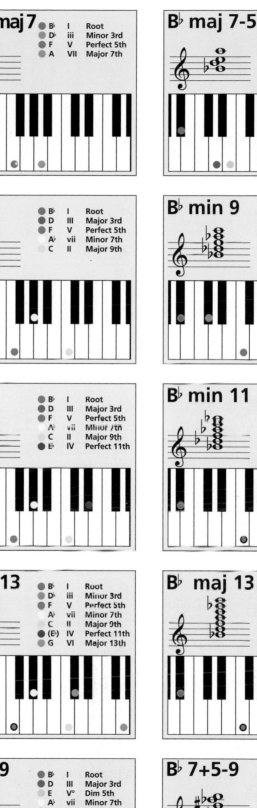
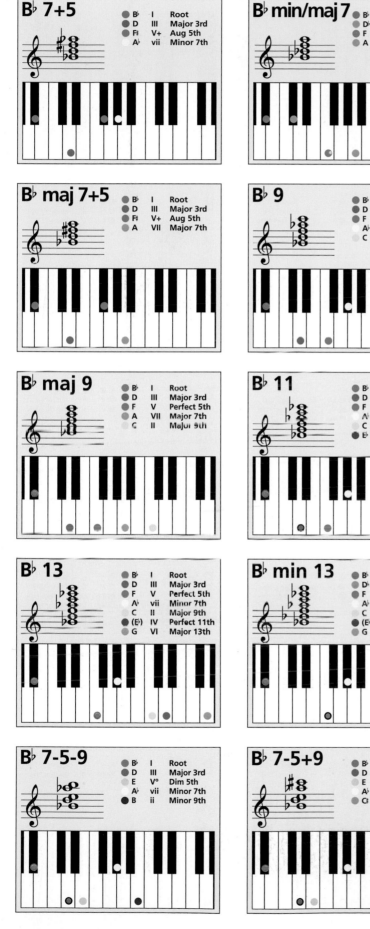
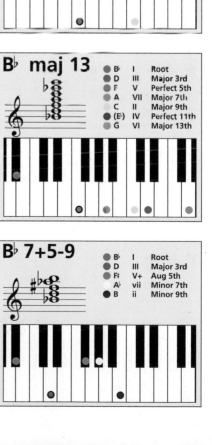

B

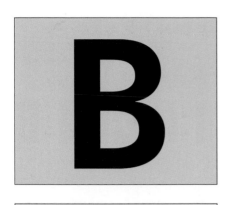

I	II	III	IV	V	VI	VII	I
B	C#	D#	E	F#	G#	A#	B

B maj

● B	I	Root
● D#	III	Major 3rd
● F#	V	Perfect 5th

B m

● B	I	Root
● D	iii	Minor 3rd
● F#	V	Perfect 5th

B 7

● B	I	Root
● D#	III	Major 3rd
● F#	V	Perfect 5th
○ A	vii	Minor 7th

B min 7

● B	I	Root
● D	iii	Minor 3rd
● F#	V	Perfect 5th
○ A	vii	Minor 7th

B maj 7

● B	I	Root
● D#	III	Major 3rd
● F#	V	Perfect 5th
● A#	VII	Major 7th

B sus 4

● B	I	Root
● E	IV	Perfect 4th
● F#	V	Perfect 5th

B sus 2

● B	I	Root
● C#	II	Major 2nd
● F#	V	Perfect 5th

B 6

● B	I	Root
● D#	III	Major 3rd
● F#	V	Perfect 5th
● G#	VI	Major 6th

B min 6

● B	I	Root
● D	iii	Minor 3rd
● F#	V	Perfect 5th
● G#	VI	Major 6th

B aug

● B	I	Root
● D#	III	Major 3rd
● G	V+	Aug 5th

B dim 7

● B	I	Root
● D	iii	Minor 3rd
● F	V°	Dim 5th
● A♭	vii	Dim 7th

B 7-5

● B	I	Root
● D#	III	Major 3rd
● F	V°	Dim 5th
○ A	vii	Minor 7th

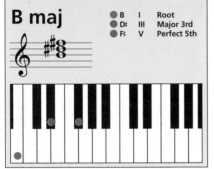
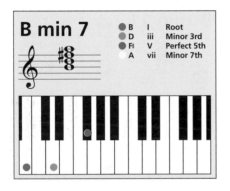
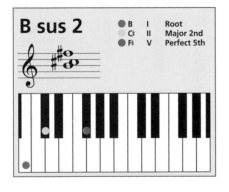
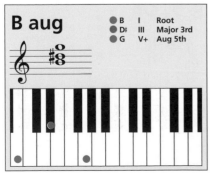
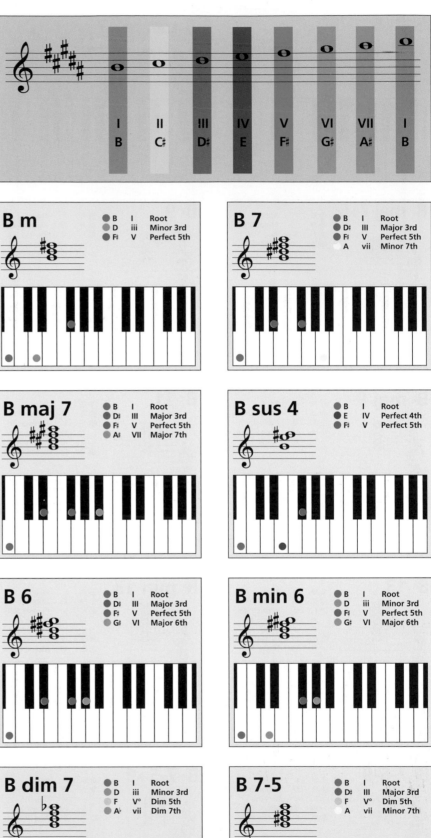
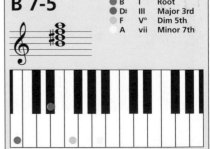

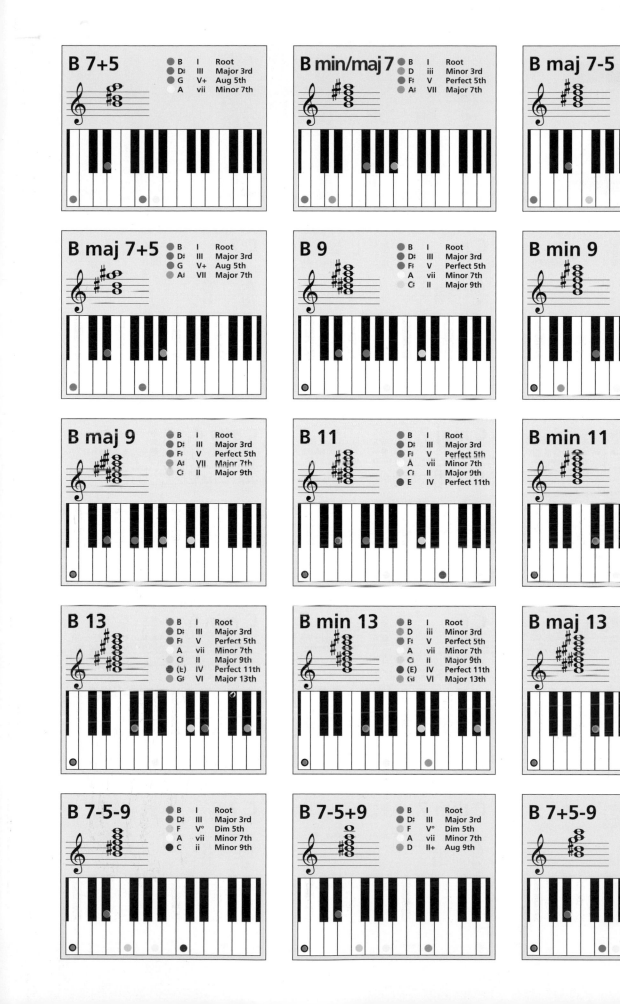

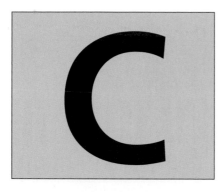

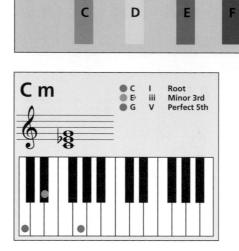

I	II	III	IV	V	VI	VII	I
C	D	E	F	G	A	B	C

C maj
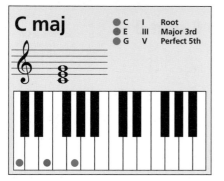

C	I	Root
E	III	Major 3rd
G	V	Perfect 5th

C m
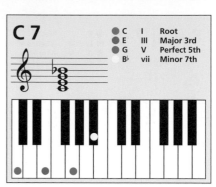

C	I	Root
E♭	iii	Minor 3rd
G	V	Perfect 5th

C 7
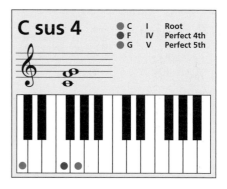

C	I	Root
E	III	Major 3rd
G	V	Perfect 5th
B♭	vii	Minor 7th

C min 7
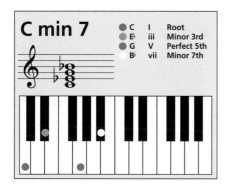

C	I	Root
E♭	iii	Minor 3rd
G	V	Perfect 5th
B♭	vii	Minor 7th

C maj 7
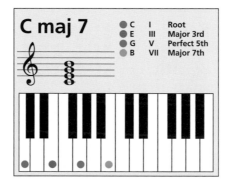

C	I	Root
E	III	Major 3rd
G	V	Perfect 5th
B	VII	Major 7th

C sus 4
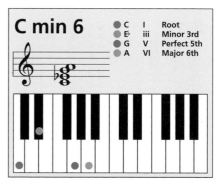

C	I	Root
F	IV	Perfect 4th
G	V	Perfect 5th

C sus 2
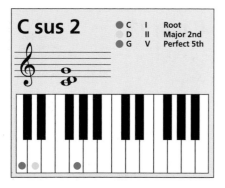

C	I	Root
D	II	Major 2nd
G	V	Perfect 5th

C 6
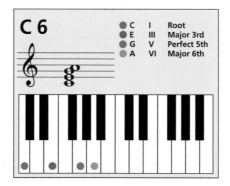

C	I	Root
E	III	Major 3rd
G	V	Perfect 5th
A	VI	Major 6th

C min 6

C	I	Root
E♭	iii	Minor 3rd
G	V	Perfect 5th
A	VI	Major 6th

C aug
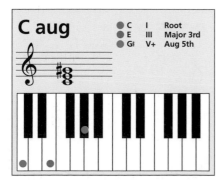

C	I	Root
E	III	Major 3rd
G♯	V+	Aug 5th

C dim 7
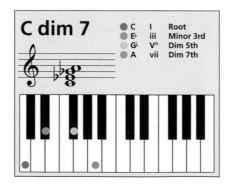

C	I	Root
E♭	iii	Minor 3rd
G♭	V°	Dim 5th
A	vii	Dim 7th

C 7-5
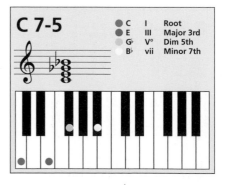

C	I	Root
E	III	Major 3rd
G♭	V°	Dim 5th
B♭	vii	Minor 7th

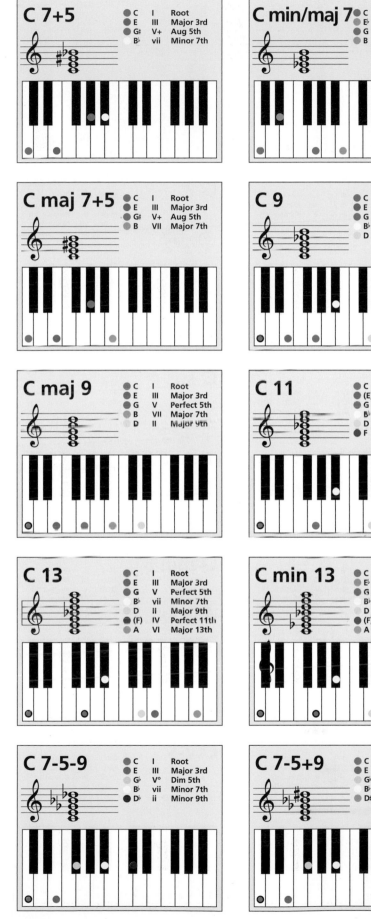
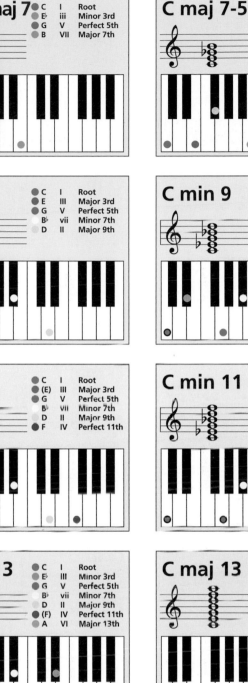
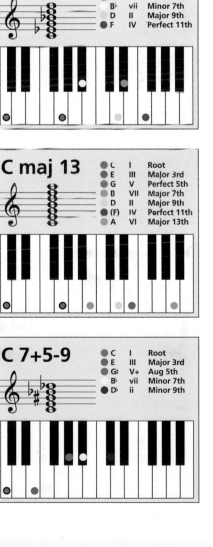

C 7+5
C	I	Root
E	III	Major 3rd
G♯	V+	Aug 5th
B♭	vii	Minor 7th

C min/maj 7
C	I	Root
E♭	iii	Minor 3rd
G	V	Perfect 5th
B	VII	Major 7th

C maj 7-5
C	I	Root
E	III	Major 3rd
G♭	V°	Dim 5th
B	VII	Major 7th

C maj 7+5
C	I	Root
E	III	Major 3rd
G♯	V+	Aug 5th
B	VII	Major 7th

C 9
C	I	Root
E	III	Major 3rd
G	V	Perfect 5th
B♭	vii	Minor 7th
D	II	Major 9th

C min 9
C	I	Root
E♭	iii	Minor 3rd
G	V	Perfect 5th
B♭	vii	Minor 7th
D	II	Major 9th

C maj 9
C	I	Root
E	III	Major 3rd
G	V	Perfect 5th
B	VII	Major 7th
D	II	Major 9th

C 11
C	I	Root
(E)	III	Major 3rd
G	V	Perfect 5th
B♭	vii	Minor 7th
D	II	Major 9th
F	IV	Perfect 11th

C min 11
C	I	Root
E♭	iii	Minor 3rd
G	V	Perfect 5th
B♭	vii	Minor 7th
D	II	Major 9th
F	IV	Perfect 11th

C 13
C	I	Root
E	III	Major 3rd
G	V	Perfect 5th
B♭	vii	Minor 7th
D	II	Major 9th
(F)	IV	Perfect 11th
A	VI	Major 13th

C min 13
C	I	Root
E♭	III	Minor 3rd
G	V	Perfect 5th
B♭	vii	Minor 7th
D	II	Major 9th
(F)	IV	Perfect 11th
A	VI	Major 13th

C maj 13
C	I	Root
E	III	Major 3rd
G	V	Perfect 5th
B	VII	Major 7th
D	II	Major 9th
(F)	IV	Perfect 11th
A	VI	Major 13th

C 7-5-9
C	I	Root
E	III	Major 3rd
G♭	V°	Dim 5th
B♭	vii	Minor 7th
D♭	ii	Minor 9th

C 7-5+9
C	I	Root
E	III	Major 3rd
G♭	V°	Dim 5th
B♭	vii	Minor 7th
D♯	II+	Aug 9th

C 7+5-9
C	I	Root
E	III	Major 3rd
G♯	V+	Aug 5th
B♭	vii	Minor 7th
D♭	ii	Minor 9th

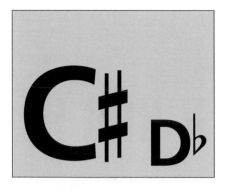

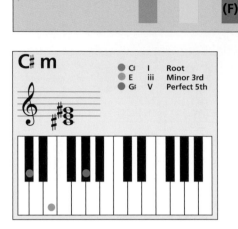

I	II	III	IV	V	VI	VII	I
C#	D#	E#	F#	G#	A#	B#	C#
		(F)				(C)	

C# maj
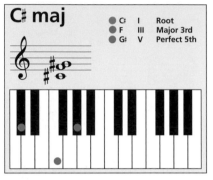

●	C#	I	Root
●	F	III	Major 3rd
●	G#	V	Perfect 5th

C# m
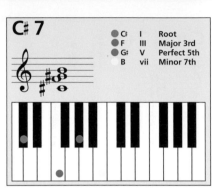

●	C#	I	Root
●	E	iii	Minor 3rd
●	G#	V	Perfect 5th

C# 7

●	C#	I	Root
●	F	III	Major 3rd
●	G#	V	Perfect 5th
○	B	vii	Minor 7th

C# min 7
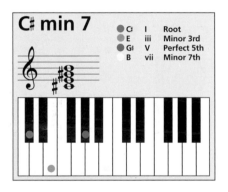

●	C#	I	Root
●	E	iii	Minor 3rd
●	G#	V	Perfect 5th
○	B	vii	Minor 7th

C# maj 7
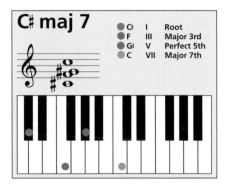

●	C#	I	Root
●	F	III	Major 3rd
●	G#	V	Perfect 5th
●	C	VII	Major 7th

C# sus 4
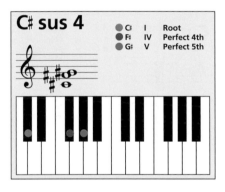

●	C#	I	Root
●	F#	IV	Perfect 4th
●	G#	V	Perfect 5th

C# sus 2

●	C#	I	Root
○	D#	II	Major 2nd
●	G#	V	Perfect 5th

C# 6
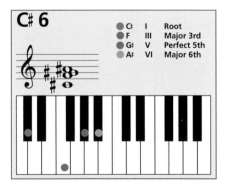

●	C#	I	Root
●	F	III	Major 3rd
●	G#	V	Perfect 5th
●	A#	VI	Major 6th

C# min 6
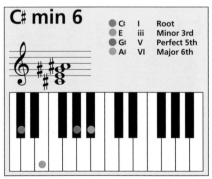

●	C#	I	Root
●	E	iii	Minor 3rd
●	G#	V	Perfect 5th
●	A#	VI	Major 6th

C# aug
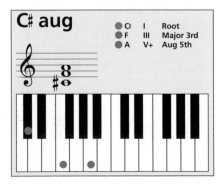

●	C#	I	Root
●	F	III	Major 3rd
●	A	V+	Aug 5th

C# dim 7
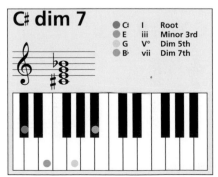

●	C#	I	Root
●	E	iii	Minor 3rd
○	G	V°	Dim 5th
○	B♭	vii	Dim 7th

C# 7-5
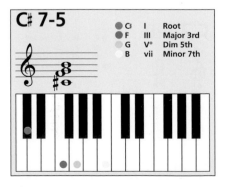

●	C#	I	Root
●	F	III	Major 3rd
○	G	V°	Dim 5th
○	B	vii	Minor 7th

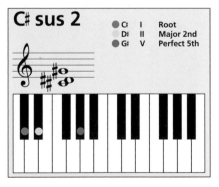

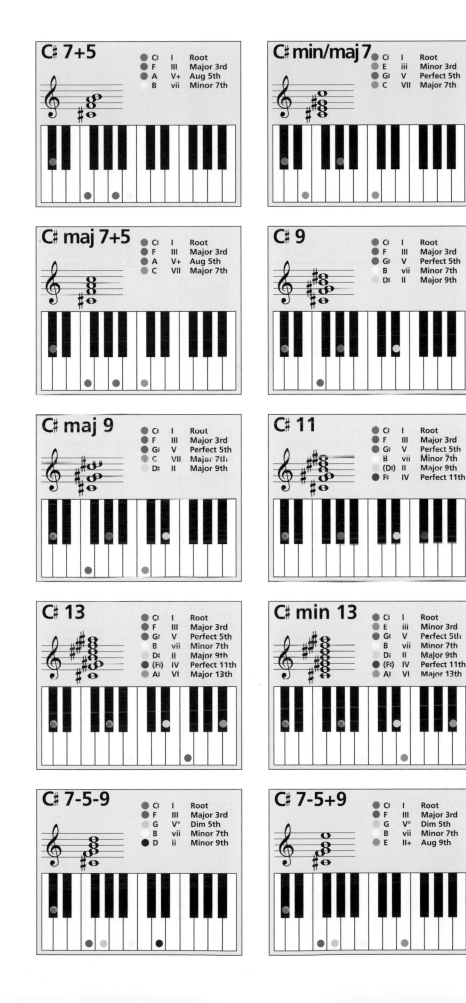
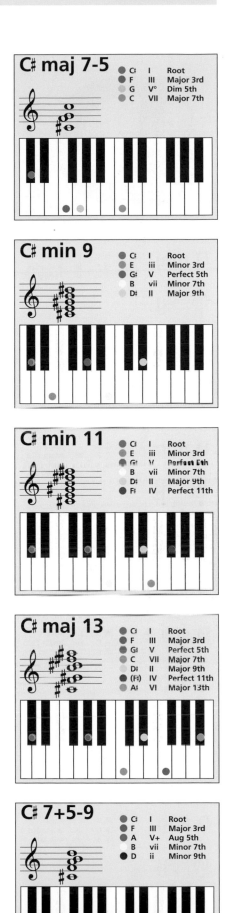

C♯ 7+5

C♯	I	Root
F	III	Major 3rd
A	V+	Aug 5th
B	vii	Minor 7th

C♯ min/maj 7

C♯	I	Root
E	iii	Minor 3rd
G♯	V	Perfect 5th
C	VII	Major 7th

C♯ maj 7-5

C♯	I	Root
F	III	Major 3rd
G	V°	Dim 5th
C	VII	Major 7th

C♯ maj 7+5

C♯	I	Root
F	III	Major 3rd
A	V+	Aug 5th
C	VII	Major 7th

C♯ 9

C♯	I	Root
F	III	Major 3rd
G♯	V	Perfect 5th
B	vii	Minor 7th
D♯	II	Major 9th

C♯ min 9

C♯	I	Root
E	iii	Minor 3rd
G♯	V	Perfect 5th
B	vii	Minor 7th
D♯	II	Major 9th

C♯ maj 9

C♯	I	Root
F	III	Major 3rd
G♯	V	Perfect 5th
C	VII	Major 7th
D♯	II	Major 9th

C♯ 11

C♯	I	Root
F	III	Major 3rd
G♯	V	Perfect 5th
B	vii	Minor 7th
(D♯)	II	Major 9th
F♯	IV	Perfect 11th

C♯ min 11

C♯	I	Root
E	iii	Minor 3rd
G♯	V	Perfect 5th
B	vii	Minor 7th
D♯	II	Major 9th
F♯	IV	Perfect 11th

C♯ 13

C♯	I	Root
F	III	Major 3rd
G♯	V	Perfect 5th
B	vii	Minor 7th
D♯	II	Major 9th
(F♯)	IV	Perfect 11th
A♯	VI	Major 13th

C♯ min 13

C♯	I	Root
E	iii	Minor 3rd
G♯	V	Perfect 5th
B	vii	Minor 7th
D♯	II	Major 9th
(F♯)	IV	Perfect 11th
A♯	VI	Major 13th

C♯ maj 13

C♯	I	Root
F	III	Major 3rd
G♯	V	Perfect 5th
C	VII	Major 7th
D♯	II	Major 9th
(F♯)	IV	Perfect 11th
A♯	VI	Major 13th

C♯ 7-5-9

C♯	I	Root
F	III	Major 3rd
G	V°	Dim 5th
B	vii	Minor 7th
D	ii	Minor 9th

C♯ 7-5+9

C♯	I	Root
F	III	Major 3rd
G	V°	Dim 5th
B	vii	Minor 7th
E	II+	Aug 9th

C♯ 7+5-9

C♯	I	Root
F	III	Major 3rd
A	V+	Aug 5th
B	vii	Minor 7th
D	ii	Minor 9th

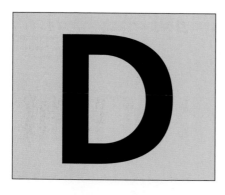

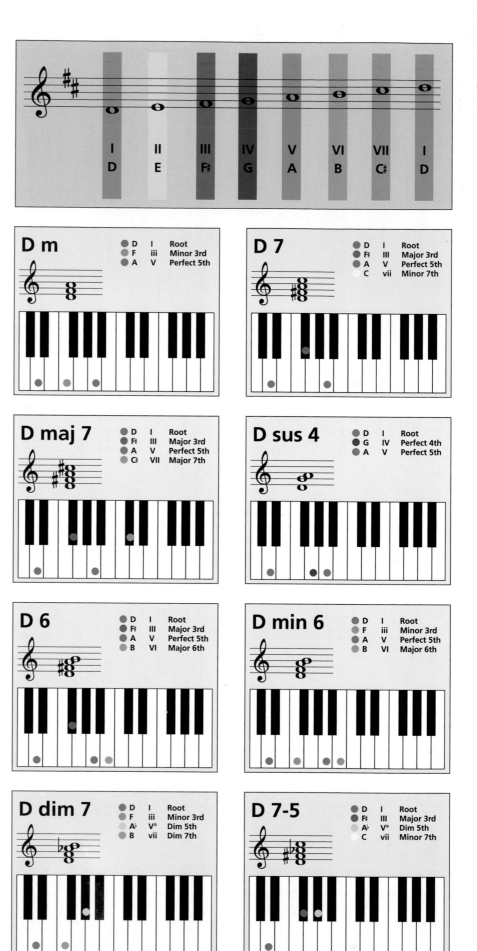

D maj

D	I	Root
F#	III	Major 3rd
A	V	Perfect 5th

D m

D	I	Root
F	iii	Minor 3rd
A	V	Perfect 5th

D 7

D	I	Root
F#	III	Major 3rd
A	V	Perfect 5th
C	vii	Minor 7th

D min 7

D	I	Root
F	iii	Minor 3rd
A	V	Perfect 5th
C	vii	Minor 7th

D maj 7

D	I	Root
F#	III	Major 3rd
A	V	Perfect 5th
C#	VII	Major 7th

D sus 4

D	I	Root
G	IV	Perfect 4th
A	V	Perfect 5th

D sus 2

D	I	Root
E	II	Major 2nd
A	V	Perfect 5th

D 6

D	I	Root
F#	III	Major 3rd
A	V	Perfect 5th
B	VI	Major 6th

D min 6

D	I	Root
F	iii	Minor 3rd
A	V	Perfect 5th
B	VI	Major 6th

D aug

D	I	Root
F#	III	Major 3rd
A#	V+	Aug 5th

D dim 7

D	I	Root
F	iii	Minor 3rd
Ab	V°	Dim 5th
B	vii	Dim 7th

D 7-5

D	I	Root
F#	III	Major 3rd
Ab	V°	Dim 5th
C	vii	Minor 7th

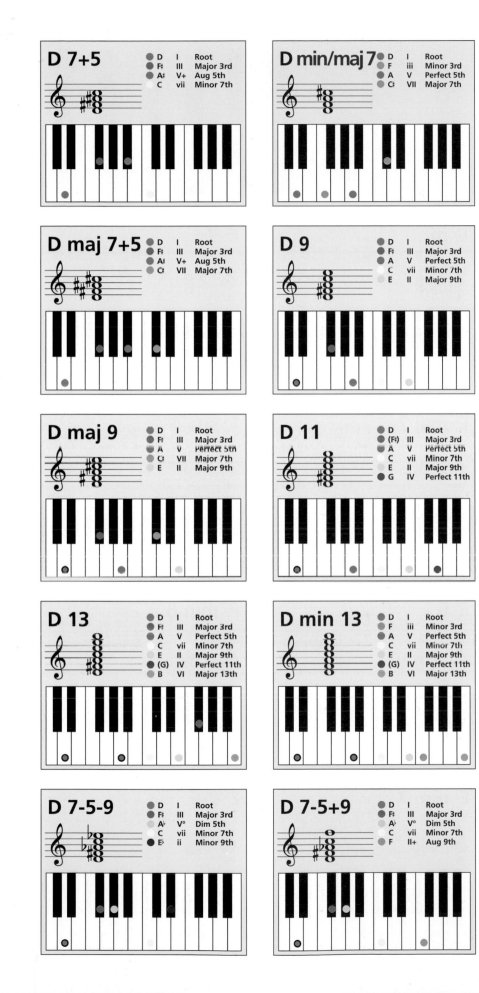
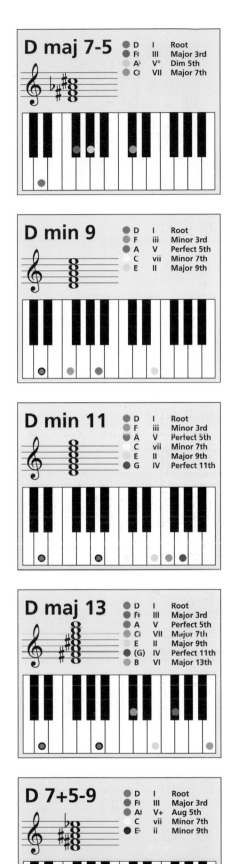

D 7+5

D	I	Root
F♯	III	Major 3rd
A♯	V+	Aug 5th
C	vii	Minor 7th

D min/maj7

D	I	Root
F	iii	Minor 3rd
A	V	Perfect 5th
C♯	VII	Major 7th

D maj 7-5

D	I	Root
F♯	III	Major 3rd
A♭	V°	Dim 5th
C♯	VII	Major 7th

D maj 7+5

D	I	Root
F♯	III	Major 3rd
A♯	V+	Aug 5th
C♯	VII	Major 7th

D 9

D	I	Root
F♯	III	Major 3rd
A	V	Perfect 5th
C	vii	Minor 7th
E	II	Major 9th

D min 9

D	I	Root
F	iii	Minor 3rd
A	V	Perfect 5th
C	vii	Minor 7th
E	II	Major 9th

D maj 9

D	I	Root
F♯	III	Major 3rd
A	V	Perfect 5th
C♯	VII	Major 7th
E	II	Major 9th

D 11

D	I	Root
(F♯)	III	Major 3rd
A	V	Perfect 5th
C	vii	Minor 7th
E	II	Major 9th
G	IV	Perfect 11th

D min 11

D	I	Root
F	iii	Minor 3rd
A	V	Perfect 5th
C	vii	Minor 7th
E	II	Major 9th
G	IV	Perfect 11th

D 13

D	I	Root
F♯	III	Major 3rd
A	V	Perfect 5th
C	vii	Minor 7th
E	II	Major 9th
(G)	IV	Perfect 11th
B	VI	Major 13th

D min 13

D	I	Root
F	iii	Minor 3rd
A	V	Perfect 5th
C	vii	Minor 7th
E	II	Major 9th
(G)	IV	Perfect 11th
B	VI	Major 13th

D maj 13

D	I	Root
F♯	III	Major 3rd
A	V	Perfect 5th
C♯	VII	Major 7th
E	II	Major 9th
(G)	IV	Perfect 11th
B	VI	Major 13th

D 7-5-9

D	I	Root
F♯	III	Major 3rd
A♭	V°	Dim 5th
C	vii	Minor 7th
E♭	ii	Minor 9th

D 7-5+9

D	I	Root
F♯	III	Major 3rd
A♭	V°	Dim 5th
C	vii	Minor 7th
F	II+	Aug 9th

D 7+5-9

D	I	Root
F♯	III	Major 3rd
A♯	V+	Aug 5th
C	vii	Minor 7th
E♭	ii	Minor 9th

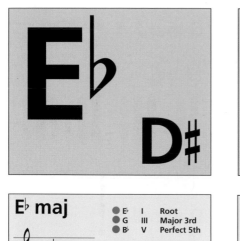

E♭ / D#

I	II	III	IV	V	VI	VII	I
E♭	F	G	A♭	B♭	C	D	E♭

E♭ maj

E♭	I	Root
G	III	Major 3rd
B♭	V	Perfect 5th

E♭ m

E♭	I	Root
G♭	iii	Minor 3rd
B♭	V	Perfect 5th

E♭ 7

E♭	I	Root
G	III	Major 3rd
B♭	V	Perfect 5th
D♭	vii	Minor 7th

E♭ min 7

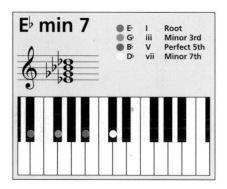

E♭	I	Root
G♭	iii	Minor 3rd
B♭	V	Perfect 5th
D♭	vii	Minor 7th

E♭ maj 7

E♭	I	Root
G	III	Major 3rd
B♭	V	Perfect 5th
D	VII	Major 7th

E♭ sus 4

E♭	I	Root
A♭	IV	Perfect 4th
B♭	V	Perfect 5th

E♭ sus 2

E♭	I	Root
F	II	Major 2nd
B♭	V	Perfect 5th

E♭ 6

E♭	I	Root
G	III	Major 3rd
B♭	V	Perfect 5th
C	VI	Major 6th

E♭ min 6

E♭	I	Root
G♭	iii	Minor 3rd
B♭	V	Perfect 5th
C	VI	Major 6th

E♭ aug

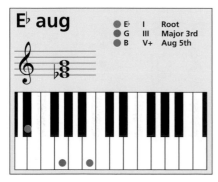

E♭	I	Root
G	III	Major 3rd
B	V+	Aug 5th

E♭ dim 7

E♭	I	Root
G♭	iii	Minor 3rd
A	V°	Dim 5th
C	vii	Dim 7th

E♭ 7-5

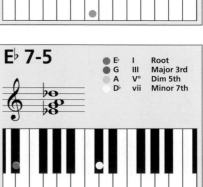

E♭	I	Root
G	III	Major 3rd
A	V°	Dim 5th
D♭	vii	Minor 7th

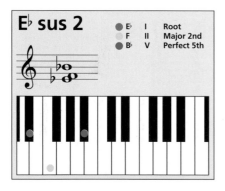
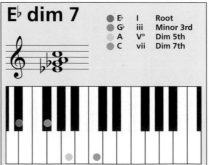

E♭ 7+5

E♭	I	Root
G	III	Major 3rd
B	V+	Aug 5th
D♭	vii	Minor 7th

E♭ min/maj 7

E♭	I	Root
G♭	iii	Minor 3rd
B♭	V	Perfect 5th
D	VII	Major 7th

E♭ maj 7-5

E♭	I	Root
G	III	Major 3rd
A	V°	Dim 5th
D	VII	Major 7th

E♭ maj 7+5

E♭	I	Root
G	III	Major 3rd
B	V+	Aug 5th
D	VII	Major 7th

E♭ 9

E♭	I	Root
G	III	Major 3rd
B♭	V	Perfect 5th
D♭	vii	Minor 7th
F	II	Major 9th

E♭ a 9

E♭	I	Root
G♭	iii	Minor 3rd
B♭	V	Perfect 5th
D♭	vii	Minor 7th
F	II	Major 9th

E♭ maj 9

E♭	I	Root
G	III	Major 3rd
B♭	V	Perfect 5th
D	VII	Major 7th
F	II	Major 9th

E♭ 11

E♭	I	Root
(G)	III	Major 3rd
B♭	V	Perfect 5th
D♭	vii	Minor 7th
F	II	Major 9th
A♭	IV	Perfect 11th

E♭ min 11

E♭	I	Root
G♭	iii	Minor 3rd
B♭	V	Perfect 5th
D♭	vii	Minor 7th
F	II	Major 9th
A♭	IV	Perfect 11th

E♭ 13

E♭	I	Root
G	III	Major 3rd
B♭	V	Perfect 5th
D♭	vii	Minor 7th
F	II	Major 9th
(A♭)	IV	Perfect 11th
C	VI	Major 13th

E♭ min 13

E♭	I	Root
G♭	iii	Minor 3rd
B♭	V	Perfect 5th
D♭	vii	Minor 7th
F	II	Major 9th
(A♭)	IV	Perfect 11th
C	VI	Major 13th

E♭ maj 13

E♭	I	Root
G	III	Major 3rd
B♭	V	Perfect 5th
D	VII	Major 7th
F	II	Major 9th
(A♭)	IV	Perfect 11th
C	VI	Major 13th

E♭ 7-5-9

E♭	I	Root
G	III	Major 3rd
A	V°	Dim 5th
D♭	vii	Minor 7th
E	ii	Minor 9th

E♭ 7-5+9

E♭	I	Root
G	III	Major 3rd
A	V°	Dim 5th
D♭	vii	Minor 7th
F♯	II+	Aug 9th

E♭ 7+5-9

E♭	I	Root
G	III	Major 3rd
B	V+	Aug 5th
D♭	vii	Minor 7th
E	ii	Minor 9th

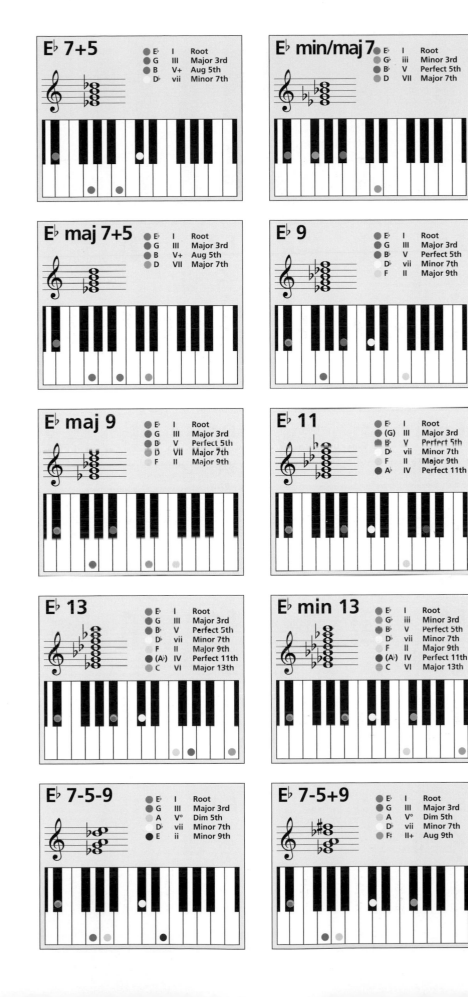
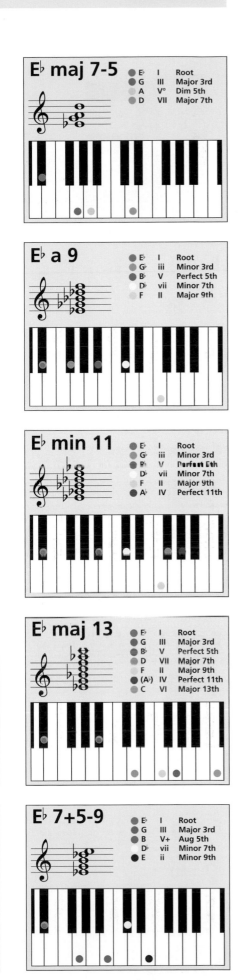

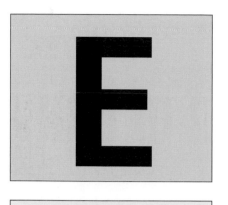

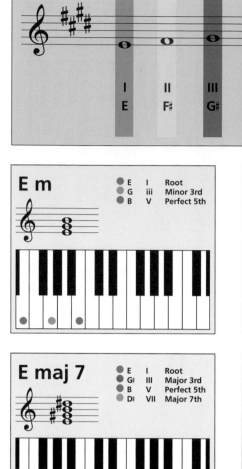

I	II	III	IV	V	VI	VII	I
E	F#	G#	A	B	C#	D#	E

E maj

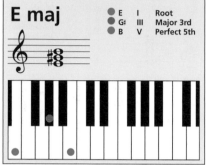

● E	I	Root
● G#	III	Major 3rd
● B	V	Perfect 5th

E m

● E	I	Root
● G	iii	Minor 3rd
● B	V	Perfect 5th

E 7

● E	I	Root
● G#	III	Major 3rd
● B	V	Perfect 5th
○ D	vii	Minor 7th

E min 7

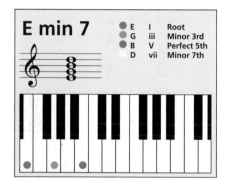

● E	I	Root
● G	iii	Minor 3rd
● B	V	Perfect 5th
○ D	vii	Minor 7th

E maj 7

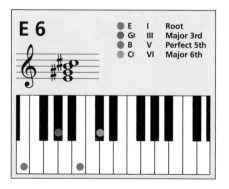

● E	I	Root
● G#	III	Major 3rd
● B	V	Perfect 5th
● D#	VII	Major 7th

D sus 4

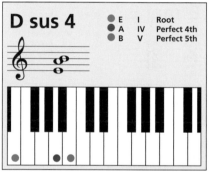

● E	I	Root
● A	IV	Perfect 4th
● B	V	Perfect 5th

E sus 2

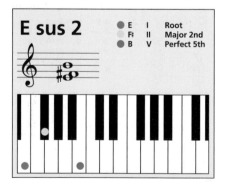

● E	I	Root
○ F#	II	Major 2nd
● B	V	Perfect 5th

E 6

● E	I	Root
● G#	III	Major 3rd
● B	V	Perfect 5th
● C#	VI	Major 6th

E min 6

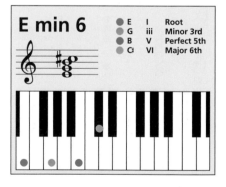

● E	I	Root
● G	iii	Minor 3rd
● B	V	Perfect 5th
● C#	VI	Major 6th

E aug

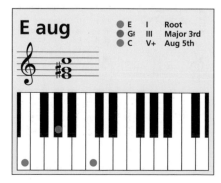

● E	I	Root
● G#	III	Major 3rd
● C	V+	Aug 5th

E dim 7

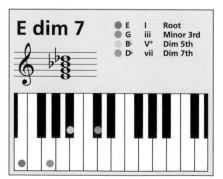

● E	I	Root
● G	iii	Minor 3rd
● B♭	V°	Dim 5th
○ D♭	vii	Dim 7th

E 7-5

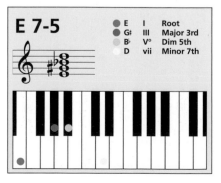

● E	I	Root
● G#	III	Major 3rd
● B♭	V°	Dim 5th
○ D	vii	Minor 7th

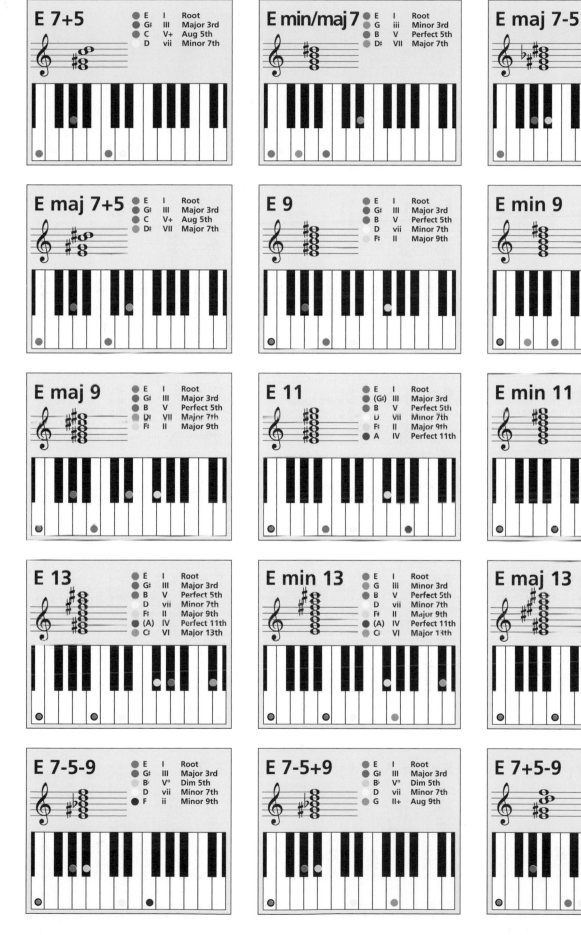

E 7+5
E	I	Root
G#	III	Major 3rd
C	V+	Aug 5th
D	vii	Minor 7th

E min/maj 7
E	I	Root
G	iii	Minor 3rd
B	V	Perfect 5th
D#	VII	Major 7th

E maj 7-5
E	I	Root
G#	III	Major 3rd
B♭	V°	Dim 5th
D#	VII	Major 7th

E maj 7+5
E	I	Root
G#	III	Major 3rd
C	V+	Aug 5th
D#	VII	Major 7th

E 9
E	I	Root
G#	III	Major 3rd
B	V	Perfect 5th
D	vii	Minor 7th
F#	II	Major 9th

E min 9
E	I	Root
G	iii	Minor 3rd
B	V	Perfect 5th
D	vii	Minor 7th
F#	II	Major 9th

E maj 9
E	I	Root
G#	III	Major 3rd
B	V	Perfect 5th
D#	VII	Major 7th
F#	II	Major 9th

E 11
E	I	Root
(G#)	III	Major 3rd
B	V	Perfect 5th
D	VII	Minor 7th
F#	II	Major 9th
A	IV	Perfect 11th

E min 11
E	I	Root
G	iii	Minor 3rd
B	V	Perfect 5th
D	vii	Minor 7th
F#	II	Major 9th
A	IV	Perfect 11th

E 13
E	I	Root
G#	III	Major 3rd
B	V	Perfect 5th
D	vii	Minor 7th
F#	II	Major 9th
(A)	IV	Perfect 11th
C#	VI	Major 13th

E min 13
E	I	Root
G	iii	Minor 3rd
B	V	Perfect 5th
D	vii	Minor 7th
F#	II	Major 9th
(A)	IV	Perfect 11th
C#	VI	Major 13th

E maj 13
E	I	Root
G#	III	Major 3rd
B	V	Perfect 5th
D#	VII	Major 7th
F#	II	Major 9th
(A)	IV	Perfect 11th
C#	VI	Major 13th

E 7-5-9
E	I	Root
G#	III	Major 3rd
B♭	V°	Dim 5th
D	vii	Minor 7th
F	ii	Minor 9th

E 7-5+9
E	I	Root
G#	III	Major 3rd
B♭	V°	Dim 5th
D	vii	Minor 7th
G	II+	Aug 9th

E 7+5-9
E	I	Root
G#	III	Major 3rd
C	V+	Aug 5th
D	vii	Minor 7th
F	ii	Minor 9th

F

I	II	III	IV	V	VI	VII	I
F	G	A	B♭	C	D	E	F

F maj

F	I	Root
A	III	Major 3rd
C	V	Perfect 5th

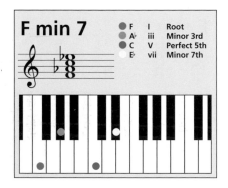

F min

F	I	Root
A♭	iii	Minor 3rd
C	V	Perfect 5th

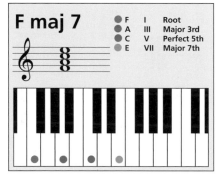

F 7

F	I	Root
A	III	Major 3rd
C	V	Perfect 5th
E♭	vii	Minor 7th

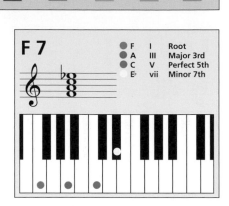

F min 7

F	I	Root
A♭	iii	Minor 3rd
C	V	Perfect 5th
E♭	vii	Minor 7th

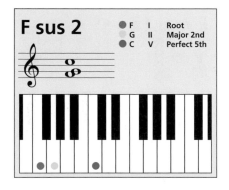

F maj 7

F	I	Root
A	III	Major 3rd
C	V	Perfect 5th
E	VII	Major 7th

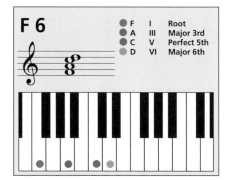

D sus 4

F	I	Root
B♭	IV	Perfect 4th
C	V	Perfect 5th

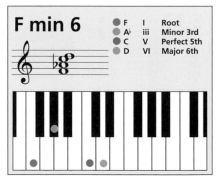

F sus 2

F	I	Root
G	II	Major 2nd
C	V	Perfect 5th

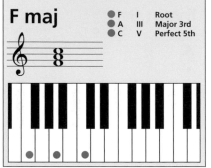

F 6

F	I	Root
A	III	Major 3rd
C	V	Perfect 5th
D	VI	Major 6th

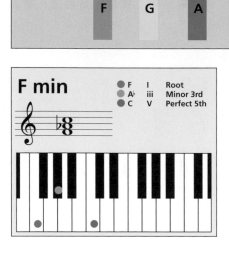

F min 6

F	I	Root
A♭	iii	Minor 3rd
C	V	Perfect 5th
D	VI	Major 6th

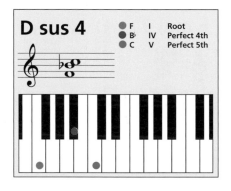

F aug

F	I	Root
A	III	Major 3rd
C♯	V+	Aug 5th

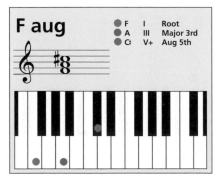

F dim 7

F	I	Root
A♭	iii	Minor 3rd
B	V°	Dim 5th
D	vii	Dim 7th

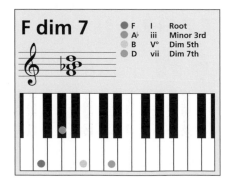

F 7-5

F	I	Root
A	III	Major 3rd
B	IV+	Aug 4th
E♭	vii	Minor 7th

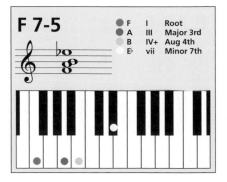

F 7+5

F	I	Root
A	III	Major 3rd
C♯	V+	Aug 5th
E♭	vii	Minor 7th

F min/maj 7

F	I	Root
A♭	iii	Minor 3rd
C	V	Perfect 5th
E	VII	Major 7th

F maj 7-5

F	I	Root
A	III	Major 3rd
B	V°	Dim 5th
E	VII	Major 7th

F maj 7+5

F	I	Root
A	III	Major 3rd
C♯	V+	Aug 5th
E	VII	Major 7th

F 9

F	I	Root
A	III	Major 3rd
C	V	Perfect 5th
E♭	vii	Minor 7th
G	II	Major 9th

F min 9

F	I	Root
A♭	iii	Minor 3rd
C	V	Perfect 5th
E♭	vii	Minor 7th
G	II	Major 9th

F maj 9

F	I	Root
A	III	Major 3rd
C	V	Perfect 5th
E	VII	Major 7th
G	II	Major 9th

F 11

F	I	Root
(A)	III	Major 3rd
C	V	Perfect 5th
E♭	vii	Minor 7th
G	II	Major 9th
B♭	IV	Perfect 11th

F min 11

F	I	Root
A♭	iii	Minor 3rd
C	V	Perfect 5th
E♭	vii	Minor 7th
G	II	Major 9th
B♭	IV	Perfect 11th

F 13

F	I	Root
A	III	Major 3rd
C	V	Perfect 5th
E♭	vii	Minor 7th
G	II	Major 9th
(B♭)	IV	Perfect 11th
D	VI	Major 13th

F min 13

F	I	Root
A♭	iii	Minor 3rd
C	V	Perfect 5th
E♭	vii	Minor 7th
G	II	Major 9th
(B♭)	IV	Perfect 11th
D	VI	Major 13th

F maj 13

F	I	Root
A	III	Major 3rd
C	V	Perfect 5th
E	VII	Major 7th
G	II	Major 9th
(B♭)	IV	Perfect 11th
D	VI	Major 13th

F 7-5-9

F	I	Root
A	III	Major 3rd
B	V°	Dim 5th
E♭	vii	Minor 7th
G♭	ii	Minor 9th

F 7-5+9

F	I	Root
A	III	Major 3rd
B	V°	Dim 5th
E♭	vii	Minor 7th
G♯	II+	Aug 9th

F 7+5-9

F	I	Root
A	III	Major 3rd
C♯	V+	Aug 5th
E♭	vii	Minor 7th
G♭	ii	Minor 9th

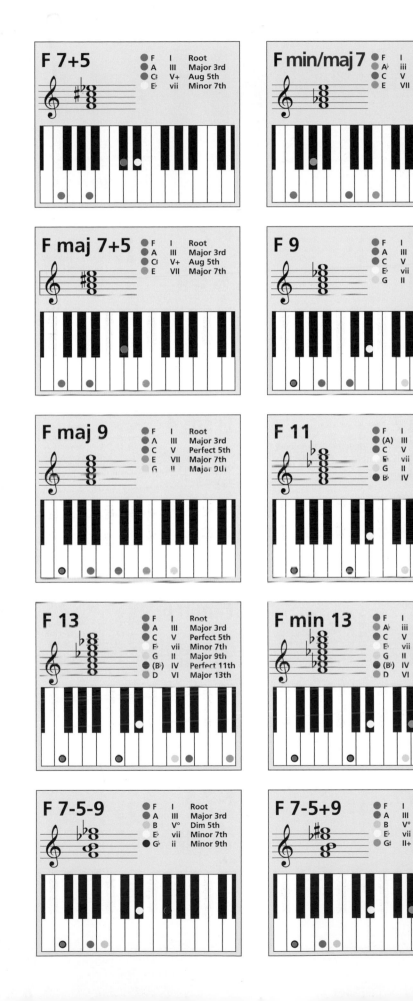
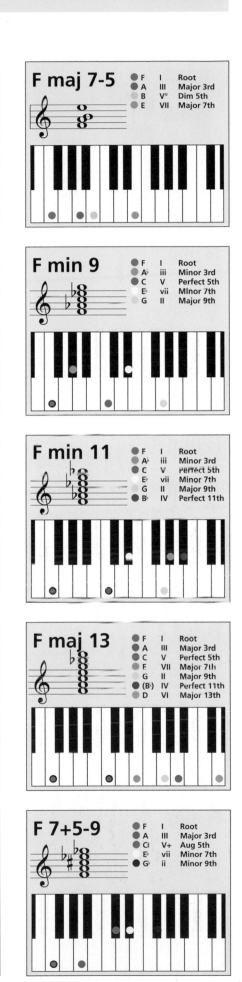

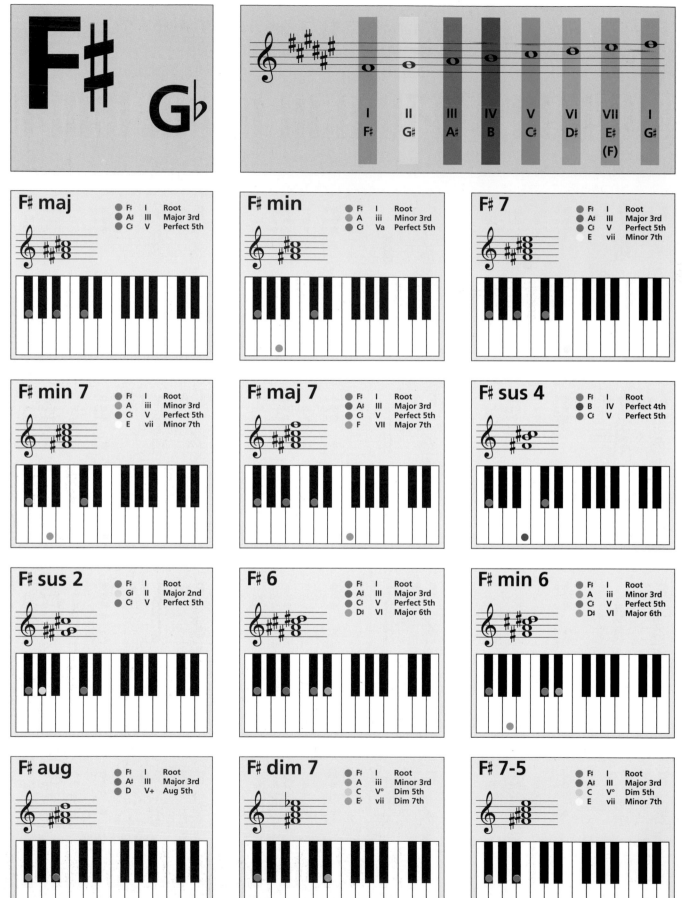

F# Gb

I	II	III	IV	V	VI	VII	I
F#	G#	A#	B	C#	D#	E# (F)	G#

F# maj

F#	I	Root
A#	III	Major 3rd
C#	V	Perfect 5th

F# min

F#	I	Root
A	iii	Minor 3rd
C#	Va	Perfect 5th

F# 7

F#	I	Root
A#	III	Major 3rd
C#	V	Perfect 5th
E	vii	Minor 7th

F# min 7

F#	I	Root
A	iii	Minor 3rd
C#	V	Perfect 5th
E	vii	Minor 7th

F# maj 7

F#	I	Root
A#	III	Major 3rd
C#	V	Perfect 5th
F	VII	Major 7th

F# sus 4

F#	I	Root
B	IV	Perfect 4th
C#	V	Perfect 5th

F# sus 2

F#	I	Root
G#	II	Major 2nd
C#	V	Perfect 5th

F# 6

F#	I	Root
A#	III	Major 3rd
C#	V	Perfect 5th
D#	VI	Major 6th

F# min 6

F#	I	Root
A	iii	Minor 3rd
C#	V	Perfect 5th
D#	VI	Major 6th

F# aug

F#	I	Root
A#	III	Major 3rd
D	V+	Aug 5th

F# dim 7

F#	I	Root
A	iii	Minor 3rd
C	V°	Dim 5th
E♭	vii	Dim 7th

F# 7-5

F#	I	Root
A#	III	Major 3rd
C	V°	Dim 5th
E	vii	Minor 7th

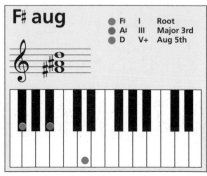
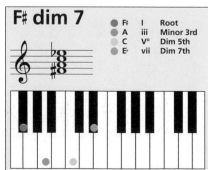

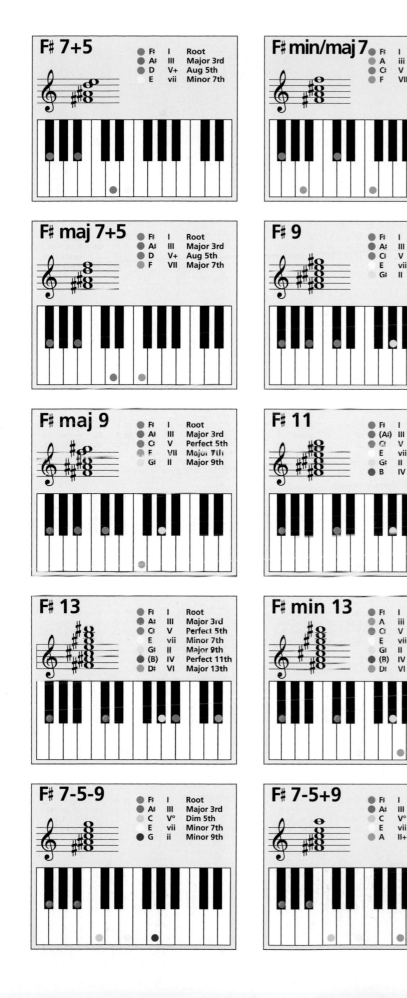
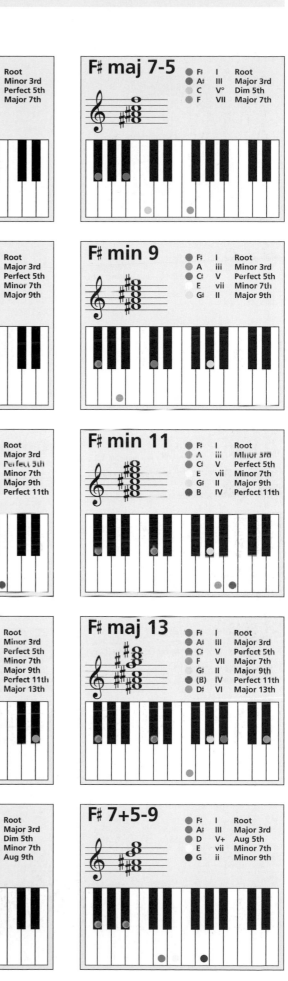

F# 7+5

F#	I	Root
A#	III	Major 3rd
D	V+	Aug 5th
E	vii	Minor 7th

F# min/maj7

F#	I	Root
A	iii	Minor 3rd
C#	V	Perfect 5th
F	VII	Major 7th

F# maj 7-5

F#	I	Root
A#	III	Major 3rd
C	V°	Dim 5th
F	VII	Major 7th

F# maj 7+5

F#	I	Root
A#	III	Major 3rd
D	V+	Aug 5th
F	VII	Major 7th

F# 9

F#	I	Root
A#	III	Major 3rd
C#	V	Perfect 5th
E	vii	Minor 7th
G#	II	Major 9th

F# min 9

F#	I	Root
A	iii	Minor 3rd
C#	V	Perfect 5th
E	vii	Minor 7th
G#	II	Major 9th

F# maj 9

F#	I	Root
A#	III	Major 3rd
C#	V	Perfect 5th
F	VII	Major 7th
G#	II	Major 9th

F# 11

F#	I	Root
(A#)	III	Major 3rd
C#	V	Perfect 5th
E	vii	Minor 7th
G#	II	Major 9th
B	IV	Perfect 11th

F# min 11

F#	I	Root
A	iii	Minor 3rd
C#	V	Perfect 5th
E	vii	Minor 7th
G#	II	Major 9th
B	IV	Perfect 11th

F# 13

F#	I	Root
A#	III	Major 3rd
C#	V	Perfect 5th
E	vii	Minor 7th
G#	II	Major 9th
(B)	IV	Perfect 11th
D#	VI	Major 13th

F# min 13

F#	I	Root
A	iii	Minor 3rd
C#	V	Perfect 5th
E	vii	Minor 7th
G#	II	Major 9th
(B)	IV	Perfect 11th
D#	VI	Major 13th

F# maj 13

F#	I	Root
A#	III	Major 3rd
C#	V	Perfect 5th
E	VII	Major 7th
G#	II	Major 9th
(B)	IV	Perfect 11th
D#	VI	Major 13th

F# 7-5-9

F#	I	Root
A#	III	Major 3rd
C	V°	Dim 5th
E	vii	Minor 7th
G	ii	Minor 9th

F# 7-5+9

F#	I	Root
A#	III	Major 3rd
C	V°	Dim 5th
E	vii	Minor 7th
A	II+	Aug 9th

F# 7+5-9

F#	I	Root
A#	III	Major 3rd
D	V+	Aug 5th
E	vii	Minor 7th
G	ii	Minor 9th

I	II	III	IV	V	VI	VII	I
G	A	B	C	D	E	F#	G

G maj

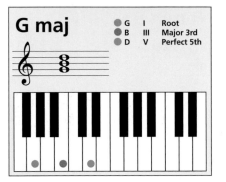

G	I	Root
B	III	Major 3rd
D	V	Perfect 5th

G m

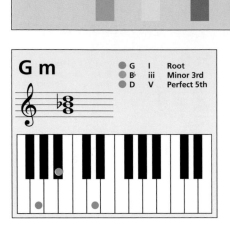

G	I	Root
B♭	iii	Minor 3rd
D	V	Perfect 5th

G 7

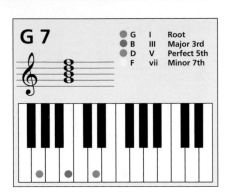

G	I	Root
B	III	Major 3rd
D	V	Perfect 5th
F	vii	Minor 7th

G min 7

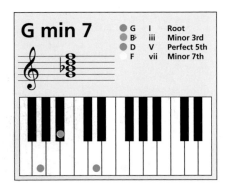

G	I	Root
B♭	iii	Minor 3rd
D	V	Perfect 5th
F	vii	Minor 7th

G maj 7

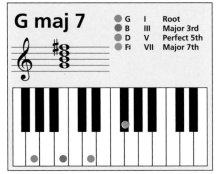

G	I	Root
B	III	Major 3rd
D	V	Perfect 5th
F#	VII	Major 7th

G sus 4

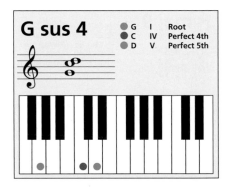

G	I	Root
C	IV	Perfect 4th
D	V	Perfect 5th

G sus 2

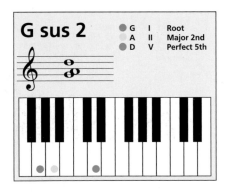

G	I	Root
A	II	Major 2nd
D	V	Perfect 5th

G 6

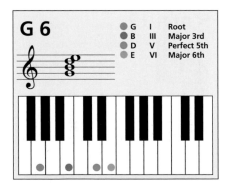

G	I	Root
B	III	Major 3rd
D	V	Perfect 5th
E	VI	Major 6th

G min 6

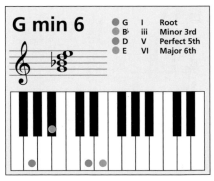

G	I	Root
B♭	iii	Minor 3rd
D	V	Perfect 5th
E	VI	Major 6th

G aug

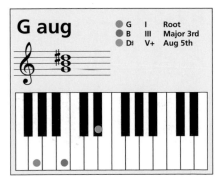

G	I	Root
B	III	Major 3rd
D#	V+	Aug 5th

G dim 7

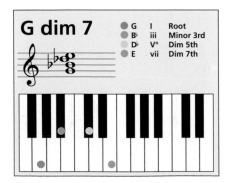

G	I	Root
B♭	iii	Minor 3rd
D♭	V°	Dim 5th
E	vii	Dim 7th

G 7-5

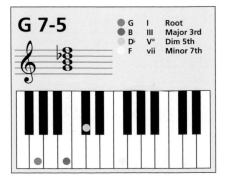

G	I	Root
B	III	Major 3rd
D♭	V°	Dim 5th
F	vii	Minor 7th

G 7+5

G	I	Root
B	III	Major 3rd
D♯	V+	Aug 5th
F	vii	Minor 7th

G min/maj 7

G	I	Root
B♭	iii	Minor 3rd
D	V	Perfect 5th
F♯	VII	Major 7th

G maj 7-5

G	I	Root
B	III	Major 3rd
D♭	V°	Dim 5th
F♯	VII	Major 7th

G maj 7+5

G	I	Root
B	III	Major 3rd
D♯	V+	Aug 5th
F♯	VII	Major 7th

G 9

G	I	Root
B	III	Major 3rd
D	V	Perfect 5th
F	vii	Minor 7th
A	II	Major 9th

G min 9

G	I	Root
B♭	iii	Minor 3rd
D	V	Perfect 5th
F	vii	Minor 7th
A	II	Major 9th

G maj 9

G	I	Root
B	III	Major 3rd
D	V	Perfect 5th
F♯	vii	Major 7th
A	II	Major 9th

G 11

G	I	Root
(B)	III	Major 3rd
D	V	Perfect 5th
F	vii	Minor 7th
A	II	Major 9th
C	IV	Perfect 11th

G min 11

G	I	Root
B♭	iii	Minor 3rd
D	V	Perfect 5th
F	vii	Minor 7th
A	II	Major 9th
C	IV	Perfect 11th

G 13

G	I	Root
B	III	Major 3rd
D	V	Perfect 5th
F	vii	Minor 7th
A	II	Major 9th
(C)	IV	Perfect 11th
E	VI	Major 13th

G min 13

G	I	Root
B♭	iii	Minor 3rd
D	V	Perfect 5th
F	vii	Minor 7th
A	II	Major 9th
(C)	IV	Perfect 11th
E	VI	Major 13th

G maj 13

G	I	Root
B	III	Major 3rd
D	V	Perfect 5th
F♯	VII	Major 7th
A	II	Major 9th
(C)	IV	Perfect 11th
E	VI	Major 13th

G 7-5-9

G	I	Root
B	III	Major 3rd
D♭	V°	Dim 5th
F	vii	Minor 7th
A♭	ii	Minor 9th

G 7-5+9

G	I	Root
B	III	Major 3rd
D♭	V°	Dim 5th
F	vii	Minor 7th
A♯	II+	Aug 9th

G 7+5-9

G	I	Root
B	III	Major 3rd
D♯	V+	Aug 5th
F	vii	Minor 7th
A♭	ii	Minor 9th

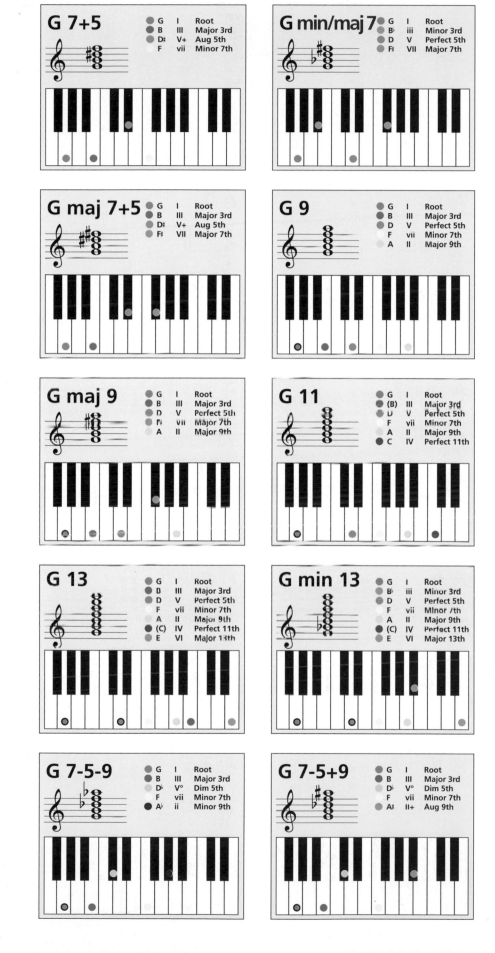
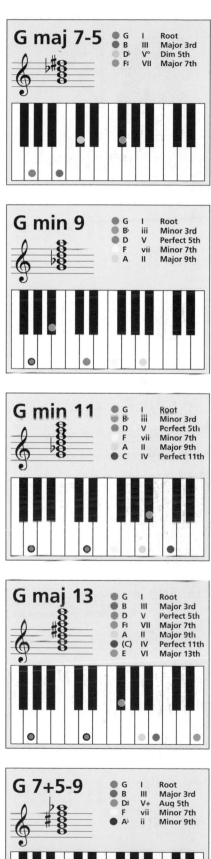

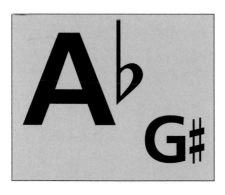

I	II	III	IV	V	VI	VII	I
A♭	B♭	C	D♭	E♭	F	G	A♭

A♭ maj

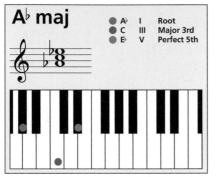

● A♭	I	Root
● C	III	Major 3rd
● E♭	V	Perfect 5th

A♭ m

● A♭	I	Root
● B	iii	Minor 3rd
● E♭	V	Perfect 5th

A♭ 7

● A♭	I	Root
● C	III	Major 3rd
● E♭	V	Perfect 5th
○ G♭	vii	Minor 7th

A♭ min 7

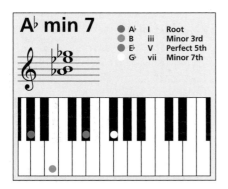

● A♭	I	Root
● B	iii	Minor 3rd
● E♭	V	Perfect 5th
○ G♭	vii	Minor 7th

A♭ maj 7

● A♭	I	Root
● C	III	Major 3rd
● E♭	V	Perfect 5th
● G	VII	Major 7th

A♭ sus 4

● A♭	I	Root
● D♭	IV	Perfect 4th
● E♭	V	Perfect 5th

A♭ sus 2

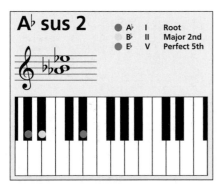

● A♭	I	Root
● B♭	II	Major 2nd
● E♭	V	Perfect 5th

A♭ 6

● A♭	I	Root
● C	III	Major 3rd
● E♭	V	Perfect 5th
● F	VI	Major 6th

A♭ min 6

● A♭	I	Root
● B	iii	Minor 3rd
● E♭	V	Perfect 5th
● F	VI	Major 6th

A♭ aug

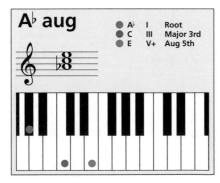

● A♭	I	Root
● C	III	Major 3rd
● E	V+	Aug 5th

A♭ dim 7

● A♭	I	Root
● B	iii	Minor 3rd
● D	V°	Dim 5th
● F	vii	Dim 7th

A♭ 7-5

● A♭	I	Root
● C	III	Major 3rd
● D	V°	Dim 5th
○ G♭	vii	Minor 7th

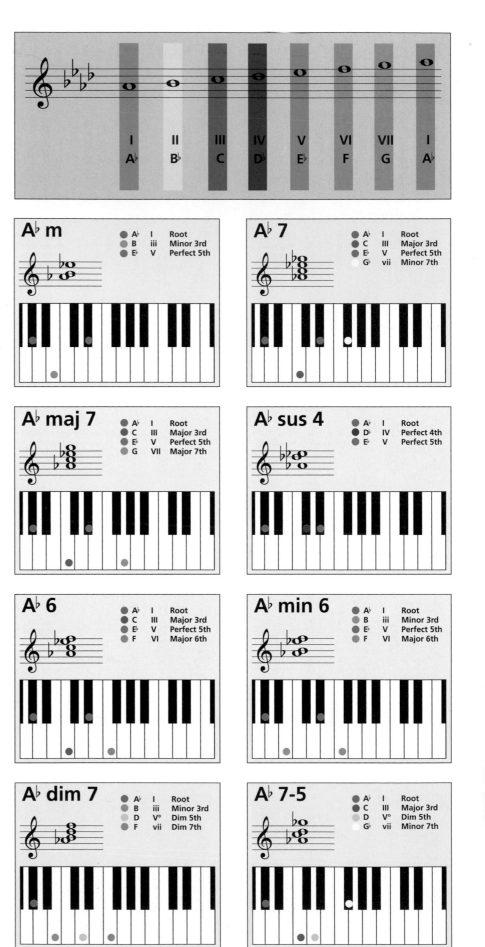

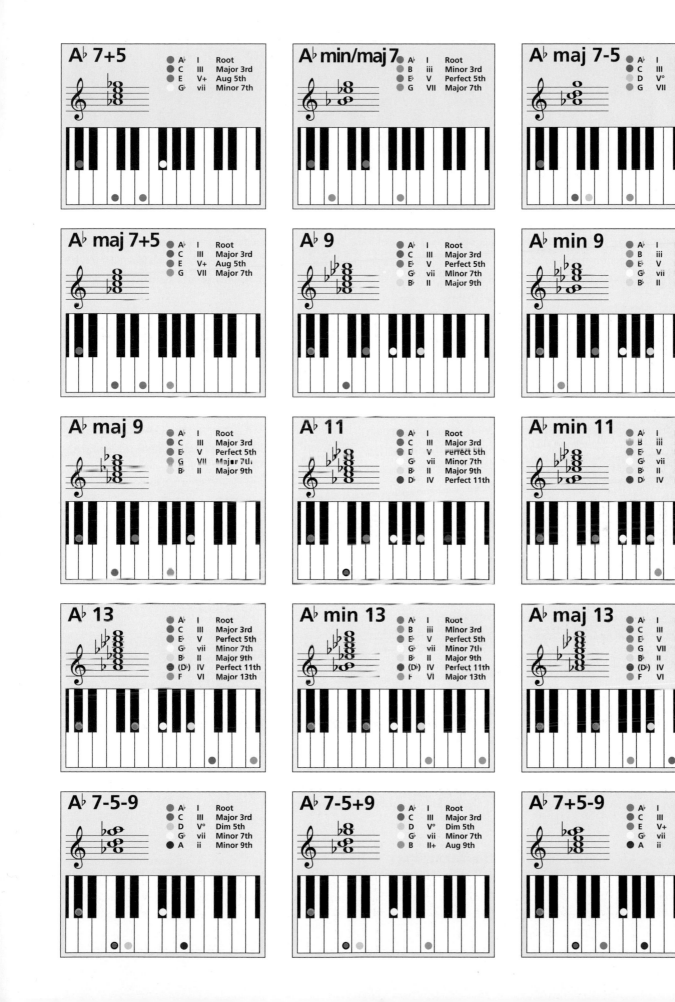

GLOSSARY

ACCENT

A dynamic playing effect that places an emphasis on specific notes of chords within a sequence, making them louder or creating rhythmic effects.

ACCIDENTAL

Symbols used in written music to raise or lower the pitch of a note by one or two semitones. A sharp (♯) raises the pitch by a semitone; a double sharp (𝄪) raises the pitch by two semitones; a flat (♭) lowers the pitch by a semitone; and a double flat (♭♭) lowers the pitch by two semitones. The effect of sharps and flats can be "switched off" with the use of a symbol known as a natural (♮).

ADAGIO

Performance mark literally meaning "at ease," a slow tempo that is faster than *andante* but slower than *largo*. Its diminutive form is *adagietto*, which is slightly faster than *adagio*.

AIR

A tune – vocal or instrumental.

ARPEGGIO

The notes of a chord played in quick succession rather than simultaneously. Commonly notated using a wavy line. Also known as a "broken chord."

ARTICULATION

The attack with which single notes or chords are played and the length of time over which they are allowed to decay. Articulation symbols can include the slur, which marks out phrases, and staccato, which shortens the length of a note.

AUGMENTED

Interval created by raising a perfect or major interval by a semitone.

BAR

Sometimes referred to as a "measure," a unit of musical time in which the notes contained within total a fixed combined value defined by the time signature. Bars are separated by bar lines.

BEAT

A metrical pulse grouped together to form recurring patterns or rhythms.

BIND

See "Tie".

BRACE

Symbol used to join together staves that are to be played simultaneously. Piano music usually shows a treble staff and a bass staff played by the right and left hands respectively.

CADENCE

A musical phrase that creates the sense of rest or resolution at its end.

CHORD

The sound of three or more notes of different pitch played simultaneously. A chord made up from three notes only is called a triad.

CHROMATIC SCALE

A scale that includes all twelve pitches from tonic to octave with each degree separated by a semitone.

CIRCLE OF FIFTHS

Closed circle of all twelve pitches arranged at intervals of a perfect 5th. First devised by Johann David Heinechen in the eighteenth century.

CLEF

Symbol placed at the beginning of a staff or bar line that determines the pitches of the notes that follow. Three types are commonly used: the G or treble clef; the F or bass clef; and the C clef. The C clef is termed the ALTO CLEF and when centred on the fourth line it becomes the TENOR CLEF.

CODA

The concluding passage of a piece of music.

COMMON CHORD

A major triad.

COMMON TIME

Alternative name for a piece of music written with a time signature of four-four. Can be shown by the symbol "𝄴" instead of the traditional two numbers.

COMPOUND INTERVAL

An interval – a semitone gap between two notes – of greater than an octave.

CONCERT PITCH

The set of reference tones to which all non-transposing instruments must be tuned. A common scientific definition is that the note "A" below "Middle C" is measured as having a frequency of 440 cycles per second.

COUNTERMELODY

A subordinate melody that accompanies a main melody.

COUNTERPOINT

Two or more lines of melody played at the same time.

CRISTOFORI, BARTOLOMEO

Harpsichord-maker, generally credited with having invented the piano.

DA CAPO

Literally meaning "from the head," *da capo* is an instruction that the performer must return to the beginning of the piece. The term is usually abbreviated as ***D.C.***

DAL SEGNO

Literally meaning "from the sign," is an instruction that the performer must repeat a sequence from a point marked by the sign "𝄋." Abbreviated as ***D.S.***

DIATONIC

The seven-note major and minor scale system.

DIMINISHED

An interval created by lowering a perfect or minor interval by a semitone; also a term applied both to a minor chord with a lowered 5th note and a chord that comprises minor 3rd intervals.

DISCORD

The description given to note intervals that are deemed to be dissonant in character. Specifically this refers to the intervals between the root note (1st) and the second and seventh notes respectively.

DOMINANT

The fifth degree of a major or minor scale. The triad built on this degree is the dominant triad; the seventh built on this degree is the dominant seventh.

DOTTED NOTES

A dot positioned after any type of note that increases its value by half. A second dot can be added to increase the value by a quarter; a third dot added increases the value by an eighth.

DOTTED RESTS

A dot positioned after a rest to increase its value by half. Most commonly found in compound time.

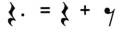

DOUBLE BAR

Two vertical lines drawn through the staff to indicate the end of a piece of music or a movement.

DYNAMIC MARKS

Terms, symbols and abbreviations used in written music to indicate different levels of volume or a transition from one level to another.

ENHARMONIC

A set of different names that may be applied to the same pitches. For example, the notes C♯ and D♭ are deemed to be enharmonic equivalents, even though they share the same pitch

EXPRESSION MARKS

Words or symbols written on a score to guide the player on matters other than pitch or rhythm – dynamics, articulation and tempo, for example.

FORTE-PIANO

An instruction to play loud then soft. Shown in a stylised script as ***fp***.

GATHERING NOTE

The note given by an organist to provide a choir with a reference tone for the singing of hymns.

GLISSANDO

A continuous sliding movement between two different pitches. On a piano keyboard the effect can be produced by running the nail of a finger along the black or white notes, creating a very fast scale of discretely pitched notes.

GRAND PIANO

The largest of the piano family, with a range of over seven octaves.

HALF-STEP *(US)* **or SEMITONE** *(UK)*

The smallest interval between two notes.

HARMONIUM

Reed organ in which sound is generated by foot-pedal-operated bellows.

HARMONY

The effect of a set of notes played simultaneously, and the way in which these intervals and chords sound in relation to each other.

HARPSICHORD

Precursor of the piano; keyboard instrument in which a mechanism plucks rather than hammers the strings.

INTERVAL

The relationship between two different note pitches numbered in terms of the degrees of the diatonic scale system.

INTONATION

The degree to which tuning and pitching is accurate among the musicians in an ensemble.

INVERSION

The order of notes in a chord from the lowest pitch. If the root is the lowest note, the chord is said to be in the root position. If the third note is the lowest, the chord is a first inversion; if the fifth note is the lowest, it is a second inversion.

KEY SIGNATURE

An arrangement of sharps and flats on the staff that defines the key.

LEADING NOTE

The seventh degree of the diatonic major scale.

LEDGER LINE

A short line that allows notes to be transcribed outside of the range of the five-line staff.

MELODY

A pattern of single notes that forms a coherent musical sequence. Often simply described as a tune.

METER

Alternative term for tempo.

METRONOME

Mechanical device used to denote the tempo of a piece of music.

MIDDLE C

The centre note on a piano keyboard that is also an important reference tone for other orchestral instruments. It is notated on a ledger line below a staff anchored by a treble clef.

MODE

A series of fixed scales that were predominant during the Middle Ages. The modern-day diatonic system of major and minor scales evolved from their existence. The seven modes that can be built from the major scale are Ionian (I), Dorian (II), Phrygian (III), Lydian (IV), Mixolydian (V), Aeolian (VI) and Locrian (VII).

MODULATION

Movement from one key to another within a section or piece of music. Often wrongly confused with transposition, in which a complete piece of music is moved to an alternative key.

MORDENT

An ornamental instruction to play a single note as a "trill" with an adjacent note. An upper mordent alternates with the note a semitone higher; the lower mordent is played with the note one semitone lower.

NATURAL

See "Accidental".

NOTES

Symbols used in written music to indicate the pitch and duration of a sound. The principal note names are: whole note, half note, quarter note, eighth note, sixteenth note, thirty-second note and sixty-fourth note. In Europe, an alternative naming system is used, based around centuries-old terminology: semibreve, minim, crotchet, quaver, semiquaver, demisemiquaver and hemidemisemiquaver.

OCTAVE

An interval in which pitches share the same note name but the frequency of the lower note is half that of the upper note.

ORNAMENTATION

The alteration of a piece of music to make it sound more effective or beautiful, usually through the addition of notes or dynamic changes.

PEDALS

Foot controls on a piano. The "loud" pedal releases the dampers inside the piano, increasing the volume; the "soft" pedal pushes a piece of cotton between the hammer and strings, damping the sound. A third pedal can be found on a grand piano that "undamps" the keys being played when the pedal is pressed.

PEDAL TONE

A bass note that sustains beneath any shifting harmonic structure, such as the bass "drone" produced by bagpipes.

PENTATONIC

A set of scales based around five notes. Among the oldest of scaler systems, pentatonic scales can be heard in musical cultures all over the world. The minor pentatonic "blues scale" is commonly used in jazz, R&B and rock music.

PERFORMANCE MARKS

Words or symbols written on a score to indicate aspects of performance not covered purely by pitches on the staff.

PHRASE

A self-contained musical sentence that can be viewed as a coherent and identifiable "whole" within the context of composition. Usually no more than a few bars in length, phrases are identified in written music within a slur.

PIANOFORTE

The formal term for the piano.

PITCH

The frequency of a note in terms of the number of times it vibrates each second.

POLYPHONY

Any type of music that simultaneously combines a number of parts.

PRIMARY TRIADS

Term describing the three triads built from the tonic, subdominant and dominant degrees of a diatonic scale.

REGISTER

The range of pitches playable by a voice or instrument.

RELATIVE MAJOR/RELATIVE MINOR

The relationship between major and natural minor scales: the pitch of the notes and chords built on any major scale are the same as those on a natural minor scale built from the sixth degree of the major scale.

REPEAT/REITERATE

An instruction to reiterate a piece of music within the bars specified by repeat symbols.

REST

A symbol placed on the staff to indicate a period in which no notes are played. Each of the different note types has its own equivalent rest.

RHYTHM

A pattern of musical sounds, principally according to duration and accents.

SCALE

A collection of notes laid out in a predefined sequence from the lowest pitch to the highest pitch.

SCALE DEGREES

The position of each note within a scale. Can be shown numerically using Arabic or Roman numerals. Each degree can also be named: tonic (I); supertonic (II); mediant (III); subdominant (IV); dominant (V); submediant (VI); and leading note (VII).

SCORE

The notation of an entire piece of music for an ensemble written out so that the simultaneous parts are aligned in a vertical manner.

SEGNO

Literally meaning "sign." The symbol ("𝄋") is used to mark the beginning or end of a repeated section. The sign must be paired with either a *dal segno* instruction, "from the sign," or an *al segno* instruction, meaning "to the sign."

SEGUE

A term indicating that the next piece of music follows immediately with no interruption.

SEMITONE *(UK)* **or HALF STEP** *(US)*

The smallest interval between two notes.

SPACE

The gap between the lines of a staff.

STACCATO

Literally meaning "detached," staccato notes or chords are dramatically reduced in length, creating a "stabbing" effect. Usually shown in notation by a dot or an arrow head above or below the note.

STAFF

A group of horizontal parallel lines and spaces on which notes are placed to define their pitch. Sometimes also called a "stave" in the singular, but always "staves" in the plural.

STEM

The vertical line attached to the head of the note. The value of the note can be progressively halved by adding a tail (or flag) to the tip of the stem.

STEP *(US)* **or TONE** *(UK)*

Two half steps or semitones.

SYNCOPATION

A rhythm that runs against the prevailing meter or pulse, emphasising the off-beats.

TEMPO

The speed at which the music is performed, usually measured in beats per minute for a specific note type; see also *Metronome*.

TIE

A curved line joining two notes of the same pitch that indicates the value of the second note must be added to the value of the first, and that the second note itself is NOT played. Mostly used to sustain notes across bar lines. Also known as "binds."

TIME SIGNATURE

The numerical symbols positioned at the beginning of a staff to indicate its meter. The upper number indicates the number of beats in the bar; the lower number shows the type of note that makes up those beats.

TONE *(UK)* **or STEP** *(US)*

An interval of a major 2nd (two semitones), known in the US as a "step"; a description of the colour or quality of a sound.

TRANSPOSITION

A piece of music rewritten at a different pitch from the original. Usually defined in terms of the difference in interval between the two.

TRIAD

A chord made up of three notes separated by intervals of a third. There are four fundamentally different forms: major triad; minor triad; diminished triad and augmented triad

TRILL

A rapid alteration of two notes over a distance of a tone or semitone.

TRIPLET

A group of three notes played in the time of two.

TUNE

A melody; adjusting an instrument to concert pitch.

ANSWERS

PAGE 73

1. Major 2nd.
3. Minor 3rd.
5. Major 7th.
7. Augmented 5th.
9. Minor 6th.
11. Perfect 5th.
13. Augmented 5th.
15. Major 6th.
17. Minor 3rd.
19. Augmented 4th.

2. Perfect 5th.
4. Minor 6th.
6. Augmented 5th.
8. Diminished 2nd.
10. Perfect 4th.
12. Augmented 4th.
14. Minor 3rd.
16. Major 2nd.
18. Diminished 5th.
20. Diminished octave.

21. Major 6th.
22. Augmented 4th.
23. Perfect 5th.
24. Augmented 5th.
25. Perfect 4th.
26. Major 3rd.
27. Major 3rd.
28. Dimished 2nd.

PAGE 87

1. G major.
2. F major.
3. D major.

BIBLIOGRAPHY

Derek Bailey
Improvisation
(Moorland, 1980)

David Bowman and Paul Terry
Aural Matters
(Schott, 1993)

Terry Burrows
Total Guitar Tutor
(Carlton, 1998)

Terry Burrows
How To Read Music
(Carlton, 1999)

Terry Burrows
Total Keyboard Tutor
(Carlton, 2000)

Charles Osborne
A to Z of Classical Music
(The Bodley Head, 1977)

Don Randall
The New Harvard Dictionary Of Music
(Harvard University Press, 1986)

Darryl Runswick
Rock, Jazz and Pop Arranging
(Faber and Faber, 1992)

Erik Satie
A Mammal's Notebook: Collected Writings…
(Atlas, 1996)

Jeremy Siepman
The Piano
(Smithmark, 1996)

Nicolas Slonimsky
Thesaurus of Scales and Melodic Patterns
(Scrivener's, 1947)

Eric Taylor
The AB Guide to Music Theory
(Associated Board, 1989)

ACKNOWLEDGEMENTS

The author would like to thank Claire Richardson and Adam Wright at Carlton Books for their help with this project. And, of course, SJ, JSJ and the strange and wonderful Junoir.

The soundtrack to this project:

John Adams
    Violin Concerto/Shaker Loops
Daft Punk *Discovery*
Philip Glass
    Concerto for Violin and Orchestra
The Hives *Your New Favourite Band*
Yo-Yo Ma *Bach: Complete Cello Suites*
Eric Parkin
    John Ireland: Piano Works, Vol.1
András Schiff *Plays Schumann*
Artur Schnabel
    Beethoven: Piano Concertos
François-Joël Thiollier
    Debussy: Piano Works, Vol.1
Tom Waits *Alice*

PICTURE CREDITS

The publishers would like to thank the following sources for their kind permission to reproduce the pictures in this book:

Kawai: 14b, 15t;
Lebrecht Collection: 8br, 9t, 17tr, 20b, 47bl, 62br, 79c, 106tr, 119tr;
B. Chaliapin: 21tr;
Topham Picturepoint: 10t, 18tr, 94c;
Associated Press: 18bl,
PAL/Clive Barda: 16br, 19b, 22b, 23t,
PAL/Jonathan Fisher: 10b

Every effort has been made to acknowledge correctly and contact the source and/or copyright holder of each picture, and Carlton Books Limited apologises for any unintentional errors or omissions which will be corrected in future editions of this book.